De'Lure

I0535534

TAKE MY BREATH AWAY

DE'LURE

DE'LURE PUBLICATIONS PRESENTS

TAKE MY BREATH *Away*

ORLANDO NIGHTS

INTERNATIONAL BESTSELLING AUTHOR

DE'LURE

De'Lure Publishing

De'Lure

Take My Breath Away Orlando Nights
All Rights Reserved. Copyright © 2015 De'Lure
 De'Lure Publishing
Cover Image by De'Lure

PRINTED IN THE UNITED STATES OF AMERICA

Author Quotes

*"Always remember that the **trouble** in your past is already done and it never changes... so in turn never be discouraged when fighting a battle that you've already fought so many times before, look instead to your inevitable future."*

"I will die a dreamer... A dreamer with the heart and the talent to realize their dream is more powerful and blessed than the richest man on the planet..."

*"Once you recognize the fact that **NOTHING** in your past be it lies or truth, can discount your present accomplishments, or the things you will achieve in the future, life becomes much simpler."*

*"We are taught to believe that our **names** and our **images** are everything... If so that's a good thing because **we are in control** of **all of the above**..."*

"To read my work... is to peek inside of my very heart and experience my vivid rainbow of imagination"

*"When people can't compete with your **present,** and they fear your **future,** they have no choice but to bring up and attempt to distort your past"*

*"We are not who **THEY** say we are... but exactly who we choose to be"*

"If we let the ghosts of our past affect our present and our future... well then, we were much better off dying, along with those nagging ghosts of long ago..."

Foreword

Every mother gave birth to a child… except his. Mike's
mom gave birth to a legend. I've known Michael
De'Lure for a year now and he's my best friend. If I had
to sum him up in one word it would have to be driven.
He's the most non-stop, hard working person I've ever
met. If he's not writing, running his store, or brain
storming on his next big project, he's lost in deep
conversation with someone trying to convince them they
can be their own boss. He always says, "If you're working
for anybody other than yourself, you're working
backwards." The more I watch him, I'm inclined to agree.
I see him almost every day and there's always something
going on, he never rests. This new book is very different
from every other urban novel on the market. The reason
so many people love, "Take my Breath Away", is
because you have a writer with the imagination and the
depth to create a fantasy novel, who just wrote an urban
novel. That has to be rare because the two genres are
worlds apart. I have never met anyone like Mike before
and doubt that I ever will again. He's definitely one of a
kind. I can assure you that anything he touches is going to
be magical. I can honestly say that knowing him has truly
been an honor.
K. Brown

Dedication

This novel is dedicated to all of my dreamers out there, and even the people that are scared to dream. I'm living my dream every day, and with everything I've been through… if I can do it so can you.

"If you're scared of becoming *great* just attach yourself to somebody who already knows how to fly. You'll never learn how to *soar* until somebody shows you how to grow your own *wings*…"

M.L. De'Lure

Acknowledgments

First and foremost, I thank GOD for giving me the drive and the strong mind to stay focused long enough to bring this project to completion. Mentally I'm in a good place right now, and I know I'm doing what He created me to do. I don't have a clue where these stories come from, but they are so real to me. When I create, I don't sit down at my lap top with an outline or a writing plan. I just start typing and let my characters tell their stories themselves. I thank Him every day for the feeling I get when his hand is on me, as these stories bleed through my fingertips. I also want to acknowledge my godmother Ms. Carol Burton, my friend Valerie Olivier, and my friend Twaneshia Powell who all worked really hard on the

De'Lure

editing of *"Take My Breath Away."*

The events and the characters you will read about in this story are all fictional. The things I write about are always born through pure imagination.

(The first three chapters serve as introductions to the initial perspectives of the three main characters in this novel)

Prologue

Love

Love is the only reason we live and breathe. We do simple and complex things throughout our lifetimes to better and at time worsen who we already are as naturally compassionate human beings. But it's all for love. Sadly, when we lose a love, fall out of love, or just plain get our hearts broken we begin to change.

Some of us are blessed enough to get our hearts broken more than once. I know it sounds strange to say that heartbreak is a blessing but it truly is. As the age-old adage goes, "It's better to have loved and lost than to have never loved at all".

Getting hurt is a terrible feeling but at least with that pain you can feel... The worst thing ever is to not know what it is to feel real love at all. And just because the person who broke your heart may not have ever truly loved you, that doesn't mean your love for them was any less real.

When your heart gets broken you have no choice but to change. That change is usually not one you can feel or detect at first. In most cases the change in you can only be noticed by the people closest to you.

In time, you begin to adapt and alter the way you deal with people based on the love's you've had and the love's you've lost. This adaptation is unavoidable but when you undergo it don't allow yourself to become cold and bitter.

If you do, in the future you may block yourself from the very love you were meant to have in the first place. Your first love is usually never your last love. So never panic, let your heart protect itself, and live to love another day.

Chapter 1
First Love...

It's a beautiful, calm, sunny morning in Orlando, Florida. The birds outside are happy but respectfully quiet for the most part. In a decent sized house, in the back corner of a peaceful cul de sac lives a beautiful young black woman who believes her new happiness is eternal.

He makes her feel like she's so full of *love* and *life*, but sadly she doesn't have a clue what either of those entities truly entail. She's lost in a strong and beautiful moment. The young woman's name is

Cameron and right now she's lying in her still warm bed, completely naked, and alone reminiscing about the night before.

(Cameron Candice Jiles)
I woke up to the breathtaking aroma of a home cooked meal and the melodious sound of my man's baritone singing voice. He spent the night last night for the first time in weeks, and it was wonderful. Mmmm, he must be in the kitchen cooking me a nice breakfast.

And he should be, because last night I gave him all of me. I was so nervous and anxious, and scared and happy all at the same time. He didn't believe me at first but now

he knows he was my first and I'm so glad I waited so he could be the one.

My name is Cameron Candice Jiles. I'm 23 years old and I live in Orlando, Florida. I work as a waitress at the Bahama Breeze restaurant on International Drive. I'm also in school for cosmetology.

I graduate this summer. But enough about me, the gorgeous chocolate god in my kitchen is Keldrick Jermaine Cole, but everybody calls him K.C. for short.

We met two months ago at my job. He was with some cute yellow bone chick, and I was their server. While she was in the bathroom he slipped me a business card and asked me to call him.

I agreed reluctantly. Honestly speaking though, he had me from hello. I knew I was going to call him at some point, I just didn't know when. He swiftly punctured my eardrums with his deep raspy voice, and I drowned willingly in the soft caramel pools of his perfect eyes. When I saw him smile, I lost all train of thought and melted on the spot. As his date returned to their table, I had to try to regain my composure. I finished serving them and they left. He tipped me fairly well and complimented my service to my manager. That night, I dreamed about him. It was so real… we were at my job and I was his server again. But this time he was alone, in fact we were the only two people in the entire restaurant. He had on a soft baby blue polo shirt with the two top buttons undone, khaki corduroy pants and light brown Prada shoes. I had on nothing but my apron. Needless to say, the dream was unforgettable.

"Good morning beautiful, I hope you're hungry."

K.C. walks in with a tray full of food flashing his infectious smile.

"Yes sir... I'm starving." Cameron responds sitting up, while still clutching her blanket close to her chest as not to expose her naked breasts.

"You cold baby... Wait I got you." K.C. sits the tray down on her bed and quickly takes his 2XL shirt off and delicately puts it over her head. Staring at his chest and stomach that look like they're made of chiseled black concrete, Cam loses her train of thought. This happens often when she's around him.

"I gotta head out baby you good?" he asks. "Yea... um, will I see you tonight?" Cam asks as she hops out of bed and follows him to the door.

K.C. opens the door and takes a couple steps out of the house and then turns around to admire Cameron's impressive little dark skin frame one last time. Stepping close to her he says, "I love you, and you make me want to be the man you need me to be."

With her head tilted to the side in awe, Cam searches his eyes. "How many girls have you said that line to K.C.?" she smiles at him bashfully. Just before he turns to leave, K.C. kisses her softly on the forehead and says, "You're my one and only baby."

Cam closes the door and then rushes to the window to secretly watch him walk away. As he makes it to the corner of the house, he reaches down in his dark blue shorts and snatches the condom off from the night before and throws it into the bushes.

K.C. didn't bother to call or stop by for the next two days. That was six months ago, everything has been up

3

and down since then. He moved into my house, started driving my second car, and refuses to find a real job. Don't get it twisted though, I have a good man with a pure heart, he's just a little lost right now. And I know I'm his main woman, but I want to know if I'm his only woman.

I mean, I do so much for him. I even watch his niece Jazemene for him three times a week. I've had her so much I feel like she's my daughter.

And I don't mind because I know her mother is very busy and she doesn't have a father. It's really cool that she calls K.C. her dad, and he treats her like she's his biological child. All in all, he's a really good man, I know he is.

Sometimes I wonder about that light skinned girl though. The one he brought to my job the night we met. Who was she? Does he still talk to her? Did I break up a happy home? All of these questions haunt me constantly.

Not that I really care because, deep in my sub conscious, I've always had some hatred towards light skinned girls anyway. Ever since I was young, I've always felt like I had to take a back seat to them.

I started to feel like a black stain in their perfect little light skinned world. They were so powerful, and it seemed absolutely effortless.

I know I was a lot prettier than quite a few of them but it didn't seem to matter because my skin was too dark to be considered legitimately pretty at my school.

The light skinned girls dated all the cutest guys and had all the other guys chasing them too, even though they knew they never had a chance with them.

I was so angry, because they made it so hard for a girl like me, a beautiful, strong, classy dark-skinned woman. I

4

stopped trying to make those little boys see my worth; because I knew one day a man would come and make everything feel the way it's supposed to. I promised myself when I was fifteen I would save myself for whoever my husband was going to be. And that was an easy task until I met him, he changed everything.

(A month later)

I worked all day today. My feet were hurting, my head was killing me, but I never once was tired because I know I'm working for more than just me. My tips and my check are cut in half every two weeks, because half of everything I own belongs to my man.

K.C. is struggling, so it's my job to be everything he needs. I'm going to be just that. If my man is down and out, so am I, until we can both climb back up together.

Yesterday was different to say the least. I blindfolded K.C. and made him ride in my car with me. I took him down a few roads and then came to a stop. We were riding for the better part of fifteen minutes.

K.C. was asking questions the entire time we were riding, he had no clue where we were going but he was definite our excursion was going to end up being something sexual.

Finally, we arrived. After I parked my car, I walked around and opened the passenger side door to let Keldrick out of the car. I took him by the hand and let him down a long grassy path. As we walked he continued to ask me questions. I didn't respond I just held his hand calmly and continued to lead him down the path.

Life is all about paths. In most relationships one

5

person is usually following the other down the path of their own choosing. It's very rare to find a relationship, be it marriage or otherwise in which both people are leading each other down the same exact path.

My grandmother before she passed away used to always speak of marrying someone you're equally yoked with. It's a beautiful thing to be equally yoked, and of the same mind as the one you love... That is the epitome of true happiness, and it can lead to a long-lasting relationship. For what it's worth as Keldrick held my hand yesterday and walked with me... in that moment we were walking down the same path at the same time.

When we reached the place, I wanted to lead him to I stopped. I smiled down at the beautiful ground. I let go of his hand and bent down low to the ground and kissed it softly. Then I stood up, and turned around to remove K.C.'s blindfold. He looked around and obviously began to panic.

"Calm down baby." I told him as I tried to hold his hand. "What the hell are we doing here," he said pulling away from me, "What are you trying to do to me?"

"Keldrick calm down please," I said, "There's no need to panic." "Don't call me that," he said, "Nobody calls me Keldrick! And I am panicking. You're trying to kill me!"

"Whoa, whoa, whoa," I said, "Trying to kill you though? Why would I be trying to kill you? Do I have a reason to be trying to kill you? You must be doing something you have no business doing behind my back..."

"Who the hell are you talking to?" he asked me.

"You..." I said. "I'm a grown ass man," he told me,

"Do you think I have to tell you every move I make? Because if that's what you think, you got me and life fucked up!"

"Really, K.C...." I said. "Yeah *really* Cameron," he yelled at me, "You know what, you're starting to sound like somebody." "I'm starting to sound like who K.C.?" I asked. "Don't worry about it!" he growled back.

"Baby," I said, "All I'm saying is, if we're together I should at least have an idea what you're doing when we're not around each other."

"Fine," he said, "Now stop jumping around and away from the real subject. Why the fuck did you blindfold me and bring me to this dirty old graveyard?"

I looked at him and waited for him to take it back. He stared back at me and didn't seem to ever even consider recanting his question.

I put my head down as the tears rushed my regretful eyes. I knew then he wasn't listening to me the other night when I was talking to him. I meant every word I said. My request to him was so real and important to me. My tears continued to shield me from him for that moment.

"Oh no," he said, "Baby... I'm so sorry." I looked up and he was staring at the grave and the tombstone in front of him.

"Is this..." he started.

"Yes," I said, "this is my father's grave. I told you I wanted to bring you here to..."

"To promise him I will always take care of you," he interjected, "I remember baby. I'm sorry I don't know how I forgot. It's just I thought you were trying to be freaky and spontaneous with this little journey and then you take the blindfold off and all I see is graves. I apologize to you Cameron."

Then I took him by the hand and walked with him to Daddy's headstone. He kneeled down with me and prayed. Then he promised Daddy he would never leave me, and that he would always love and protect me. I believed every word.

(One late night)

I knew K.C. wasn't even planning on coming back home tonight. I'm so tired of crying myself to sleep wearing his oversized clothes on those nights he doesn't come home.

When I'm alone I wear his shirts to sleep because the scent of his cologne lulls me to sleep like a baby, and I wear his pants to sleep because the small .22 he keeps in his back-left side pocket makes me feel protected. It's hard but I do eventually fall asleep once I fool myself into believing he's lying right behind me sound asleep.

I love K.C. but ignorance and denial had never been commonplace to me until I met him. It has to stop, so tonight when he slipped out to "go wash the car," I followed him.

He stopped at the McDonald's on Sandlake Road first. I waited in the side parking lot where he couldn't see me as he went through the drive-thru line.

It felt like I was waiting for an hour for this dude to get the two-cheese burger meal, a large fry, and a large coke to drink. I'm sure that's what he ordered, that's what he always orders from McDonald's. Yeah, K.C. doesn't particularly like variety he's comfortable doing the same things over and over again. My man is insanity in its purest form.

Next, he drove to the Wal-Mart on S. John Young Parkway. I waited outside in the parking lot for the better part of thirty minutes.

While he was inside, I text his cell phone and asked what he was doing. At first, he didn't respond at all.

He finally texted me back as he was walking out of the store and said he couldn't find a car wash that was still open.

As he walked out of Wal-Mart he had a huge box of Pull Ups, and several plastic bags filled with groceries. He undoubtedly bought all of these things with my damn bank card.

After putting it all in the backseat of my other car, that I have been letting him use, K.C. jumped in the driver's seat and drove off.

I continued to follow his black ass until he pulled up to the Vintage Lakes apartment homes. He parked quickly and then disappeared inside an upstairs apartment with all the items he purchased at Wal-Mart.

I parked across the parking lot from the apartment so I could watch the door. I stayed up all night, until I finally lost track of time.

(7 hours later)

There he is finally. Cameron sees her man coming out of the upstairs apartment. She believes in him one last time… maybe it's his cousin's place or an old friend from high school.

But all hope and belief dies when a short thick light skinned

female follows him a couple of steps out of the doorway. Cameron's eyes double in size as she witnesses the ease in his untrustworthy swagger.

K.C. turns around, hugs the light skinned lady and kisses her ever so softly on the forehead. Cameron tries to read what his perfect deceitful lips are saying. ***"I love you boo. You make me want to be who you need me to be"***. The exact words he told Cameron not long ago.

The warm tears start to rush from Cameron's eyes down her beautiful black face. Jazemene walks out of the door and hugs K.C.'s legs from behind. K.C. turns around, picks her up high in the air, and then kisses her on the lips before giving the child to the lady. He kisses them both one more time and then heads down the stairs to leave.

Cam shakes her pounding head as she realizes Jazemene must be K.C.'s daughter, not his niece. He lied.

After the light skinned lady and Jazemene disappear inside the apartment, K.C. begins his descent down the stairs.

As Cameron watches him joyfully prance down the stairs like a sick fairy, everything inside her begins to shatter. Her heart is turning a deep, hard, shade of black.

At the bottom of the steps, K.C. reaches down into his bright blue sweat pants and snatches an old stale condom off and throws it in the nearby bushes.

Cam almost throws up inside her mouth at the sick consistency of this man's disrespectful behavior. As much as Cameron loves K.C. she hates him so much more right now, and she truly believes she always will.

Cameron opens her door and painfully turns her small body sideways to exit her car. K.C. is still smiling in light skin bliss, ecstasy, and ignorance as if Cameron's love never even existed. In Cameron's back pocket is a tiny twenty-two caliber handgun.

As she approaches him, she knows she's about to break the law and probably his face. But that's ok right, because he broke her heart.

So that justifies everything she plans to unleash on him now. As
K.C. unlocks the car, he can feel someone behind him but he's too scared to turn around.

In the reflection of the dirty car window he sees who it is. He turns around quickly now, buck-eyed like a deer caught in headlights. Before Cam's eyes his face appears to transform, he looks so demonic to her.

He doesn't speak; he just stares in frightened amazement. He's trying to figure out if this is some kind of sick set up or just a terrible coincidence. She's crying slowly now and her face appears to be lifeless.

As two tears slowly cascade down her pain stricken face, everything in her, all the power she ever had is all manifested in one tiny arm and one tiny hand as she slaps him as hard as she possibly can.

She's not even looking at him now she's looking straight through him. Cam wipes her face one time, then she looks deeply in his eyes and finally she speaks.

"Let me smell your breath." She demands. K.C. doesn't respond. "Oh, so now you're deaf huh?" Cam continues.

"Boy you must be out of your damn mind," Cam says with a sadistic smile on her tear stained face, "I saved your life K.C... You had nothing without me; I saved you from your damn self. Or at least I thought I did. But noooo... you don't give a damn about any of that shit, because to you I'm just another piece of *ass*, another short phase in your pitiful life. I'm just another random chick."

Stepping closer to him Cam says, "***Now lemme smell your breath***.
Open your mouth K.C..."

He's still silent. Pushing her way past him Cam finds a small blue plastic bag underneath the driver's seat of the car containing a tooth brush and a tube of toothpaste.

The same kind of bag he used to keep in the same exact spot in his car, when he used to come spend the night at Cam's house before he moved in with her.

This was before his car got repossessed of course. Cam snatches the blue bag out of the car and flings it wildly across the parking lot. "Let me smell your breath Keldrick!" she exclaims pulling the small gun out of her back pocket.

"Wait, Cam. Please, don't do this." He speaks. The foul smell of his hot breath, still lingering in her heartbroken nostrils tells Cam everything she needs to know.

Chapter 2
Save Me from Myself

The Vintage Lakes apartment homes at Lake
Orlando are not the fanciest apartments the city has to
offer, but a home is a home.
It's not so bad really. The apartment complex as a whole is
very beautiful and the residents do have access to several
lakes on the property.

Lake Orlando, the largest of the resident lakes is 175
acres. It's easily big enough for just about any water
activities you can imagine. Other than the country club,
and the lakes, the best thing about the
Vintage Lakes apartment homes is the fact that
downtown Orlando is less than ten miles away from the
property.

All in all, Vintage Lakes is not perfect, but it's good
enough for a young family to find itself, and begin
building a life together on its more than safe property.

(Inside apartment 210
a tall dark skinned man is sitting alone)
(K.C.)

Another day stuck inside the filthy prison of my own
mind. I've been out of prison for two years now and I still
don't feel free. My name is Keldrick Jermaine Cole, but

everybody calls me K.C. for short. I'm twenty-five years old and completely lost.

It is so hard to even try to pick up the pieces of a life that's always been broken anyway. My daughter Jazemene doesn't respect me and it used to be very awkward every time I was with her.

It's getting better with time, but I still feel like something is missing. Her mother, Whitney is a very good woman. She cooks, cleans, and works two jobs to take care of me, and my baby.

I do what I can to help out, but it's rough because I never had a real job before. In high school, I was the star player on the football team, and everybody expected me to go pro.

After my injury though, everybody's big hopes for me, and all my own dreams died instantly. I even dropped out of school. No matter what, my high school sweetheart, Ms. Whitney Powell never left my side.

She's always there to cater to my every need and desire. Whitney is so good at this; she's a hardworking woman, a Christian, a good mom, and she would make any man a great wife.

All she's ever wanted was me. I don't have to do anything. She takes care of me like I'm her king.

I wonder though sometimes, if maybe my fantastic perception of Whitney is all just a fantasy. When you've been through extremely tragic things in life, I guess it becomes easy to want all the seemingly great things that appear in your life to be real and lasting.

Whitney is that real thing for me. I know full well that I have the potential to be a very good man, and I believe she deserves the man that I can become. Likewise, my daughter Jazemene deserves the wonderful father, provider, and protector I could be.

I never really got to know my dad that well, but whoever my father's, father was he grew up in a time when men took care of their women, and their children. Somewhere along the way that rule, and that chain was broken.

So many women today grew up watching their mothers take care of grown ass men, so likewise the younger women follow suit. I don't want to be one of those men.

In the same respect, I refuse to let my baby girl grow up with that mindset. I'm going to train her to love herself first. I want her to know, once she is of age that there is absolutely nothing wrong with wanting to be with a man, but I don't want her to ever feel like she can't survive without one. Daddy will always be there to supplement her wherever she's lacking.

Whomever my wife ends up being, I don't want her to have to settle for less. I want to be her man; her friend, her rock, her everything. But it's so hard to do the right thing, especially when you've never seen anybody else do it.

Whit knows we're not together, but she'd much rather have me here living with her, than to not be with me at all.

"Daddy." a tiny voice squeals from behind the La-Z-Boy chair. "Yes princess." K.C. replies. "What you doing…" she asks in a cute little sing-song voice.

"Oh, daddy's just sitting here thinking baby…"

"Thinking about what Daddy?" she asks stepping around to the front of the chair to face him.

"Life, baby girl…" he playfully picks his beautiful

15

daughter up in his dark masculine arms and hugs her tightly. K.C. blows into her tiny belly button to tickle her.

They both laugh happily. "Daddy…" Jazemene says lying in his arms as he rocks her back and forth.

"Yes Jazemene?" K.C. replies. "Do you love my mommy?" she says.

"Of course, I do," he tells her, "Do you know why?"

"Why…" she asks. "Because," he kisses her on her tiny forehead, "Your mommy is gorgeous… *just like you.*"

Jazemene smiles happily. Then she closes her eyes, and continues to rock safely, in her father's loving arms.

As K.C. watches his tiny daughter rocking back and forth he's more than intrigued by how comfortable and protected she seems to feel in his care.

It wasn't easy getting his daughter used to being around him on a regular basis at first, but this is a beautiful contrast that makes his big heart smile.

He remembers when he was a kid, and how much he wishes he could have had a constant adult comfort zone similar to what he has become for Jazemene. A loving thoughtful mother, or at least and overbearing overprotective father. Keldrick Cole had neither.

(Date Night)
(K.C.)

I love my daughter but it's always good to get a night out with her mother whenever we can find a good sitter.

Whitney paid her little sister Audrey to watch Jazemene for the night, because she wanted me to take her out to eat. When I walked in our room, she had my outfit already laid out for me, ironed perfectly.

I was trying not to linger in the moment too long because we were already late so I started putting my clothes on. After I was fully dressed I sprayed on some of the YSL cologne Whitney bought me for my last birthday.

I don't know if it's the real YSL fragrance or not, but I don't really care. My baby bought it for me, because she wanted me to smell good, and I do. I'm not one of those people that have to spend thousands of dollars on ridiculous things that really don't matter.

Even if I was rich, I like to think I would still keep things reasonably simple. These Prada shoes she bought me are the definition of style and comfort, but they're a little much for my taste.

Before leaving the room, I stopped to check myself out in our full body mirror.

"Damn!" I looked pretty good. *She bought me a baby blue polo shirt; khaki corduroy pants, and a matching Prada belt, to go with the light brown Prada shoes.*

In my left pocket, I found a hundred-dollar bill. This didn't surprise me though because she does this every time we go out, so I can at least feel like I'm paying for the evening myself.

We decided to go to her favorite restaurant, the Bahama Breeze on International Drive. The drive there was quiet at first, but once we got close she tried to break the ice. I guess it was a little too quiet in the car. I was lost in my own thoughts so deeply that I had forgotten to cut the car radio on.

"Have you been putting in those job apps I brought

home to you baby?" she asked. "No point." I replied. "And why is that?" she asked with seemingly genuine concern. "I'm an ex-felon baby," I told her, "If people don't absolutely need employees, they are not going to even consider hiring me."

I parked the car near the front door of the restaurant, and then I hopped out and made it around to her door to let her out. Hand in hand we made our way to the front of the busy seafood joint. We walked in and were immediately greeted by a charming young white hostess.

As she led us to our table, I was walking behind Whitney and I couldn't help but notice how she's getting more gorgeous year after year.
She walks so eloquently, like a real queen. Her body is flawless, she's not skinny but she's nowhere near fat.

The way, her behind moves in her dresses as she walks is absolutely intoxicating. My baby had on a sheer pink lace summer dress with pretty green floral print all over it. Her toes and finger nails were painted the same shade of green. Pink and green, have been her two favorite colors ever since she became a member of the Alpha Kappa Alpha Sorority Incorporated.

It smells so good in the Bahama Breeze. Whitney and I both really love seafood. Looking around me, none of the other couples I saw that night seemed to be happy; they just looked like their being there was just a part of a scheduled routine. I hope Whit and I never get like that.

"Good evening and welcome to Bahama Breeze," our server said
as she approached our table, "my name is Cam and I'll be

your waitress for the evening."

Our server was a gorgeous little dark-skinned woman. Her voice was soft and genuine. She's very well spoken but I could tell she was originally from the hood, like me.

Her face was absolutely angelic like a perfect black china doll. I don't know if her hair, her eyelashes, or her nails were real, but it doesn't even matter they all look damn good on her. I'd tried hard not to stare at Cam, because I know how jealous Whitney can get. The last thing I wanted was for her to cause a big ignorant scene.

"Baby, I have to pee. I'll be right back." Whitney said as she left the table quickly. While Whitney was in the bathroom, I slipped Cam an old business card and asked her to give me a call.

She was hesitant at first, and then she seemed to get lost just as in my eyes as I was in hers. She eventually agreed to call me. I must admit she's not my usual type, I'm already dark skinned myself so I usually only date light skinned women like Whitney. But there's something very different about Cam, and was gonna find out what it was. As Whitney made her way back to the table and sat down, Cam and I played everything off real smooth. Whit never had a clue about what happened. After we finished eating, we paid, Cam gave me the change and we left.

Lord knows I didn't want to leave yet, because I didn't know if I would ever see my beautiful thoughtful waitress again. But it was necessary that Whit and I leave before I ended up openly disrespecting her with all the attention I could feel myself giving to Cameron. Before I left the table I slid a crisp twenty-dollar bill underneath my empty wine glass for Cam, hoping that it would entice her a little bit more to make that call.

I stayed up late that night expecting at least a simple greeting text. Then I woke up early that next morning and my cute waitress had still not reached out to me.

After about five days I decided she wasn't going to call at all. Of course, I was racking my brain trying to give her all kinds of excuses as to why she had not called or texted me.

Like maybe she was married, or maybe she was a lesbian, or even easier maybe she just lost my card. No matter how many grand notions I came up with in my mind, nothing ever took her completely off my mind.

This feeling was significant to me because I usually forget about females rather quickly; whether I've slept with them, dated them, or just met them in passing.

It took her a full seven-day week to call me, but I was so glad when she finally did. When we spoke, she admitted to me that she never stopped thinking about me since that first night.

She swore the only reason she waited as long as she did to contact me was because she didn't want to come off as desperate. I told her I would never had looked at her as being desperate, hell I was the one who pursued her.

After that initial conversation, we started texting each other throughout each day. Our text conversations always flowed so easily just like our initial phone call.

Cam just seemed like a natural fit in my life, she just felt necessary. I wasn't sure exactly what her purpose was going to be in my life, but she definitely felt necessary.

After a couple weeks, I started spending the night with Cam a couple nights out of the week. I always carried my little overnight survival kit with me; it consists of a small blue plastic bag containing a toothbrush and a tube of toothpaste.

Cam claims she's a virgin so I never even tried to have sex with her. I mean of course in today's society it's kind of farfetched to believe in twenty-three-year-old virgins.

But for some reason, I believe everything this girl tells me. Cam might be the one to change my world. Life with Whitney isn't bad but it has become redundant to put it mildly.

I don't want to leave or hurt Whitney and our daughter Jazemene so I'm taking my time before making any definite decisions.

But I must admit being with Cam, who is a few years younger than Whitney, has been very refreshing. There are so many things we talk about, and deal with that I know how to handle because I've been there and lived it all before with Whitney.

I remember I asked Cameron one time, why she's waited so long to have sex. She looked me in my eyes and told me she wanted her first time to be perfect, and with the perfect man.

She told me not to laugh at her, but in her mind her first time, will happen late one night after the perfect movie/dinner date.

The man would pick her up from home dressed exquisitely and take her to see a good movie. Then afterwards, they would go downtown for a candlelit dinner.

Once the dinner was over, he would take her home and run her a hot bubble bath with pink and red rose petals floating calmly in the steamy water.

The brim of the tub would be laced all around with scented candles. After her relaxing bubble bath, she would make her way to the bedroom and climb up in the bed next to him.

She said she knew it was probably corny, but the only music she could ever imagine playing in the background during her first sexual experience was, "First Time" by IMX. I don't know if she realized it, but I was paying close attention to everything she told me that night, but then again, I always do. I love her lips and her voice, it's very hard for me to miss anything she says to, or around me.

Weeks later I took Cameron to the movies to see, "Onyx Cielo" 1 (The Tree of Transformation). It was really inspiring. I feel myself growing and changing the more I'm with this woman.

Before, I wouldn't have even considered watching a fantasy movie, and I definitely wouldn't have paid to see one. But Cam said this entire series was written by De'Lure, a black man.

That fact alone let me know that this movie wasn't going to be anything like "Harry Potter," or the "Twilight" series. After listening to her tell me about the book, I had to see the movie. "Onyx Cielo" is about a little girl named Onyx.

Onyx is the only black girl on her planet. The planet Delure, where she lives, is fueled by an ancient prophecy that says she is the Chosen One. The prophecy basically says Onyx and her friends, the Children of the Light, are the only ones who can save the planet from the Evil Ones.

In the movie, Onyx, a.k.a. the Beautiful One fights

strange creatures as she searches for the forbidden fruit of the Tree of Transformation, and also the truth about her biological parents.

"So, how'd you like the movie baby?" Cameron asks, as she steps out of the bathroom into the bedroom wearing nothing but some panties and one of K.C.'s oversized T-shirts. Peeping from behind his book K.C. responds, "Girl that had to be one of the best movies I have ever seen. That man's imagination is out of this world. I mean
look at me. I'm even reading the book; I ain't read a book since like... the 10th grade."

With a satisfied grin on her face Cameron pulls the covers back so she can slide into the bed next to her man.

"I'm glad you enjoyed it," she smiles in pure satisfaction, "the book is even better than the movie. And thanks for my candle lit bubble bath baby." "You're welcome Cameron, I wonder when "Onyx Cielo" book two will be released." he says.

Climbing on top of him, grabbing the book from him, and placing it on the table beside the bed Cam says, "I don't know, but right about now I need you to take me on a journey of my own... for the very first time."

"Say what," K.C. asks, "are you sure you're serious baby?" Cameron doesn't respond to the question, but from the look in her eyes he knows she's ready.

So, he leans over and plugs his phone up to the speakers next to the bed and presses play. The soothing scintillating sounds of Marques Houston's voice come blasting through the speakers, *"La la la la la la...la la la la... la la la la la la la... See, normally a brother wouldn't talk about his first time... But I'll just be real*

23

with y'all and say what's on my mind."

Cameron giggles lightly as he rolls over on top, and lays her on her back softly. Biting playfully on his left ear lobe, she whispers, "That's my song... baby you remembered."

"Girl I could never forget anything you say." he confesses. The deep sensual sounds of his baritone voice vibrate her eardrums perfectly as they send shocking chills down her anxious spine.

Oh my God she smells so sweet. Her intoxicating aroma is obviously a concoction of the bath oils and soaps I laid out for her mixed with the scent of the pure Amberella candles I placed around the tub. We made sweet love all night long...

Last month Cam enrolled me in some online classes so that I can finally get my G.E.D. She also gave me the key to her second car, a key to her house, and she even got me some part time work with her uncle installing tile floors.

Cameron Jiles is a God send, my own personal guardian angel. I violated my probation by not reporting on time, because I didn't want to ask Cam or Whit for the money to pay my P.O. So, he had me locked up for two weeks.

The two weeks I was gone Whit came to visit me three times, and she kept money on my books so I could eat, just like she did the entire time I was in prison. When I got out I didn't want to tell Cam where I had been because I was afraid she'd give up on me.

So, I allowed her to believe I'd been out running the streets hustling, because in my mind that sounds better than I was locked up again. I spent that first night with

Whit, because I couldn't face Cam yet.

Before I went to sleep I texted Cam, and said, "I love you boo, you still make me want to be who you need me to be." Cam didn't text back. Part of me wanted to call her or just continue to text her until she responded, but I didn't.

Damn, is it morning already? Yeah, it must be, because Whit's already gone to work, and Jazemene must be at daycare because this apartment is way too quiet. It's storming pretty bad outside too.

(K.C.'s phone vibrates)

It's a text from Cam. It reads, "Good morning boo, I hope you have a great day even in the mist of the rain."

K.C. is certain Cam meant to say, "In the midst of the rain," but either way it just felt good to know she still cares. He texts her back, "Damn I miss you girl, and I must admit that even in the *mist,* and the *midst* of the rain I could never get as wet as your body gets when I'm inside you... lol."

I gotta find a way to leave Whit without her putting me on child support, but I know if she ever sees me out with Cam that's exactly what she's gonna do.

(Weeks later)
(Cam's house)

"Baby..." Cam walks into the bedroom dressed nicely carrying a long silk black headscarf in her left hand.

"Wassup baby," K.C. replies laughing at the television, "Cam, have you ever seen this old episode of

25

Good Times?" "I think so," Cam sits next to him on the edge of the bed in front of the T.V., "Which one is this?"

"It's the episode," K.C. starts, "When J.J. is trying to win the art contest. And he painted the picture of Black Jesus…"

"Oh yeah," Cam laughs aloud, "And his Mama didn't know J.J. modeled Black Jesus after *Ned the wino…*"

"Yeah," K.C. laughs with her, "But they kept the painting hung up in the apartment for a while anyways, because James Sr. thought it was bringing the family good luck." "Yeah this is one of my favorite episodes of *Good Times*." Cam admits.

"I'm glad I don't need a good luck charm." K.C. tells her. "And why is that?" Cam asks staring at him curiously. "Who needs luck when they have a blessing like you in their lives," Kel asks her, "I'm in love with my biggest blessing ever. I can't ask for much more than that."

"Awe," Cam stands up to kiss him, "That's the sweetest thing I ever heard baby…" "It's true." K.C. tells her.

"Okay," Cam pats his shoulder, "Now turn around so I can blindfold you."

"Wait," Kel looks at her with concern, "What the hell? How do you just segue into some weird shit like that?"

"Keldrick, would you just turn around so I can blindfold you please." Cam repeats with a sexy smile.

Kel can see that glow in her eyes and he knows now that whatever his girlfriend has in mind can only end well for him. "You don't have to blindfold me to…" he starts.

"I want to." Cam flashes a genuine smile as she turns

his body around and blindfolds him tightly. "Well damn you think it's tight enough?" Kel says reaching up to try to adjust the blindfold.

"Stop it," Cam playfully slaps his hands away from the blindfold, "No peeking." "Yes ma'am." Kel replies with a smile of his own. K.C. can tell from the way her voice sounds she has her back turned to him now. He reaches out in front of him and begins caressing her firm bottom.

"Mmmm," she moans as she reaches forward to turn off the T.V., "You like that Daddy…" "I do." he replies. "I bet." she says turning around to face him. Kel pulls her into his powerful arms. Cam bends down and kisses him softly.

"Follow me." she takes him by the hand. "Slow down baby," K.C. insists, "I can't see remember."

"I got you boy," she smiles back at him, "Trust me." Cam walks

K.C. outside to her car and helps him into the passenger seat and closes his door. Then she jumps in the driver's side, cranks up, and drives off.

"Where are we going Cameron?" he asks. She doesn't respond. "Baby," Kel says, "You know we could have done whatever you're trying to do back at the house." Cam turns the radio up just a little to drown out his questions.

"Cam," he says, "Cam, I know you hear me."

The car stops twenty minutes later. Cam walks around and opens the passenger side door to let Keldrick out of the car. She takes him by the hand and begins to lead him down a long grassy path.

As they reach the place Cam wanted to bring him to,

she stops walking. Cam looks at Kel and then she smiles down at the ground. Cam lets go of Kel's sweaty hand and bends down low to kiss the ground. Then she stands up, and turns around to gently remove the blindfold. Kel looks around and begins to panic instantly.

"Calm down baby." Cam tries to hold his hand. "What the hell are we doing here," Kel asks pulling his hand away from her, "What are you trying to do to me?"

"Keldrick calm down please," Cam says, "There's no need to panic." "Don't call me that," K.C. demands, "Nobody calls me Keldrick! And I am panicking. You're trying to kill me!"

"Whoa, whoa, whoa," Cam raises calming hands, "Trying to kill you though? Why would I be trying to kill you? Do I have a reason to be trying to kill you? You must be doing something you have no business doing behind my back."

"Who the hell are you talking to?" K.C. asks. "You..." Cam replies.

"I'm a grown ass man," he assures her, "Do you think I have to tell you every move I make? Because if that's what you think, you got me and life fucked up!"

"Really K.C..." she replies. "Yeah *really* Cameron," he screams, "You know what, you're starting to sound like somebody."

"I'm starting to sound like who K.C.?" she asks. "Don't worry about it!" he growls.

"Baby," Cam says, "All I'm saying is, if we're together I should at least have an idea what you're doing when we're not around each other."

"Fine," he says, "Now stop jumping around and away from the real subject. Why the fuck did you blindfold me and bring me to this dirty old graveyard?"

Cam looks at K.C. She's waiting for something but he clearly doesn't know what. He just continues to stare back at her still lost and confused.

Cam looks defeated. She slowly drops her tired head and begins to cry.

K.C. feels terrible now. He still doesn't know why he's here, but whatever the reason is, it's obviously important to the woman he loves. Kel begins to look around himself for a clue. Directly in front
of him Kel notices the large letters at the top of the tombstone. "Jiles..." he whispers.

"Oh no," he says, "Baby... I'm so sorry." Cam looks up with her puffy face covered in regretful tears.

"Is this..." Kel starts. "Yes, this is my father's grave," Cam tells him, "I told you I wanted to bring you here to..."

"To promise him I will always take care of you," Kel interjects, "I remember baby. I'm sorry I don't know how I forgot. It's just I thought you were trying to be freaky and spontaneous with this little journey and then you take the blindfold off and all I see is graves. I apologize to you Cameron."

Down on his knees on the large grave plot Kel listens to Cam pray. After she finishes her prayer she looks at her man. Kel nods.

"Mr. Jiles," he says looking directly at the beautiful gray tombstone, "Sir, I am not a perfect, or even a good man. But I do love your daughter. I swear to you that I will always do my best to protect her heart, body and soul from the world. Thank you, sir for blessing the world with this stunning example of a young, beautiful, strong, black woman."

Kel looks over at Cam. She's still staring at him with new tears in her eyes. "I uh," Kel stutters, "Baby, I don't know what to say…"

"Keldrick… that was perfect." she cries wrapping her arms around his strong body.

(Months later)
(K.C.)

I left Cam's house last night and came home to sleep with Whit because she started back threatening to put me on child support. I don't have the thousands of dollars of back child support I would owe and I'm not trying to get locked up again.

So, I did what I had to do to stay free. I told Cam I was leaving to go wash the car or some lie like that, and then I came home late last night to sleep with Whitney.

I know it's wrong but I still have sex with Whitney ultimately because I don't want her to feel unattractive, and then allow her insecurities to affect our daughter. I want my daughter to always see me adore her mother, so hopefully that's the type of man she'll seek one day to be in her life.

I realize my baby's still a baby, but you'd be surprised at how early kids pick up on the traits and habits that will direct their adult lives. I'm very conscious of this, so until I find a better solution, I'm gonna keep doing what I'm doing.

When I got to Whit's apartment, I walked in and she looked kind of nervous like she had done something wrong, but I had other things on my mind so I didn't bring it up.

I gave Whit the business for about two hours straight. Cow girl, missionary, doggy, froggy, and monkey style... That last one I swear I think we created it just last night.

This morning I know Whit would love to just sleep in together, but I gotta get back to Cam's crib to get my paperwork to go take my G.E.D. test today.

"I gotta go baby, I'll be back tonight." K.C. says unable to look Whit in her eyes as he stands up and begins putting his clothes on from the night before to leave.

"No, you won't Keldrick," she says, "can you please stop lying to me? We've been through way too much. Whenever you're lying to me you can't look me in my eyes. Why is it so easy for you to lie to me?"

With that said, Whitney storms into the bathroom, slamming the door shut behind her. Whitney hears K.C. making his way out of the front door. She leaves the bathroom and follows him outside.

He turns around, kisses her on the forehead softly and says," I love you boo. You make me want to be who you need me to be."

Jazemene walks out of the door and hugs her daddy's legs from behind. K.C. turns around picks her up high in the air and then kisses her before putting her safely in her mother's arms. He kisses Whit and Jazemene one more time and then heads down the stairs to leave.

Man, I gotta hurry up and get to Cam's house, the G.E.D. test starts in 20 minutes. Damn I forgot to take this damn condom off. I hope nobody's looking...

K.C. throws the condom in the bushes near the bottom of the stairs and heads towards Cam's spare car. A few footsteps later he makes it to the car. Looking in the reflection of the car window, he can see Cam standing right behind him.

Chapter 3
Holding On

S ometimes the brightest sunniest days can feel dark and gloomy. It's a shame how some people can without conscious destroy the light inside of other people. Spiraling into a deep lonely depression is a very frightening thing. She decided long ago that Cupid's pointy and blind arrows are painful and unnecessary.

(An attractive light-skinned woman is walking down a busy sidewalk talking to herself about her man.)

"Why me Lord? Why me? I just don't understand. As obedient as I am, how did I end up like this? When did I become one of those sad and desperate women that would do anything just to have a man around? I love Keldrick more than I love myself, more than I love my child. And I know that's wrong, but at least I can admit it, and there are a lot of other women just like me. Lord, as many times as you've allowed him to be stripped away from my life, how does he always find his way back in. And I know I'm not supposed to question you Lord, but I can't help it, and I just keep holding on, and holding on... hoping and praying that one day maybe he will understand that I'm all he will ever need. Most people don't know how intelligent he is

because he hides it so well. And I help hide his intellect as well because I'm afraid of losing him. If he becomes successful and self-sufficient, he won't need me anymore. I'm the mother of his child. I protect him and care for him when nobody else will. I'm so tired of crying and my migraines have become unbearable. Men just don't get it. Finding a good woman is something they should be proud of, something they should cherish forever. I'm still young but I know I'm getting older and my body is changing. He doesn't have to look at me twice anymore when I walk by. Hell, most times he doesn't even look once, but it's okay. I'm not gonna cry anymore. And I can't just die because the only man I've ever loved doesn't love me anymore. I have to be strong for my baby. Jazemene has to be my main focus. I have to make sure that when she's of age, she doesn't make the mistake of talking to little boys that are gonna grow up into sorry men just like her father. K.C. is just…"

Whitney accidentally bumps into an attractive young light skinned guy as she's talking to herself. "I'm so sorry." Whitney acknowledges that she's at fault for their collision. Bending down in unison with the young man to pick up her belongings she dropped,

Whit continues to mumble to herself. As she stands back up, she notices the young man is laughing as he hands her the portion of her belongings that he picked up for her.

"Thank you," Whitney begins, "but what's so funny?" she asks. Realizing that his laughter must appear rude he apologizes. "Oh

I'm sorry ma'am. I wasn't laughing at you, but whoever K.C. is, he's a very lucky man." he says.

"Wait… How do you know K.C.?" Whitney asks

wrinkling her eyebrows with her head tilted to the side.

Holding his head down, the young man begins to laugh to himself again. Now with his hands positioned behind his back he looks back at Whitney.

"No ma'am. I don't know K.C.," he explains, "but you did just mumble his name like five times in the past seven seconds."

As the two of them enjoy a good laugh together, Whitney realizes the young man is very handsome. He stands about 5'8, he's built like an athlete, and his dark well-kept dreads are pulled up in a winding pony tail.

At the ends of his dreads that are protruding from his perfect ponytail Whit can see the tips of his locks are bright blond. He's covered in beautiful artistic tattoos, and judging from the tight workout shirt, and basketball shorts he's wearing, she figures he must have just left the gym.

"It's very nice to meet you my name is Love, and what's yours?" the young man smiles taking her tiny yellow hand in his.

Her beautiful face begins to glow. "My name is Whitney," she smiles back at him, "But Love, is that like... your real name?"

"Well, my name is Lance Orlandis Vinson," he admits, "so people usually call me Love for short. But you can call me Lance, or Orlandis, or hell girl, you can call me whatever you want to."

"No, I like Love..." She tells him focusing closely on his soothing green eyes.

"I just wish it liked me back." she mumbles to herself looking away sadly. Completely perplexed by her last comment, Love is at a loss for words. "Um, are you talking to yourself again or… am I missing something?"

"What did I say this time?" Whitney asks snapping out of her private mental moment. "Well," Love says with one hand across his lean stomach, and the other inquisitively holding his chin, "you just said you wished Love liked you back. And I mean you seem cool Whitney, but I don't even know you."

"I said that out loud?" she asks as her soft yellow cheeks turn bright red,

"Yeah, you did." Love smiles trying to hide his confusion. Whit leans forward to grab his arm softly as she explains herself, "I wasn't talking about you Love. I was talking about true love. A real passionate emotional attachment, that lasts forever. The type that no man, no woman, no hater… can ever sever." "Damn girl was that a poem? It was kinda nice…" Love laughs to himself.

"Well thanks I guess," she smiles, "but it wasn't a poem… just something every girl dreams of at some point in her life." Love is observing her body language very closely. "Oh, I see," Love finally speaks, "your man ain't acting right…" With a comforting smile on his face, Love holds his chiseled arms out to the prettiest woman he has seen in a while.

"Come here," he beckons for her, "You look like you need a hug boo. Can I give you a hug Whitney…?"

She hesitates briefly, then steps forward into his chiseled arms and body. They're both surprised by how comfortable they feel together.

Her body feels so soft in his hands, and she smells delicious. His well-trimmed goatee tickles her forehead as she tries to reposition herself to look up into his emerald eyes.

The short light skinned woman is breathless as she allows herself to be showered in the raw power of his pure emerald gaze.

In her mind Whitney hopes Love never lets her go, but the moment is halted as K.C.'s dark, 6'4 body frame forces its way into her thoughts.

Pulling away from him suddenly, and simultaneously looking at her rose gold Michael Kors watch Whitney says, "Oh my God we've been standing here talking for almost fifteen minutes. I gotta go I'm sorry."

"Wait Whit, don't leave like that girl," he says, holding his mouth to the side in disappointment, "we were having a good… comfortable conversation."

Looking back at his handsome face, she shakes her head, "Boy I gotta go I'm married. Well I'm not married, but if I ever want to be I gotta go *now.* You are way too fine to be playing with, you're gonna get me in trouble."

Still not accepting defeat, and realizing from her conflicting body language she doesn't really want to leave, Love steps towards her. Taking her tiny hand in his for the second time he says, "You don't want to leave yet, I can tell. Look Whitney, if that man is not already the man you want, you can't mold him or make him be that. That's the problem with so many women they treat men like science experiments. Like, let me take this one and mix him with a little bit of this, and a little bit of that. Then hopefully in the end he will be what I want him to be."

"I'm sorry, here's my card," she says reaching in her pocket, "I'll be a lawyer soon, so if you're ever in need of any legal advice give me a call. It was nice meeting you, Love." Whitney walks away and doesn't look back.

(Date Night)

I paid my little sister Audrey to watch Jazemene for the night, because I want to go out to eat. Stepping into her closet, Whitney tries
to decide what she wants K.C. to wear to tonight. Half of the clothing in this closet he's never even worn before. It's like he doesn't even notice when I buy him things anymore. Okay, let's start with the shoes. He's never worn these light brown Prada shoes before. Let's do these with this pair of khaki corduroy pants, and this baby blue polo shirt. Because I know my baby loves blue.

I ironed everything, and laid it all out on the bed for him. In his left pants pocket, I put a hundred-dollar bill. I always do this anytime we go out, so he can pay for the evening himself. I want my man to feel like he's important, because he is… to me.

That was two hours ago when I laid his clothes out, but he's still not home.

Looking at her cell phone Whitney thinks to herself, *I wonder what Love is doing right now.* The door opens.

"Sorry I'm late baby," K.C. says as he walks in quickly and kisses Whitney on the forehead, "I got your text message. Let me take   a quick shower then we can go eat wherever you want. As he reemerges from the room thirty minutes later, Whitney can tell K.C. is feeling himself.

"Damn! You look good baby." she says. "And you look gorgeous Love." he responds. Whit grabs her cell phone swiftly. ***"Love...* Wait, what are you talking about Keldrick?"** Whitney asks *Nope, no new text messages that he could have read in my phone while I was in the kitchen.*

Blushing bright red, she realizes her mistake, as she looks back at K.C., who is completely confused. "Oh, you mean me." she says.

"Of course, I mean you Whitney," he replies, "You know you're my one and only love. Are you feeling okay?"

"Yeah, I'm fine," she claims, "are you ready to go?" "Yeah let's ride," he responds.

We decided to come to our favorite restaurant, the Bahama Breeze on International Drive. Some short, ugly, black lady is our server.

"Good evening and welcome to Bahama Breeze," she says in a fake articulate voice, "my name is Cam and I'll be your waitress for the evening."

If I didn't know any better, I would say K.C. is checking this chick out right in front of my face. Hmm, he better watch himself because I'm looking for a reason to find "Love," in all the right places. Okay, that's it I'm going to test him.

"Baby, I have to pee. I'll be right back." Whitney excuses herself from the table. Standing near the back wall where the bathrooms are Whitney looks on as K.C. flirts openly with the server, and then hands her a business card.

Whit watches the two of them talk for several

minutes. Amazingly she keeps her cool instead of causing a scene as she has done many times before due to her raging jealousy.

After she walks back from the bathroom Whit sits back down at the table, and never mentions what she saw.

After we finished eating, he paid, and he left that bitch a twenty-dollar tip. Twenty dollars of my money!

For the next few weeks I noticed him doing a lot of extra texting. Then he started staying gone all night long. I'm not stupid I know what's going on. But I can't just put him out, because then I would really be alone. He's the father of my child, and one day he'll be my husband. I hope...

(6 months later)

I've been threatening to put K.C. on child support for three days straight. But obviously he doesn't care anymore, because he knows by now I'll never actually do it. But if I ever do get up the nerve to do it, he's going back to jail because he owes over four thousand dollars, in back child support. Maybe I don't need him. He hasn't even called me or text me in four days.

On late nights like this; when there's a light drizzle outside tapping at my bedroom window, and the moon is full and bright, every woman needs to be held and caressed in that special way. I figured out about a week ago that when I'm in that mood and K.C. is not around, I have other options. Hell, I can take care of myself.

"Ooh that feels so good," Whit moans, "Right there. Please don't ever stop." Whitney hears the front door open unexpectedly. She jumps up in a panic and quickly points towards the bathroom door. Then she hurriedly gathers up everything laid out on the bed and stashes it all in the top drawer of the dresser next to her bed.

As K.C. walks in she can tell he knows she was up to something, but from the look in his eyes he's so horny he doesn't even care right now.

For about 35 minutes that boy was an animal. After that he fell straight to sleep. Now that he's snoring loudly, I know he's in a deep sleep. So, if he stops snoring I'll know he's awake, but he usually doesn't wake back up until about nine in the morning.

With that assurance Whitney quietly slips on her pink silk robe, and creeps into the bathroom. Closing and locking the door behind her she quickly makes her way toward the shower.

Pulling the shower curtain all the way back slowly, I laid eyes on my light-skinned lover. He's standing here staring straight through to my soul. His emerald eyes are wide open, as he's obviously nervous because K.C. is right in the next room.

"Did you know he was coming?" Love asks.

"No." she responds admiring his perfect nude body from head to toe. Reaching up behind his head she begins to break the bands that are holding his dreads in place.

One by one the beautiful locks begin to fall down around his face, shoulders, and chest. Love shakes his dreads twice to reposition them. His eyes and his colorful tattoos appear fluorescent, from the glow of the bright

41

moonlight shinning in through the bathroom window.

Whit almost can't breathe as she revels at how perfectly his body is contoured. Stepping forward inside the tub, Love grabs her soft behind and pulls her close to him so he can kiss her soft pink lips.

Whitney is on the tips of her dainty well pedicured toes right at the edge of the tub. After the kiss is done, Love's raw sexual adrenalin is soaring through the roof.

Stepping back from her, Love slowly unties her silk robe. Then he pushes the robe off over her shoulders slowly, as her robe falls to the floor she's left in nothing but some cute pink boy short panties. With his gentle hands Love reaches around behind Whitney and pulls her closer so that he can carefully taste both of her almost perky breasts.

Her soft moans send instant shock waves through his young hard body. As Love sucks one of her breasts he gently squeezes the other. His technique is more than soothing to Whitney to say the least.

He's ready now. Love picks Whitney up as she wraps her legs around his waist. Then he walks her towards the bathroom sink.

After he sits her down on the edge of the long white sink, he gets down on his knees on the soft black rug at the foot of the sink. Looking up into her anxious eyes, Love is savoring every moment of her openness to him.

Pulling her panties aside he begins to taste her fully. Whitney arches her back slightly and leans her head back against the cold mirror.

Love continues to taste her as he explores her body

with his tongue flowing in a specific circular motion.

Biting her bottom lip in complete ecstasy, she closes her eyes tightly as she holds on to his soft dreads for dear life. With her tiny feet now on his shoulders, she begins to grind to the rhythm of his talented tongue.

After thirty minutes of rapid orgasms, Whitney leans forward towards Love. After eating her, in impressive fashion Love finds his neck beginning to feel sore.

As he stands up, he snatches Whitney off the sink, and turns her around facing the mirror. After wildly pulling her panties down to her ankles, he pushes her face down on the sink and enters her body hard from the back. After about 20 pumps he speaks, "this is how he did it right?"

"What baby? Who…" Whitney whispers. Continuing to go as hard as he possibly can Love speaks again, "K.C… I sat in this bathroom all night thinking about how I had to watch him do whatever he wanted to the woman I love."

"Oooh ooh ooh… Wait *baby*. You gone make me… screaaaam." she whispers passionately.

"I'm sorry you had to watch that… *I swear I'll make it up to you*, I promise." Whit tells him. "No need to apologize," Love moans continuing to drill her at the same pace, "what I'm saying is… Watching you with him… *turned me on.*"

Reminiscing on what he saw the night before Love gives her one last strong stroke. After a moment, he falls back on the soft black rug exhausted. As Whitney stands up straight, she feels the warm moisture running down her left leg.

Climbing on top of him Whitney kisses him passionately several times, before falling forward on his hard body. "I wish I could lay here with you forever..." she admits.

"I wish you could too baby." he replies. After the better part of twenty minutes Whit climbs off of his body and puts her panties and robe back on. Then she leaves him lying there on the floor as she makes her way back to the bed to lay with K.C.

The next morning K.C. stands up and begins putting his clothes on from the night before to leave. "I gotta go baby, I'll be back tonight." K.C. says unable to look Whit in her eyes.

"No, you won't Keldrick. Can you please stop lying to me? We've been through too much. Whenever you're lying to me you can't look me in my eyes. Why is it so easy for you to lie to me?" With that said Whitney storms in to the bathroom, slamming the door shut behind her. Once inside the bathroom, Whitney smiles at Love as she sees him asleep in the tub. K.C. makes his way out of the front door. Whitney leaves back out of the bathroom and quickly follows K.C. out of the front door to the apartment.

He turns around, kisses her on the forehead softly and says," I love you boo. You make me want to be who you need me to be." Then Jazemene walks out of the door and hugs her dad's legs from behind.

K.C. turns around, picks her up high in the air, and then kisses her before putting her safely in her mother's arms. He kisses Whit and Jazemene one more time and then heads down the stairs to leave.

After he leaves, Jazemene happily runs back to the T.V. to continue watching cartoons. Whitney closes and locks the door behind him, and then rushes back to the bathroom.

"Wake up baby, he's gone." Whitney whispers with her soft pink lips close to Love's ear.

Love opens his eyes. "Finally…" Love says as he yawns lazily. "Shut up boy." Whit says playfully.

"So now what round two?" Love asks sitting up in the tub with an anxious grin on his perfect yellow face.

Whitney takes him by the hand and leads him to her bed and they begin making sweet love all over again.

Love is digging as deeply inside of Whitney's body as he possibly can. His full intent is to legitimately take her away from K.C once and for all.

BANG! A loud gunshot rings out; Whitney feels as if her eardrums have been permanently damaged. She pushes Love off of her

quickly, and then she falls to the bedroom floor.

She feels like she's been shot, but there's no blood. Whitney crawls slowly towards her bedroom window. Love is watching every move his lover is making with obvious confusion.

With the little strength, she has left in her body Whit pulls herself up just high enough to look out of her window. What she sees takes her breath away. That little black bitch from the restaurant is standing over K.C.'s limp body holding a gun. Whit passes out cold.

Chapter 4

We're All Alone… Together

(Cam)

I didn't sleep much last night, lately I don't sleep much at all. The past eight days have felt like they were longer than my entire life. I can't sleep… I can't eat. All I do is smoke and drink. Alcohol and weed have become the only two things I can consume.

I woke up this morning and made a huge bowl of Apple Jacks cereal. I scrambled some eggs, made some French toast, and poured a tall glass of pure orange juice.

After I finished cooking, I cleaned the kitchen, washed the dishes, and set the table perfectly. I walked outside to get the newspaper and check the mailbox. When I walked back in, I set the newspaper right next to his plate.

Finally, I went into the bedroom to wake him up, and tell him his breakfast was ready. I stood there for a moment and fantasized about his perfect body lying there under the covers, and I smiled. Slowly I began pulling the covers down so I could see his strong black physique, and his dark handsome face.

But as the cover started to come down all I saw was pillows. I kept pulling the covers, down, down, down. But there was nothing there but pillows. I fell down on my knees still clinging to the cover, my face covered in tears.

Reality was setting in again. I must have lined those

pillows up last night and covered them up with blankets. I guess I do this every night to pretend that he's still here. But he's not, he's gone. It's my fault but it was a mistake. It wasn't supposed to happen like that. It wasn't supposed to happen at all.

All I did was, confront him. I just wanted to scare him and maybe make him feel at least some of the pain I felt. That's all I wanted to do, but then he grabbed the gun. I didn't mean to pull the trigger, but my finger was already on it and I panicked.

Then I went deaf instantly, as he fell hard to the ground. I know I'm overtly dramatic, but it seemed like his blood was everywhere. It was on the car, on the ground, and even on me. I remember looking up into the window of the apartment he had spent the night before in, and seeing the light skinned chick beating on the window screaming and crying her eyes out.

I felt exactly the way she looked, but I couldn't move, I couldn't even breathe. I was stuck, so frozen without him. My body got cold and numb and then everything went black.

I woke up the next day to a rude overweight nurse and stale coffee. Soon everything that happened the morning before all came rushing back to me at once. My chest got tight, my forehead and palms began to sweat, and then I started shaking uncontrollably.

I was having a seizure, the very first one of my 23 years on this earth. As several nurses held me down, I saw the light skinned chick from the restaurant standing over me. She said, "You better hope he makes it, or you're going to die next bitch." *Then everything went black again.*

When I woke up, there was a man standing next to my

bed, wearing all white. "Good afternoon beautiful," he said in a thick English accent, "my name is Dr. Sanchez."

This man looked like Enrique Iglesias, with a body like Channing Tatum, and he sounded like Idris Elba.

"How are you feeling now?" he continued. "I… I, I…" *I couldn't say a damn thing. No man has ever made me stutter. I guess I can't say that anymore.*

"That's okay Cameron," he began, "just rest. You'll be just fine in a day or so." *With that said, he tucked me in tightly turned and walked away. The way he said my name was absolutely gorgeous. Hell, he almost made me forget about K.C.'s ass all together.*

(Hotel Lobby)
(Whit)

"What am I going to do Love?" Whitney asks still in tears. "You *live* baby," he says wrapping his comfortable arms around her, "people die every day Whitney. And he's not even dead yet. He might not even die. I know this is hard, but I don't want you sitting out here stressing, going through an array of desperate emotions that may not even be necessary. I've been back and forth and basically living in this waiting room with you in this hospital, for the past eight days. Whitney, this has to stop. Your life has to go on."

Pulling away from him abruptly, with her yellow forehead wrinkled tightly, and her pretty pink top lip curled she says, "What the hell does that mean?"

"Baby…" Love starts to speak, but Whit cuts him off

quickly. "Lance," she begins, "*boy*, do **not** baby me right now…"

"Whitney, all I'm saying is most people that go into comas after being shot… never wake up." Standing up and stepping away from him with a disgusted look on her face Whitney says, "So, what are you saying, I should just give up on the life of my daughter's father?" "No Whitney," Love shakes his head, "all I'm saying is life goes on. I mean damn Whitney; you haven't even taken a good shower in seven days."

"What the hell are you talking about?" Whitney asks as she rolls her neck aggressively, and places her hands firmly on her hips.

"Every time I drive you home," Love says, "I get you a couple of towels, turn the shower on for you, and I even put you in the tub. And Whitney, you only stay in there for maybe two minutes."

"So, what the fuck were you doing, timing me?"
Whit

asks.
"No, but I just don't understand what's going on with you." he responds. "How can you be so damn insensitive," Whitney asks Love, "the father of my only child is in there *lying* on his death bed. That man represents the only love I have *ever* known."

Leaning forward in his chair Love looks deeply in her eyes, and then he speaks. "Really, **he** represents *the only* love you have ever known?" "Lance, you know what I mean." Whitney cries throwing her hands up in frustration.

Love stands up and walks towards her. "No, Whitney I

can honestly
say I have no idea what you mean. See, because since the day
I met you, I've been your brother, your best friend, your
counselor, your lover and everything in between. But see
now... Now I finally understand that no matter what I do...
in your eyes I'll ***never... ever*** be as great as K.C." Whitney
steps towards Love trying to put her arms around him.

Love gently pushes her away with one hand, as he
wipes several tears off his yellow face with the other.
"I'm hurt, but I'm not even mad," he says, "Because I
already knew what I was getting myself into. I never
really had a chance. How was I supposed to compete
with a man, not even a man but a fantasy, somebody who
in your mind will always have the potential to be your
ideal match. Me, I was just somebody to help you pass the
time when he wasn't around." Grabbing both of his arms
firmly she pulls Love towards her.

"That is not true! Baby... Please you know that's not
true..." Whitney says. "You know what," Love says after
taking yet another step away from her, "I really do love
you, but you gave your heart away a ***loooong*** time ago."

Falling down to her knees, Whitney breaks down and
begins crying hysterically. Love looks down at her with
no sympathy at all. After a moment, he begins to laugh
harshly.

"See, now that's sad," he says, "because now you're
about to lose me too, and I don't even know if those tears
are for me or for him. Man, I've really reached an all-
time low, because now I'm fighting a *dead man* for his ***side
hoe***!"

"Don't do that Love..." she cries. "Don't do what
Whitney!" he

barks at her. "Don't call me... a side hoe." She tells him. Love shakes his head at her.

Without another word Love turns around to leave. "Wait," Whitney screams out, "Lance, please don't leave me like this!" "What am I staying for Whitney?" he asks.

"What," he continues, "What Whitney? What do you want? Do you need moral support? You need another shoulder to cry on?
Hmm...Well fuck that! I can't be your shoulder anymore. I'm more than just tear stained shoulders, and a pretty face. And I'm not just some sex toy, I have a heart too... and it's breaking. You got me standing out here in this waiting room being all emotional in front of all these *fucking* people. It's time for me to go."

Still on her knees in tears oblivious to the people around her, Whitney screams out, "Wait Lance you *are* my brother, you're everything to me! You're just not..."

Holding his head down Love says, "I'm just not K.C., right?" "That's not what I was going to say." Whitney claims. "No, you weren't going to say it out loud, but that's exactly what you were thinking. Goodbye Whitney."

(Inside Cam's hospital room)

"Are you awake, Ms. Jiles?" Dr. Sanchez asks. Cameron opens her eyes slowly as they adjust to the bright sunlight shining in through the hospital window.

"K.C.?" she whispers. Stepping closer to her bedside Dr. Sanchez says, "Um no ma'am. My name is Dr. Sanchez, but you can call me Carlos. You may not remember me but we met before... you know the last time you were conscious?" He smiles at her.

"What are you talking about," she inquires, "and what am I doing in the hospital? Where is my man?" Looking solemnly towards the ground, knowing what he has to tell her, Carlos chooses his words wisely.

"Ms. Jiles," he begins, "I don't really know how to tell you this, because obviously you're having some type of slight memory loss. Your man, your boyfriend, or whoever that guy is to you... you shot him and he's dying. So, I don't want to seem harsh but if by some miracle he does recover I don't think your relationship has even a fighting chance."

Ignoring the excruciating migraine, she has as a result of the head injury she suffered when she fainted after the gun went off Cameron tries frantically to sit up straight in her hospital bed.

Unable to make her way up into a vertical posture, Cam slides back down into her original position. Stepping forward quickly trying to cradle her, Dr. Sanchez tries to ease her pain.

"It's okay," he says, "stuff happens. At least you're not in any serious trouble. The judge dropped all charges; he said this was a crime of passion, that in itself should be something to celebrate, most people probably think you deserve the death penalty."

"I remember now." She says. "I remember everything," she continues, "Where is he now? Take me to his room, he needs me."

"No," Carlos begins, "what that man needs is an organ donor, a blood transfusion, and a special prayer from God himself. I've seen God, and baby you're not him. Besides, his family doesn't want you near him anyway."

"Family," she says, "what family, his whole family left him for dead years ago. I am his only family."

"I'm not talking about his mother or his father Cameron," Carlos explains, "I'm talking about his wife, Whitney Powell."

"His wife?" she whispers somberly. "When did he get, who is, how long has he been…" swallowing painfully she continues to ramble, "Married… How can K.C. be married? He lives with me. Who is Whitney Powell; she must be the blindest, deafest, dumbest woman on the damn planet."

Shaking his head in disbelief Dr. Sanchez responds, "Really… no offense Ms. Jiles, but she could say the same thing about you. I mean think about it; you moved a married man into your house, you've been having sex with him, and taking care of him like he's your child. Keldrick is older than both of you."

"Don't judge me!" Cameron shouts, finally able to sit up vertically with a pillow cushioned comfortably behind her back. Dr. Sanchez can hear the venom in her voice.

"Wait a minute Ms. Jiles, "he starts, "I said no offense. I'm not trying to judge you. I'm just making sure you fully understand what the complete situation is. K.C., whom I'm sure seems like a really nice and smooth guy, lied to you both. So, don't be angry at Whitney Powell, if you're angry at anybody be angry at him. What's more, be angry at yourself."

Cameron exhales deeply with annoyance. "So, what happened to 'I'm not trying to judge you'?" she asks.

"One thing you're going to learn about me Ms. Jiles," he says, "I'm a very honest man, I sugarcoat nothing."

"First of all," Cameron snaps, "stop calling me **Ms. Jiles** I'm not that old. My name is Cameron. Second of all, none of this is your business." "Look Ms. Jiles, I mean Cameron... as your treating physician, this *is* my business. You obviously don't have any family either because we weren't able to contact anyone to come see about you." "What the hell is that supposed to mean?" Cam slams her fist down hard on the bed.

"Calm down," Dr. Sanchez says, "all I'm saying is, I'm your first and only point of contact. So, it's my duty to relay the specifics of your situation to you. If I don't tell you everything that's going on, how else are you going to find out?" Looking down into her lap blankly, Cameron remains silent.

"I'm sorry if I seem harsh," Dr. Sanchez says as he walks over to close her hospital room door to talk privately with her.

"The truth is," he continues, "I don't understand why you're with him in the first place. I mean, you seem like an intelligent woman. So, I don't understand why you would choose to be with a lowlife like K.C. I don't know the man, but he doesn't sound like that great of a catch to me."

"You're right about one thing," she says, "You don't know him. Yeah, he may not be perfect, and he may not be rich like you, but he's still a good man."

Laughing to himself Carlos says, "Oh okay... So that's what a good man is?"

Crossing her arms in childish defense Cameron says,

"He may not even be a good man, but he's good to me."

Sitting down on the edge of her bed, Carlos looks deeply in Cameron's eyes. "Can I be honest with you?" he asks. "If you must." She replies.

"Wow, okay." Dr. Sanchez laughs to himself. "Say what you were gonna say." Cam tells him. "No," he tells her, "I'd rather not."

"And why not," she asks, "you were just so amped to tell me whatever it was a second ago." "Yes, I was," he agrees, "I changed my mind." "And my question to you Dr. *Asshole*," she says, "is why?"

He laughs at her obvious disposition again. "I make it a point to never waste words on people, who I know aren't going to listen to what I have to say in the first place." He tells her.

"If I wasn't going to listen," she sighs loudly, "I wouldn't still be asking you what you had to say sir."

"Fine," Carlos replies, "I hate women who date broke men based on their own insecurities. I mean damn, it's like the blind leading the deaf and dumb. And what I mean by that is no woman should ever be forced to run her own household. If she so chooses to run her own house that's fine, but it shouldn't be a burden placed on her because some asshole wasn't man enough to stand up and accept his own responsibilities to her and his children."

Not even slightly changing the position her body is in, Cameron says, "So every woman should be with a man like you, right? We all need to live in a fantasy world and believe that one day we'll meet some rich, gorgeous doctor, with a British accent. Your way of thinking is wrong on so many levels Dr. Sanchez. Of course, women want to marry somebody rich and attractive, with goals and ambitions, but sooner or later, reality catches up to you. Yes, I am still very young, but I know sooner or later reality does catch up to you. I've dated rich guys before, but it never lasts. I always end up feeling like they see me as just another potential notch in one of their expensive designer belts."

"First of all, my accent is English," he explains, "There is no such thing as a British accent. Britain is made up of multiple countries that do not share a common accent, so therefore a British accent does not exist. Secondly, not all rich men are the same. And last but not least, you think I'm gorgeous…"

Unable to resist his infectious smile, Cameron begins to blush. "Yeah, you're kind of cute I guess." She admits.

"No, you said gorgeous," Carlos reminds her, laughing lightly. "So, let me ask you a question Ms. Cameron." He says. "Sure."

She replies as she focuses in on the wavy curls of his sandy brown hair. After a calculated pause, Carlos says, "If I wasn't your doctor, and I was interested in dating you… what would you say?"

"Well now, Dr. Sanchez that depends." She says. "And what does it depend on?" he asks. Smiling playfully, she replies, "Are you actually interested, or you just like asking people out on hypothetical dates to make conversation?"

"It depends on what your response would be Ms. Jiles." He replies with a playful smile of his own. Their conversation is halted by a loud knock at the door.

A young Asian nurse rushes into the room. "Dr. Sanchez, they need you in ICU stat!" she tells him.

"What is it, Nurse Huengo?" he asks as calmly as he possibly can. "It's Mr. Cole. He's fading fast." She says grabbing his arm tightly and leading the doctor towards the door.

"Wait," Cameron exclaims, "Is she talking about K.C.? I thought you said you never met him."

Half way out of the door he turns around and says, "Well, technically I haven't, the man is in a coma." Without another word, he leaves.

(K.C.)

Clutching his chest and gasping loudly for air K.C. has finally awakened from his coma, surrounded by several nurses. "Oh my God, it's a miracle!" a cute twenty-three-year-old nurse named Sasha screams.

"It is, and he's even more handsome when he's awake," an overweight thirty-seven-year-old nurse, named Caroline replies, "he's in shock. But, Dr. Sanchez is on the way".

"Hmm, you mean Dr. Do every nurse in the building?" The first nurse replies. "No ma'am," the second nurse laughs loudly, "Just because he did you, and all your nasty sisters and cousins that work up here, does not mean he does everybody in the building. He only does those willing to be done."

"Whatever Ms. Caroline," Sasha says with her hands on her tiny hips, "don't act like you don't want him.

Because he would've gotten you to, if menopause didn't get to you first."

Together they burst out in hysterical laughter. "Little girl, you better watch your mouth." Caroline says playfully. "Girl you know I'm just playing," Sasha smiles at her, "but for real though Dr. Sanchez is only playing with these other hoes. You know he gone be my baby daddy one day."

The door to the ICU swings open violently. "How is he?" Dr. Sanchez inquires. "We don't know," Sasha shakes her head, "you're the doctor, you tell us."

"This is a matter of life and death," Dr. Sanchez says, "and you two have been sitting in here gossiping, while this man is dying?"

"No sir." Caroline says. "I don't want to hear it, both of you get out of here now!" he screams. "Nurse Huengo, get me two other nurses in here stat!" he continues.

"But baby..." Sasha says. Cutting her off quickly, Carlos says, "Nurse Williams, I am not your baby, and if you want to keep your job, I suggest you leave the hospital right now."

The two dismissed nurses leave the ICU with their heads held low. After they're gone, Carlos does everything he can to save K.C.

(Hours later Cameron is laying in her hospital bed thinking)

What do I do now? Lord I know I've never been the type to pray but I think I'm ready to start. God, am I crazy... am I? I shot and almost killed the only man I have ever been in love with. He's in a room, on another floor, at the end of a cold dark hallway fighting for his life. The judge may have deemed this a crime of

58

passion, but I realize that means I'm crazy. I went temporarily insane based on my emotions. How is it that I fell so deeply in love with this man that I would rather kill him, than allow him to live and hurt me? I mean, when people ask me about it, I'll tell them that he grabbed the gun and I panicked and pulled the trigger. I've even forced myself to believe that this was true. But now that I'm becoming fully coherent again, thinking back, I knew once I smelled his breath I was going to shoot him. That's how I know I was insane. I focused on something as ludicrous as his foul morning breath to determine whether or not I was going to take his life. I sat in my car for seven hours outside that girl's apartment, waiting for him to come out. So, I already knew what he did inside her apartment that night. But I didn't want to believe it. I was shaking, and hurting. I was so lost. I felt broken, because the only man that I ever loved or believed in was turning out to be a liar, just like all the rest of them before my very eyes. I couldn't focus, nothing else mattered. When I saw him, everything inside of me cracked and shattered, I felt beaten and battered. I didn't know if I was going to allow him to live or make him die, but I was leaning towards the latter. There wasn't enough common sense left in me to gather, but even then, I was still flattered by the look in his eyes… I thought maybe I mattered. That made me even sadder, but then he reached, and I shot… then blood started to splatter. Lord, am I still crazy? My thoughts are like poetry, with dangerous rhythm and rhyme. How do I even…

"Are you ok Cameron?" Dr. Sanchez asks. "I'm fine Carlos," she snaps out of her makeshift prayer, "Why?"

Sitting down at the edge of her bed, Carlos says, "Because, you looked like you were in really deep thought." Sliding out of her hospital bed she says, "I was praying Carlos, don't you pray?"

"Yeah, I do," he watches her curiously, "what are you doing now?" Smiling back at him holding the back of her hospital gown closed she says, "I have to pee, is that okay with you Doc?" Carlos raises both of his hands in playful surrender.

"Lord, this man is fine." Cameron whispers quietly while inside the small bathroom. *"If Keldrick "K.C." Cole is not the man for me,"* she continues to whisper, *"then Lord, please let Dr. Carlos Sanchez be the one."*

Cameron flushes the toilet, washes her hands, and then exits the bathroom. As she climbs back into her bed she finds Carlos on the far side of the room looking out of the window.

"We control nothing," he says, "We think we're in control, but that thought is really just a false idea that's been imprinted on our brains since birth. We are now, and will always be controlled by our fears, and the things we love."

With her forehead wrinkled tightly in confusion, Cameron says, "Carlos, are you okay?" Still staring out the window he says, "Yeah I'm fine. It's just I made it a rule and practice of mine, to never ever date a patient."

Leaning forward, in her bed to attempt to get a full understanding of what he's saying Cameron says, "That's a very respectable policy to have."

"Yeah, I used to think the same thing." He replies. "So, what's different now," she asks, "what happened to change the way you feel?"

Turning around to look at her he says, "You

happened, that's what's changing the way I feel. Cameron, you make me want to feel... ***something***. But I refuse to waste my time. I love black women, but so many of you are damaged goods with a whole lot of baggage."

"Well none of that applies to..." Cameron begins to speak but is quickly cut off by Carlos. "Please let me finish," he says, "I'm not saying any of this applies to you, but I do want you to know where my head is at."

"I understand," she says. "Now when are you going to get me out of this hospital, and take me on a date?"

(K.C. is out of surgery and doing considerably better. Whitney is at his bedside)

Whitney has been watching K.C. quietly for about thirty minutes as he continues to bat his brown eyes in total confusion. "What happened?" K.C. asks. "They keep telling me some girl shot me."

"No," Whitney says, "some girl didn't shoot you. The girl who shot you is claiming to be your girlfriend." With an impulsive burst of energy K.C. sits up straight in his bed.

"Cameron," he says, "you mean Cameron shot me? That doesn't make any sense why would Cameron shoot me?"

After slapping him hard across his face, Whitney stands up and begins to scold him, "I knew it!" "Girl, what's wrong with you?" K.C. asks holding the left side of his numb face in shock.

"Shut up K.C.," she says, "that's the bitch from the

restaurant!" "What restaurant," he responds, "What are you talking about baby?" Whitney slaps him again in the same exact spot. "I'm not stupid, Keldrick," she says. "I saw you, **both** of you."

"What did you see Whitney… Who did you see?" K.C. says trying to move towards the far edge of his hospital bed, so she can't slap him again.

Pacing back and forth on the white tile floor, Whitney is trying to control herself. "That night at the restaurant," she says, "the Bahama Breeze… I pretended to leave the table to use the bathroom. I stood in the back of the restaurant and I watched you. You flirted with that black bitch like I wasn't even there with you Keldrick!"

"No, I didn't," he says, "It wasn't what it looked like."

"Stop lying Keldrick," Whitney says slapping him hard on the top of his head this time, "I saw you give her a business card. If it wasn't what it looked like, then why would she shoot you? How did she even know where you were?"

Whitney attempts to strike him again.

"Okay!" he screams. "It was exactly what it looked like," he says, "Cameron is my girlfriend. I didn't want you to know because I didn't want you to put me on child-support. I don't want to go back to jail, so I'll do *whatever* I have to do to stay out. If you never want me to see her again, I won't. I'll move all my stuff back home and I'll change my cell phone number and everything."

Folding her arms tightly as she listens closely to his lies, Whitney begins to shake her head slowly. "I am so stupid," she admits, "boy I don't think you ever told me the truth about anything except your name. She loves you Keldrick."

Realizing his strategy is not working K.C. throws his hands up in surrender. "You're right," he says, "I lied to you. I've lied to you a lot. But how can you say that girl loves me, when she just tried to kill me?"

"You can't be that blind," she says, "she does love you Keldrick. That's exactly why she tried to kill you. You know what? I need some air. I'm going for a walk." Whitney storms out of the room and doesn't look back.

K.C. puts his head down in his hands and begins to sob uncontrollably because everything good that he has ever known seems to finally be falling apart like the rest of his life. About ten minutes later he hears his door open again, but he doesn't look up. He hears her footsteps getting closer and closer to the bed. "Whitney, I am so sorry." He claims.

"Baby I'm sorry," he continues, "I never meant for any of this to happen. It all happened so fast. You're right, I know that girl loves me but you're the one that has always been here for me."

Cameron stands there listening to him as her heart breaks all over again. She hears his words but her heart knows this can't be real. Every one of his deceitful words is like a cold, sharp knife slicing into her back. She feels just as frozen as she felt the moment after she shot him.

"Just stop Keldrick," she says, "you've said enough." Looking up through his tears Keldrick sees the young waitress he fell in love with at first sight. "Cameron?" he says.

"Yeah, it's me," she says, "or you know, you could just call me *that girl*. I came in here to tell you I was sorry that I shot you. But now I guess I won't have to because you're doing enough lying for the both of us."

With that said, Cameron leaves as quickly as she came. As she makes her way back down the hallway to her room, Cam walks right by Whitney. Neither one of the girls notices the other because they're both lost in their own thoughts.

Thirty minutes later, Whitney walks back into Keldrick's room. All the anger she has built up inside of her begins to fade away as she watches the strongest, toughest man she has ever known cry like a helpless baby.

Her motherly instinct comes to the forefront of her senses as she tries to console him. She puts her arms tightly around him as the large man falls powerlessly into her chest.

"Calm down *love*, I... I mean baby," she stutters, "everything is gonna work out. Isn't that what you always tell me when things get rough?"

"Yeah, but..." he starts. "No, there are no buts," she says, "I can't have you in here breaking down crying like a baby. You have a beautiful little girl at home that needs a strong father."

"His home," Cameron says as she walks back into the room, "is *where ever* I am." "No ma'am, I'm sorry you must be confused," Whitney says, "because see, this right here is my man. He may sneak out sometimes when Mama's not around, to come play with you but he will always know where home is."

"Oh really," Cameron says, "Is that true K.C.?" she asks. "Look, I don't..." K.C. is quickly cut off by Whitney.

"Shut up," Whitney tells K.C., "back to you. His

name is Keldrick, and any questions you have for him you need to direct them to me."

"Oh bitch, you got me messed up. Who do you think you're talking to?" Cameron says taking her hooded jacket off. "Oh… what you thought I was gonna be scared of you because you black as hell," Whitney says stepping away from K.C. as she takes her jacket off as well, "Girl just because you ugly don't mean you can fight."

"And just because you're light skinned don't mean you're pretty, you miss piggy looking bitch!" Cameron says stepping closer to Whitney. "Bitch…" Whit starts.

Before she can finish her statement both women attack each other like two rabid pit bulls. Cameron grabs Whitney's hair first. After she has a firm grasp, she tries to drag her down to the ground. Cameron soon realizes Whitney is a lot stronger than she thought she was. Whitney pushes away from Cameron trying to make her let go of her hair.

"Stop, both of you cut that shit out right now!" K.C. exclaims. But neither one of the girls pays any attention to him. Cameron still has a firm grasp on Whit's hair, so Whitney grabs Cameron's neck with her left hand and slaps her hard with the right.

Cameron immediately lets go of Whitney's hair and slaps her back as hard as she can. Then Whitney charges hard at Cameron, tackling her to the floor. Once they hit the floor, Cameron rolls over on top of Whitney and starts choking her. Even though it's hard for her to breathe with her throat being squeezed like this, Whitney continues to slap Cameron and pull her hair.

With a sudden burst of desperate energy, Whitney is able to power upward and she pushes Cameron off of her. Now down on her back, Cameron urgently tries to wiggle free. Then Whitney hits Cameron hard in the face twice, while Cameron throws a couple of powerful blows herself.

"Ms. Jiles!" Dr. Sanchez screams as he enters the room. Carlos immediately grabs Whitney and sits her in a nearby chair, where two nurses quickly hold her down.

Then he picks Cameron up like a baby and carries her out of the room to safety. Once in the hallway Cameron jumps out of Carlos' arms and scolds him.

"Why did you break the fight up," she asks, "I can handle myself." "Excuse me," Carlos says, "you didn't look like you were handling yourself too well to me, and besides this is a hospital not the *ghetto girls'* boxing gym."

Cam takes two quick strategic steps ahead of Carlos to turn around and stand face to face with him. "Oh, so now I'm ghetto," she asks, "a few hours ago I was Michelle Obama, now I'm *Frankie*, Keshia Cole's crack head mama."

"You're who…" he asks.

"Never mind Carlos," she says, "I knew you didn't take me seriously." Cam walks in her hospital room and closes the door in Carlos' face.

He surveys the hallway quickly and then walks in her room closing the door behind him. The room is dark except for a tiny bit of light trying to peak in through the window.

The air has a stale sweetness to it from the dozens of dying wild flowers that mysteriously found their way into Cam's room over the past couple of days.

"What are you doing?" she asks. "So that's the best

66

you can do?" Carlos says stepping towards Cameron.

"What," Cameron says, "Carlos what are you talking about?" Carlos laughed lightly to himself. "It was too easy," he says, "everything was a little too close to being and *feeling* right."

"Carlos, what the hell are you talking about?" Cameron asks again leaning back in her bed crossing her arms tightly in confusion. "*You*... standing in your own damn way," he says, "you were waiting for the chance, waiting for any little opportunity to be able to say I'm just like every other rich guy you ever dated, and that's why..."

Unable to finish his statement Carlos walks calmly towards the window at the back of her room. "And that's why what Carlos?" Cameron asks leaning forward in her bed.

"Never mind, I don't want to waste my time," Carlos says, "no, I know I'll regret it if I don't say this... Because I'm not black and I'm not from this country you'll probably feel like it really isn't my place to say any of what I'm about to say, but I don't care. The majority of black women in this country fall into three separate categories. In the first group, you have the black women who only date guys who don't mean them any good, the type of guys who eventually ruin them. In the second group are the black women who are chasing dreams. These women tend to date men, who they *know* will never take them seriously. They cater to these men, spoil them, and do everything in their power to try to make them happy. But they all know deep down in their hearts that one day these men are going to leave them for somebody else. Now, the women in both of these groups who never figure out how to break these dangerous patterns all end up in the last category, the bitter black woman category. Now, make sure you're taking notes Cameron, because you're listening to a true genius at work. The women in the last category look for love in all the wrong places for so long, that finally they begin to believe that love doesn't exist, at least not for them. Now, some black women get it right. They focus on the things about a man that should matter. Does he have a relationship with God? Is he stable? Is he actually interested in me? These are the things every woman on the planet should look for in a potential mate. Does he excite you, is he spontaneous? Don't waste any time ever dating a man that you could never see being your husband. This Cameron, by far is the best advice moving forward that you may ever receive."

With her eyes squinted slightly and her head tilted to the side, Cameron stares at Carlos in awe, completely speechless now. As she continues to stare at him, Carlos walks towards Cam and kneels down to be at eye level with her. Her entire body is tingling being this close to him.

"Well, professor genius," she says with a nervous smirk on her face, "since you know all these things… why haven't you been able to find Mrs. Right yet?"

Then Carlos does something he's never done before, he grabs Cameron's face firmly and kisses her passionately on the lips, staring deep into her eyes. After their hungry lips part ways, he says, "I think I have found her love."

Cameron feels her entire body getting weak now. From the look in her eyes Carlos can see how vulnerable she is. He kisses her once more, and then heads towards the door because he has no interest in taking advantage of her.

As he reaches for the door handle she calls out to him, "Carlos… Please don't leave me." As he turns around he sees she has pulled her gown up high enough to expose both of her supple breasts, in a strong attempt to entice him.

Carlos bites his bottom lip hard as his mouth begins to water. Since he first laid eyes on the gorgeous Cameron, he has dreamed of a moment like this. Carlos takes his white lab jacket off and tosses it aside on the floor. Cameron feels her tight underwear begin to moisten. Unable to stay seated she throws her sheets to the side and gets out of her bed.

With her hospital gown now hanging down at her waist like a skirt, Cam stands frozen waiting on him to make the next move. Carlos walks towards her as he undoes his tie and a few buttons at the top of his expensive yellow button-down Polo shirt.

Cam stops him at the third button and attempts to rip the shirt open. Three white buttons fall scattering to the floor. The second time she tries, the shirt rips open completely revealing his hypnotizing abs and chest. Carlos knows he will probably lose his job for this, but at this point he really doesn't care.

As Cameron enjoys the view of his perfectly sculpted body, she notices on the left side of his chest he has a tattoo that says, "*I Will Break You*". She kisses his tattoo softly as she runs her long fingernails up and down the sides of his hard warm stomach.

"You promise?" she whispers to him. "Promise what?" he asks. Cam laces his body with delicate kisses from the top of his chest down to his stomach.

Kneeling down she bites his lower stomach several times, her crafty teeth slowly driving him insane with anxiety. Now, down on her knees Cam grabs hold of him and squeezes gently, to get the blood flowing.

"What am I promising Cameron?" Carlos moans. "I want you to break me doctor…" she says carefully unbuckling his authentic Louis Vuitton belt as she looks up into his desperate eyes.

After unzipping his pants gently, she pulls them down and pulls his throbbing member out through the slit in the front of his Polo boxer shorts.

Taking it in her bare hands she kisses it twice and then says, "I want you to break me… and then I want you to put me back together again Dr. Sanchez…"

Without another word, she makes the majority of his penis quickly disappear in her mouth and the back of her throat. Carlos feels his entire body begin to tingle, as Cam showers him with undeniable pleasures on a level he's never known.

Without stopping she turns his body so that his back is to the bed. Cam can tell from the fact that Carlos was shaking he needed some support because his knees were getting weak.

She looks up into his dazed eyes with a full mouth. The fact that she's giving him pure ecstasy is turning her on even more. Unable to stand anymore he sits back on the bed, as she puts her soft left hand on his perfect abs gently forcing him to lay back.

Supported by only his two numb elbows, Carlos lies back completely. It's clear he's incapable of escaping her hungry mouth. He looks down at her briefly in amazement, as she begins to quickly flick her tongue up and down his strong shaft.

With his head to the familiar ceiling, his eyes begin to roll back in his head, as she begins to suck him as fast as she can.

Carlos has never felt as vulnerable as he does at this very moment. With every nerve in his body betraying him his toes begin to curl as his knees raise up involuntarily and his feet leave the floor.

"Stop…"he whispers as he pushes her head back as softly as he possibly can. "What's wrong Dr., I know you're not tapping out on me…"Cam says playfully resting back on her heels awaiting his next move. "No… I just want to return the favor." He says.

With his composure, almost back in tact Carlos gets off the bed, strong again and ready to take control of the situation. After kissing her softly once, he turns her around backwards pressing her body hard against his. Tenderly biting the right side of her neck, he massages her thighs and butt, as he continues to press himself against her.

Grabbing her by her waist at first, he picks her up and continues to raise her up until her knees are on his shoulders. With a firm grip on her breast, he holds her up as he tastes her body from the back.

Walking around the room, holding her up in the air he continues to hastily devour her succulent flesh. As he

reaches the opposite side of the bed from which they started on, he attempts to lay her upper body on the bed as he continues to drive her crazy with his tongue. With her arms outstretched, she grips the sheets on the bed tightly, trying to brace herself with her knees pressed tightly against his ears. After getting his fill of her orally he turns her small frame
around on the bed and makes passionate love to her.

(The next day)

"Check out time, I see." Sanchez says sounding almost American.

Smiling at the sound of his voice, Cameron turns about-face to greet him.

"Well doctor," she says, "you did give me a release, didn't you?"

"Yes, ma'am I did," he says, "I hope I see you again real soon."

Cameron flashes her bright beautiful smile as she hands Carlos her hospital bill and turns to leave. "What is this," he says chuckling to himself, "you're trying to give me bills to pay already?"

"No," she says, "I can pay my own bills Dr. Sanchez. I put my cell phone number on the back, call me later."

"Will do," he says, "but please... call me Carlos. I'm not your doctor anymore."

"That's too bad doctor," she says, "I was hoping you did house calls."

Without another word, she flashes one last smile, puts

her cheap Chanel shades on and leaves the hospital to start trying to move on, and put her life back together again.

From down the hall, Whitney smiles mischievously as she just saw the friendly exchange between Carlos and Cameron. In her mind, she's already begun formulating a plot for revenge against Cameron.

Chapter 5
Moving On

(Love)

My *name is Lance Orlandis Vinson. I'm a twenty-one-year-old loner just trying to find myself. People look at me and just automatically think my life is great and everything is so simple for me. But so much more lingers deep on the inside of a human being than what the physical eye can see. My past continues to break me but it's also making me who I'm supposed to be.*

We can't change our pasts or how they affect our ways of thinking. All we can do is try to cope with any problems we've endured and use them to make us stronger. I'm doing quite well for anybody even close to my age, but I still sleep with the demons deeply embedded in my mind every single night. I want sweet revenge on those who crossed me and ultimately changed me forever.

I'm confused about a lot of things in my life but not Whitney Powell. I know that she is everything I would have ever wanted in a woman or a wife. She has the potential to fix me and cleanse the damaging stain on the fabric of my life. She can't help that she still loves K.C...

I know that but it doesn't make it hurt any less, especially when I hate the man with everything I am. I wasn't supposed to love Whitney. I wasn't even supposed to like her. She met me long ago but she doesn't even remember me.

See Whitney and I went to school together but I look a lot different now than I did back then. She has no idea who I am or what I've set out to do. I can almost taste the satisfaction that is due to me once my mission is complete. But if I fall any deeper in love with Whitney my mission will cease to exist.

(Whit)

There comes a time in every woman's life when she has to decide whether or not a love is worth losing herself. I use to think it was, I'm not so sure anymore. I realize now that when God created the love that I feel for K.C., he didn't stop creating love.

Love comes in many forms, but you have to be ready to accept it with open arms or you will lose it. In the same respect when a love is dead, you have to be willing and able to let it die so that a new one can be born in its place.

I can let K.C. go, but I refuse to let that bitch Cam have him. I'm going to hurt her something awful. She stole something from me that has meant the world to me since I was sixteen years old. She will pay for it.

(On a plane in the coach section)
(Jacody and Tyrone)

Two childhood friends are on an airplane flying from Atlanta to Orlando to check on their other best friend who they recently found out was shot by his girlfriend.

K.C., Tyrone, and Jacody have been best friends since elementary school. Tyrone "Tyboonie" Carter is 5'10, and dark skinned, with a low haircut. He's twenty-five years old and he's one of the head managers at Six Flags over Georgia.

He also has a decade's worth of plans to build and launch his own theme park *Ride with Me Adventures*. Ty is very religious but he still stumbles hard at times, but everybody stumbles sometimes, right?

Jacody "J Milli" Miller is 5'9 he has light brown skin, and low haircut. He left Orlando after high school to pursue his dream of being a rapper. His loyalty has never been in question but the boy used to be as stingy as a fat kid in the projects. He's nowhere near as stingy as he used to be, and with a friend as cheap as Ty he can't afford to be.

"Blood of Jesus…" Tyrone says looking around the plane. "What now, Ty?" Jay asks. "This plane is nice as hell bruh," Ty says, "Big screen T.V., reclining seats, and all the nuts you can eat?"

"All the what… you know what dude I'm gone leave that alone," Jay replies, "It would have been even nicer in first class, if you didn't give those two old people our tickets."

"Blood of Jesus, stop being so stingy Jay," Ty says, "It's their 60th wedding anniversary." After shaking his head slowly Jay looks at Ty and says, "Right, so after 60 years they should be able to afford their own damn first-class tickets."

"What if it was your mama, Jay?" Ty says laughing lightly to himself. "If it was *my* mama, she would have bought first class tickets from the jump." Jay tells his friend.

"You're right," Ty agrees, "but everybody ain't able. Nigga, your parents are rich as hell." "Those that ain't able should sit their asses in coach then," Jay replies, "and my parents are not rich. They worked very hard for everything they have."

Leaning back with his eyes wide open to get a good look at his childhood friend, Ty says, "your folks have a movie theater inside their house!"

"So, what's that supposed to mean?" Jay asks. "Boy that means they're rich as hell!" Ty responds.

"Whatever, Ty." He responds. Sensing his friend is getting a little touchy about the topic, Ty attempts to change the subject.

"So, anyway, tell me what's up with Keldrick?" Jay bursts into sudden laughter. "What's wrong with you fool?" Ty asks in confusion.

"Keldrick," Jay says still enjoying his laugh, "Who is that? Bruh, when did you start calling K.C., by his government name?"

"I don't know bro," he replies, "but we're grown now so you should start calling him by his *government* name too, Mr. *J Milli*. What does that even mean anyway?"

"What does what mean?" Jay asks. "J Milli," Ty responds, "Where did you come up with that? You couldn't come up with anything better?" "Man, you stupid," Jay responds, "you gone see how hot my name is once I get this record deal."

"Ok, well let me know when that happens so I can move into your mansion and live off you for a while," Ty says, "anyway what's good with Keldrick?"

"You killing me with that name bruh," Jay says laughing to himself again, "but yeah I really don't know bruh. You remember Jessica Martin from back in high school?"

"How could I forget?" Ty says with a slick grin on his face. "Watch your mouth fool," Jay says, "you know that was my baby."

"Man, that was my baby too," Ty says, "In fact that was Robb's baby, Charvez's baby, Tabb's baby... bruh that was *everybody's* baby. You just messed up and fell in love with her ass."

"Man, here you go with this again," Jay says, "anyway Jessica posted something on Facebook about everybody keeping K.C. in their prayers because his girlfriend shot him, and he wasn't expected to make it."

"Blood of Jesus," Ty responds, "I knew it was bad when you wouldn't tell me what happened over the phone. So why did Whitney shoot him?"

"Listen," Jay says, "that's the crazy part it wasn't even Whit. It was some new girl named Cameron."

"Cameron," Ty says looking at his friend sideways, "That sounds like a man's name to me. Let me find out K.C. been trapped in the closet like *you know who*?"

"Hey Ty, leave that alone. That ain't our business man." Jay tells him. "Blood of Jesus," Ty says, "I could pray for both of them, but they're still going to Hell."

"Says who?" Jay responds, "I was always taught that no sin is greater than any other." Shaking his head Ty says, "Not true, Jay." "How…" Jay inquires.

"That's not true, Jay, I'm telling you," Ty claims, "We just went over this in my Bible study class last Wednesday." Ty says.

"So, you're telling me," Jay says, "If I kill and rape women until I die, I still have a better chance of seeing Jesus than a gay person?" "Exactly…" Ty says, nodding his head to acknowledge his friends statement.

"What?!" Jay exclaims as he burst into laughter. "Yep," Ty replies, "As long as you repent and ask for forgiveness. Enough of all that though, are you gone kill this dude Cameron or you want me to do it?"

"Wait," Jay says, "You think Keldrick, I mean K.C. is really gay?"

"Come on Jay," Ty says, "what type of female do you know named *Cameron*? It's a dude, boy I'm telling you it's *a dude*, but that's still our boy so, gay, straight, bi, whoever shot him we gone fuck them up."

"You right." Jay agrees.

(K.C. is in his hospital room alone thinking to himself)

Keldrick Jermaine Cole, it's time to grow up baby boy. The game is over; this can't last forever. I got two great women fighting for my heart, and playing both sides of the fence is a very dangerous game. It's more dangerous for me than anybody else involved obviously. Everything is out in the open now, so this has to stop now.

Whit and Cam know about each other. I have to choose which one I really want to be with now, before I lose both of them. What do I want to do? Man, this is really hard. I don't have any real history with Cam, but I know I'm in love with her.

Whit on the other hand is battle tested and proven. She has always been there for me, through thick and thin. I don't have to hide myself when I'm with her. She knows every skeleton in my crowded closet personally. She witnessed each of their creations, and never once judged me. Whitney Powell deserves to be my wife. I trust her and I

know she'll never turn her back on me. She's honest, faithful, and loving. She's never once even thought about sleeping with another man.

But even with all of that in her favor, I know I'm not in love with her anymore. So, my choice should be simple. By the end of the year, one of them is going to be my wife.

(Cam)

My house no longer feels like a home without him here, but I have to move on now. My mama always said the best medicine for when things start breaking up, is to start shaking things up and try something new and exciting. Dr. Carlos Sanchez is definitely something new and exciting for me.

He's on his way to pick me up and take me to the movies and out to eat. This will be our first real date, but surprisingly I'm not nervous at all. I don't know what it is about this man, but he's so natural at making me feel powerful and beautiful.

Over the past two days he has really awakened my

mind, body, and spirit, especially my body, thank you Jesus! The way he talks to me is so soothing. His conversation is like the perfect therapy for me. He holds me like a baby... like his baby.

He caresses me as if my skin is made of the finest silk. He's always thirsty for my kisses as if his desire for my lips is unquenchable. And he listens to me. Oh my God I mean the man actually listens to me as if my thoughts and concerns actually matter.

I barely even know this man and I already feel like he's my best friend. He's a triple threat though. I don't know which is the best his sex, his company, or just looking at him.

Ten minutes later a fire engine red *Maserati Ghibli* pulls up into Cam's cul de sac, and in front of her house. Dr. Carlos jumps out with the keys in his hand, dressed to kill.

He's wearing a pale green Michael Kors button down shirt, white silk Versace pants, and white Armani boat shoes with gold medusa head buckles on them.

The shoes match his white Versace belt with the exact same gold buckle. After a short walk to the door Carlos knocks twice and rings the doorbell once.

After making him wait a few carefully calculated minutes, Cam opens the door wearing the beautiful green flower print maxi dress Carlos bought her the night before while they were out shopping together. "Wow..." Carlos says admiring Cams frame in the new dress. "What's wrong now Dr. Sanchez?" Cam asks playfully. "Nothing," he replies, "It's just that, the mannequin was absolutely stunning in

81

that dress but I think you may have her beat my dear."

"Well, thank you sir," she says as she twirls around to give him a full view of the dress and how it fits her perfectly. "You look quite stunning yourself," she continues, "but why do you have on so many different designers at the same time?"

"Honestly," he says, "I've acquired so much clothing over the years if I don't mix them all up, I'll probably never get around to wearing them all."

"Must be nice," she says looking down at her feet laughing nervously, "I just try not to wear the same outfit twice in the same week to work. Nice car by the way. Is it new?"

"Yes ma'am," he says turning around to look at it with her, "I picked it up on the way over here. Do you like it?"

"Yes, it's gorgeous Carlos." She says, lost in a momentary daze. "I really hope you like it, because it's yours." He says holding the keys out for her to take them. "What…" she says trying to comprehend what she just heard.

"Take the keys, the car is yours." He says. "What are you talking about Carlos," she asks her eyes wide open with excitement, "You can't just buy me a car. You couldn't just… you didn't buy me a car, did you?"

Smiling in satisfaction at the joy in her recently heartbroken eyes, Carlos says, "Take the keys Ms. Jiles, it's yours."

"Call me Cameron, Dr. Sanchez." She says taking the luxurious keys in her trembling hands. Cam hasn't cried since the morning she caught K.C. coming out of

Whitney's apartment, but she feels the tears coming on strong now.

The warm salty tears rush her beautiful black face uncontrollably. Throwing her arms tightly around this unbelievably awesome man, she says, "Thank you so much Carlos. Is it my car to keep?"

"Of course, you can keep it my darling," he says in his erotic accent, "now lock up so we can go. Oh, and you don't have to worry about wearing the same outfit to work in a week, or even a year for that matter."

"Why not," she asks, "what are you talking about now Carlos?"

"I had some of my designer friends create you a whole new wardrobe," he says, "They're delivering it all to you this weekend. Now let's go, and give me the keys I'm driving."

Cam locks her door then follows Carlos down to the car. Carlos opens her door and she joyfully jumps in the passenger seat of her brand-new luxury car, the first she's ever owned outright.

Holding Carlos' right hand tightly, as he steers with his left hand Cameron can barely contain herself. But she won't show it, she promised herself she would not let him see how blown away she is by his unreal world. But even still, she can't help but wonder what this wonderful guy could possibly see in her.

(Cam)

I know he could have any woman on the planet he wants, so why is he choosing me? I mean I've heard stories about women meeting wealthy attractive men and how they get married and lead these glamorous fairytale lives. I just never thought I would have my own fairytale.

And even if Carlos didn't have a dime nothing would be different because he's just a great man, and that's rare these days. Just holding his hand feels so right, I get goose bumps every single time we touch.

I pray this feeling never fades away. Looking up into the night sky I feel like every star is shining just for me. That's the way he makes me feel.

"So, what else do you do Dr. Carlos?" Cam asks to steady her nerves from the awkward silence. "What does that mean Beautiful, *what else do I do?" he asks.*

"Well," Cam says, "I mean I know Doctors make a ton of money but you're only what 31, so you haven't been a doctor for that long. So, there must be something else you do…right?"

"Some things Cameron are better left kept secret." He says with no distinct expression on his handsome face. "Ok," she replies as her nerves begin to resurface, "Well what if I told you I don't like secrets?"

Carlos ignores her comment, as he turns the car around suddenly and then makes a sharp right turn down a dark alley. "Carlos where are we going," she asks in a panic, "the movies and the restaurants are on International drive. So why did we turn around?"

He still doesn't respond to her.

"Look Dr. Sanchez," she says raising her voice and losing all composure, "you're scaring me right now, and I don't like to be scared. If you don't want to talk to me, you can just take me back home."

"You want to know what I do right?" he asks. "I could tell you," he continues, "but I'd much rather show you."

Minutes later they pull up to a large iron gate surrounding an enormous private property. The letters on the gate read "*CS*". Carlos pulls up to the gate, waves at the camera outside of it, and the gates open instantly.

Cameron is more nervous with every silent second that passes by. The long driveway up towards the mansion is made of bright red and white gravel. It's very pretty, but it also looks like some of the gravel could be covered in old dried blood.

Instead of stopping at the monstrous house Carlos pulls around back of it and continues to drive down another path behind the mansion.

"Whose house is that Carlos?" Cam asks still a bit frightened. "It's my house Beautiful," he says, "didn't you see my initials on the gate?"

"Yes," she says, "Well why were you ignoring me earlier, and is this gravel stained in blood?"

"No," he says fighting back a laugh, "the gravel is not stained in blood. The gravel is red and white because I'm a Kappa. I don't kill people my dear... but I do live off of them."

Wrinkling her brows in confusion Cam chooses her words wisely. "What do you mean... you live off of people Carlos," she asks, "And you still didn't tell me why you were ignoring me."

Pulling up to an enormous garage Carlos says, "I didn't want to spoil the surprise." Carlos parks the car and then jumps out headed towards the side of the large garage leaving Cam all alone in the fancy car with the engine still running.

Several men dressed in dark suits begin to walk towards the car. One of them jumps in the driver's seat, another grabs all of the contents out of the trunk, and the third one opens Cam's door and holds his hand out to her. Her heart is pounding painfully loud in her ears now.

"Ms. Jiles..." he says in a very polite voice. "Yes..." Cameron responds not sure what to do next. "Dr. Sanchez is waiting for you by the hanger." The man tells her.

Clutching the loaded .22, in her new Michael Kors purse that Carlos bought her Cam exits the car and walks towards where she saw Carlos go. The man in the driver's seat reaches over, closes her door, and then drives off quickly back towards the mansion.

Cam looks back briefly at the car speeding away and then continues following the man in the suit towards the garage. As she turns the corner her heart drops. Cameron can't believe her eyes. Standing at the foot of an all-black private G7 jet smiling from ear to ear is Dr. Sanchez. "What's going on Carlos?" she asks. "We're going on a trip." He replies. "This jet... is yours Carlos?" she asks finally able to smile
again.

"Yeah," he says, "I was in the market for a space ship but this was the best they could do for me."

"What..." she says as she tries to steady her heart beat. "No, I'm just kidding about the space ship," he replies, "but yes this is my baby, I call her "Unbreakable"."

"And where exactly are we going on *Unbreakable* Dr. Sanchez?" Cam asks walking towards him. "Paris,

France Ms. Jiles, *the city of love…*" he says wrapping her in his strong protective arms. Cam feels so comfortable in his presence.

"What did I tell you… about calling me Ms. Jiles, Dr. Sanchez?" she asks lazily swaying back and forth in his arms.

"Well one day," he says pulling slightly away from her to look down into her eyes, "You might be the next Mrs. Sanchez so I guess I'm just burning myself out on your current name."

She smiles as he takes her dark hand and leads her up the shiny chrome stairs into the jet.

"Wait," she says, "What do you mean *the next* Mrs. Sanchez?"

Looking back at her with a coy grin he says, "Some things are better left kept secret."

(Three days later Whit is sitting in a chair in K.C.'s hospital room)

"So, now what Keldrick…" Whit says. "What are you talking about?" he asks. "The nurse said the doctor's going to release you in the morning." Whit reminds him.

"Yeah, I heard them Whitney," he says," but what's your point?" "What do you plan on doing once you leave," she asks, "not the same day, or the next day, for the rest of your life Keldrick?"

Furrowing his thick eyebrows Keldrick says, "Wait… for the rest of my life? What the hell does that even mean?"

"I want to know what you plan on doing forever," Whitney replies crossing her arms firmly across her chest,

"Is that a problem?"

"Um yes it's a problem girl," he says laughing sarcastically, "don't you think *forever* is a little extreme?"

Whit is not amused. "I've been giving you *my* forever since we met K.C.," she claims, "why is it so hard for you to give me yours?" He doesn't respond.

"Hello… boy I know you hear me," Whit says, "I said why, is that so hard for you?"

"Because it is!" he exclaims. "Look I realize you want to give me your forever," he continues, "I also know you have never been with another man other than me, even while I was in prison." Whit chokes due to her suddenly dry throat and mouth.

"What the hell was that?" K.C. asks. "What the hell was what," she replies, "I was coughing damn…"

"What the hell ever," he says, "you ain't start choking and shit till I said something about you sleeping with other men."

"Keldrick please," she says, "don't start that shit with me right now just finish your little damn speech."

"I didn't ask for any of this," he continues, "and I know you didn't ask for it either but damn it, it's here. Now first of all I'm a man and you're going to stop talking to me like I'm your child!"

Whit turns her head away from him and mumbles, "Then stop acting like you're my child."

"I don't act like your child Whitney," he says trying to stay calm, "but you handicap me so damn bad, what else could I ever become if I stay with you? I'm not making excuses but my circumstances are not yours. I made a lot of mistakes, and as you know one in particular changed my life forever. So, when I do apply for jobs nobody gives a damn about giving out second chances, all they see is a background that will never check out in my favor *ever* again. But it's okay I can live with that, I don't have a choice. But I will not live with you talking down to me, and feeling like you gotta micro manage my ass. You never once tried to help me get a decent job, a car, or a piece of higher education. Do you have any idea what Cameron has done in the short time I've known her?"

"No..." Whitney replies. "All of the above Whitney," he tells her, "She helped me and showed me how to do all of those things that I desperately needed to know how to do as a man. See I may not have all the degrees you have but I'm far from stupid. I know exactly why you didn't do the things for me that she did."

"And why is that Keldrick, please enlighten me..." she says. "Because you were scared..." he replies.

Whitney laughs snidely.

"Scared of what Keldrick," she asks, "Scared of you?"

"No, just scared of losing me," he tells her, "see in your mind as long as you kept my ass paralyzed you could always be my wheel chair. It's just like what Denzel said in that movie; *The Great Debaters* "keep the body, take the mind". I'm a slave to you, so you allow me to stay physically fit but psychologically weak."

"No," Whit says, "that is not true." "Yeah... yes, it is Whitney," he says with a satisfied smirk on his handsome but pale face, "I see right through you girl. I was your cripple, but *that baby*... Cameron taught me how to walk."

"Oh, so she's your baby, right?" Whit asks standing

up from her seat. "I'm not in prison anymore **Warden** Powell," he says, "I already served all my time. No parole, no probation, no nothing. So that means I don't have to answer to you or anybody else."

K.C. stuns Whitney with his painful verbal blows. Wiping away a few tears she says, "I didn't know this is how you felt about me Keldrick."

"Na, don't give me that crap…" he says throwing his hands up in rejection.

"Boy I am so serious," she says, "I just don't understand though." "Don't understand what Whit…" he inquires. "Where did all of this anger towards me come from?" she asks. "You and Cameron both had it coming." He says.

"What do you mean we both had it coming?" Whit asks. "When I was still on that anesthesia yesterday," he says, "you both handled me real fucked up. But now that I'm back in my right mind, I demand respect."

"Ok Keldrick." she says.

"See there you go with that weak sarcasm shit again," he replies angrily, "get out of my room!"

"What…" Whit says holding her hands out waiting for an explanation. K.C. notices she has two cell phones in her left hand. "What are you doing with my cell phone," he asks, "I thought you said it was dead."

Whitney looks nervously down at his phone next to hers in her sweaty palms.

"Uh," she says unable to look him in his eyes, "well…it was. It was dead, but I charged it for you babe." "You were probably looking for Cam's number," he says, "Did you get it?"

"What," she says, "get her number for what?"

"It doesn't matter, just put my phone down, and get out of my room now." He repeats coldly.

"I'm not going anywhere Keldrick," she replies, "You know you need me."

"I don't Whitney," he replies laughing sarcastically to himself, "and the funny thing is I never did. Now get your yellow ass out of my room before I call security to have them remove you." Whitney turns and walks out without another word.

(Whitney)

Cameron is messing with the right one. I'm gonna show her how to play the game though. She shot and almost killed my man, and turned him against me. When I get through with that little black bitch she's gonna be begging me to shoot her and put her out of her misery. First thing I'm going to do is break up her little fantasy love affair with Dr. Sanchez. Mmmm that man is gorgeous. This is going to be fun, but how am I'm gonna pull it off? It's going to be hard because I think he actually likes her now. I got it! I know exactly what to do.

Whitney heads to the hospital café' to grab a couple of hot coffees. Meanwhile Dr. Sanchez is in his office doing some paperwork, and trying to unwind from his short vacation with the gorgeous Cameron.

His cell phone ringtone, IMX's, "*My Very First Time"* begins to play loudly.

"Hello," Carlos says answering his phone in a deep smooth tone, "What's up baby… yeah I know. You still unpacking and hanging up your new wardrobe? You're very welcome baby."

Carlos hears somebody knocking on his office door. "Hold on baby," he says putting Cam on hold, "Yes, who is it?"

"Whitney Powell," the voice on the other side of the door replies, "can I talk to you for a minute Dr.?"

"Just a minute," he replies, "Hey baby I'm going to call you right back I have a patient at my door. Ok… bye. Come in Ms. Powell."

Whitney walks in wearing a long skin-tight body dress with a plunging neck line exposing a good portion of her breasts.

"I need to talk to you Dr. Sanchez." She says handing him a cup of coffee. "Thank you for the coffee Ms. Powell," he says as he takes a healthy sip, "Mmmm this coffee is good, but there's something… *different* about it."

Whitney quickly sips her own coffee in a panic and says, "It's just an herbal blend I added in for flavor."

"Well whatever it is it's the best coffee I've ever had. Now what can I do for you Ms. Powell?" "Well Dr.," she begins,

"You know how I asked you to come on to Cameron Jiles, and get into her head so that she would leave my husband alone?"

"Hold your voice down Whitney," he says, "or someone might hear you. And K.C. is not your husband." "Your red oak door is very thick Carlos," she says pointing towards his expensive door, "No one is going to hear me."

"We can't talk about this again Whit," he says, "This time it's too close to home. If this gets out I could lose my license to practice, this is all very unethical."

"Oh, stop crying Carlos," she says, "I'm not out to get you darling. If that was the case I would have destroyed your career years ago with that video." Whitney giggles to herself.

"I was very... very drunk," he says sipping his coffee nervously, "and that was seven years ago. Please just leave the past in the past." "Oh, I intend to," she says, "as long as you continue to play ball." "What do you want now Cruella?" Carlos says sipping his coffee and waiting on his next assignment from the devil. "It's simple Carlos,"
she says, "all you have to do is **break** her little black ass heart."

"No." he replies. "What, I must be hearing things because I know you didn't just say no to me."

Whitney says standing up from her seat. Carlos takes another sip of the strange coffee.

"The game has changed now Whitney." Carlos tells her.

"No," she says raising her voice an octave, "the game has not changed, the game never *fucking* changes unless *I* say so."

"No Whit," Carlos says, "I'm actually starting to like Cameron. I refuse to hurt her just so you can feel better about your already failing relationship."

"Oh, you will break her heart Carlos," she says, "or I'll

break you." Smiling to herself, Whitney walks towards him and begins unbuttoning his button-down polo dress shirt. Carlos feels light headed as he takes another sip of the special coffee she brought him.

Standing behind him she begins to massage his broad shoulders as she kisses the back of his strong bronze neck.

"Has Cam seen your tattoo yet?" she asks as she rubs his bare
chest. "You're sick." He replies. Whitney laughs at his discomfort. "Well... has she seen it?" she asks.

"Yes Whitney." He replies through clenched teeth. "Mmmm does she know what it means?" she asks. "Of course, she doesn't know what it **bloody** means Whitney!" Carlos growls in frustration.

"Well Dr. if you want to keep it that way," she says, "Continue to do exactly what I say, and your secrets will always be safe and sound with me."

Then Whitney pulls Carlos' chair back away from his desk and steps around in front of him. Propping herself up on his classy desk she kicks her shoes off and places her cell phone off to the side out of the way.

"What are you doing Whitney?" he asks shaking his head slowly. "Come here Carlos, you know you want to." She says pulling her long dress up to her knees.

"No." he says. Carlos' entire body feels hot and he's sweating profusely. "Whitney, what did you put in this coffee?" he asks rubbing his own chest now.

"I told you it's just a special herbal blend."

"No," he says, "that was molly. You put molly in my coffee."

"So, what are you going to do about it Dr.?" she asks

playfully. "Shut up," he grunts as he takes his Gucci loafers off and drops down to his knees in front of his desk. Carlos lifts Whitney's left foot and begins to massage her toes with his tongue.

Sucking each yellow toe one by one Carlos takes his sweet time driving her entire body insane. Feeling extremely woozy Carlos stands up trying to keep his balance as he snatches her tight dress up to her waist. Next, he snatches the top part of her dress down completely so that her dress is only covering her midsection.

Whitney has her legs spread anxiously, and her feet positioned at the edge of the table. Back on his knees Dr. Sanchez begins to bite her inner thighs softly as he makes his way to her center.

Whitney looks towards her phone sitting close by on the table and smiles. Then she reaches for it and repositions it. Grabbing a handful of Carlos' soft curly hair she pulls his face in close to her wet body, as she grinds on his face.

Carlos' heart is beating extremely fast and he knows he doesn't like this woman but he can't help but be attracted to her right now. He knows something is wrong but he's far too gone to understand what it is now.

His emotions are conflicting with his spontaneous unexplainable arousal. He can't think straight at all so as she moans he continues to give her more. Methodically licking, every sweet crack and crevice on her beautiful lower body.

His adrenaline is insane right now, he feels like he can go on like this forever. Whitney leans forward toward him and hangs her legs over his broad shoulders.

Never stopping his oral assault Carlos stands up, placing his hands under her perfect round behind and picks her up with her legs still dangling over his shoulders.

"Carlos… please, please don't stop baby." Whitney moans.

I can't understand what's wrong with me and why I can't stop. **Carlos thinks to himself.** *I don't even like this woman, so why is it that I... I can't believe she drugged me.*

Trying to fight the effects of the drug Carlos sits her back down where she was positioned originally at the edge of his desk and then falls back to his knees. The impact of her landing back on the desk knocks her phone to the floor. Regaining some composure Carlos decides to take control of the situation.

"This is so wrong," he says, "Why would you do this to me?" Smiling down at him like an evil serpent she says, "You belong to me Carlos, you will always give me what I deserve, when I want it, and however I want it."

Carlos shakes his head violently still trying to fight of his powerful high. Looking up into her eyes he says, "I hate you, but you're right I'm going to give you exactly what you deserve."

Standing up in front of her he reaches behind her head and grabs her long ponytail and twirls it harshly around his fist to get a good grip.

"You like that!" he growls harshly with his lips close to her ear. Whitney closes her eyes but doesn't respond as the pain of his grip is still new to her. Carlos yanks her head back pulling on her hair still wrapped around his strong hand.

"I said… Do you like that!" he growls at the evil light skinned woman again. "Yes…" she whines.

"You are a terrible fucking person," he whispers in her ear, "and nothing good will come to a woman like you in the end..." "I don't care..." she moans honestly.

"I know," he growls, "that's what makes you so dangerous."

Carlos roughly yanks her hair again, then he turns her around and pushes her forward making her bend over. "I'm ready Dr. Sanchez..." she moans almost out of breath. "Have you ever seen the movie 300?" he asks as he pulls her thong underwear down.

"No...why?" she moans. "Don't worry about it," he says, "Just know you're not supposed to enjoy what comes next."

After wetting two fingers with his mouth he sticks them both quickly in her behind. Whit tries to scream out in pain and outrage. The screams get caught in her throat as he continues to ram his fingers inside of her.

In his mind Carlos wants to punish Whitney and this is the best way he can think of. After he feels she's loose enough he goes in her from behind. Whitney reaches back putting her sharp green fingernails deep into his bare thighs in protest.

Carlos' thighs are bleeding but he can't feel a thing at this point, and nothing matters beyond hurting her. He knows full well nothing he could ever do to Whitney short of killing her will make up for all the pain she's caused him over the years.

After kicking each of his shoes out of the way one at a time, he wiggles out of the rest of his clothing. Carlos continues to pound her hard from the back covered in tiny beads of sweat.

Whitney still in shock is unable to make a sound. Never letting go of her hair he stands her up and walks her to the closest wall in his office and pins her against the wall.

With her body plush against the wall he continues to stroke deeper, and deeper. Whitney sighs with relief as he begins to slow down. She even arches her back forward inviting him to continue.

Hearing her moan Carlos can tell she's starting to enjoy her punishment, this turns him off and he quickly throws her to the floor. Staring down at her with his lip curled and eyes squinted, he's never hated anyone as much as he hates Whitney Powell.

"Get out of my office Whitney." He says turning away from her. Carlos makes his way to his chair and falls back in it completely nude. Whitney crawls to him slowly like a wounded cat, with a sick smile on her face.

"I can't leave yet Dr. we haven't finished." She says reaching out for his bare right leg. Carlos kicks her hand away. "You're sick Whitney you don't know what you want," he tells her, "You're not happy, and you want everybody else to be miserable just like you. Now we're quite finished here, so get out. I don't care about the video anymore do what you want with it, just leave me and Cameron the hell alone!" Whitney stands up without saying a word, fixes her clothes and walks towards where her phone is lying next to the desk. She picks her phone up, and starts towards the door. With her hand on the knob she turns around to look back at Carlos.

"So, does this mean we're through?" she asks. Unable to look at her Carlos spins his chair around backwards so she can't look at him.

Whitney looks down at herself and straightens her crooked dress. Then she turns around and says, "By the way Carlos…"

"Whitney, I don't want to hear it!" Carlos yells cutting her off quickly.

"I'm pregnant." She says. Then she walks out closing the door behind her.

Carlos spins around quickly in his chair to find Whitney already gone. Putting his head down softly on his desk, Carlos begins trying to formulate a plan of action just in case the baby turns out to be his.

Chapter 6
Homecoming

(Jay and Ty are on their way to the hospital in a taxi cab)

"Finally, back home in the O." Ty sighs. "Yeah man," Jay says, "feels pretty good to be home huh?" "Yep," Ty agrees, "Hey Jay… You ever thought about moving back here and…"

"Hell no," Jay interjects, "I mean don't get it twisted I love Orlando, this city made me who and what I am. But what I am now is a rapper, and I just don't think the city has room for me to shine and spread my music the way I can back in Georgia."

"Yeah, I feel you," Ty says, "It's just something to think about, you know…" "Not now," Jay tells him, "but maybe in a few years."

"Sounds like a plan," Ty says, "whenever you're ready to make that move I'm riding with you bro. Besides in a few years I should have all the financial support I need to launch my first theme park." The cab finally pulls up in front of the large hospital.

"You ready bruh?" Jay asks Ty.

"What you mean Jay," he replies, "Hell yeah, I'm ready, are you ready? Man, we bout to find out a lot about our boy, this might get ugly."

Both men step out of the cab after Jay hands the driver a fifty-dollar bill. "Thanks man." Jay says to the driver. "Yeah," Ty says, "we appreciate that my brother."

The driver steps out to help them get their bags out of his trunk. Ty and Jay both grab all of their belongings. "You guys all set?" the driver asks.

"Yes sir." Jay replies. "Need any help carrying your bags inside?" the driver asks. "Depends..." Ty asks with a slick smile.

"On what?" the driver asks. "Do I have to tip you again?" Ty asks. "Um," Jay says, "first of all Ty if you tip the man it will be your first time, because I paid and tipped him for us both. Now bring yo cheap ass on. Thank you, sir, but we can carry our own bags."

Ty and Jay both laugh as they make their way towards the front door of the hospital. The cab driver pulls off.

"Tell me why we didn't go to the hotel first again bro?" Ty asks.

"Because," Jay says, "we had to come check K.C.'s status first homie."

"Yeah, you're right." Ty agrees as they enter the hospital. Ty and Jay approach the front desk of the hospital. "How are you doing beautiful?" Ty says to the nurse at the front desk. "I'm fine, how may I help you?" she replies. "Yes, you are fine..." Ty compliments the woman.

"Ty get the hell out of the way," Jay says pushing

past his flirtatious friend, "yes ma'am we're looking for Keldrick Cole. Can you tell us what room he's in?"

"Sure, let me check our system." She says looking at her computer screen. "I found him Keldrick Jermaine Cole," she says finally, "He's in room 317."

"Thank you," Jay says, "Ty bring your ass on she'll still be here later on." Ty passes the nurse a business card and then reluctantly follows his friend toward the elevators.

"So, are you nervous?" Jay asks. "Hell, no I'm not nervous Jay," Ty says as they step on the elevator, "what the hell I'm gone be nervous about? I'm not lying in some hospital bed because I got shot by some sweet little light skinned dude named Cam."

Jay bursts into hysterical laughter.

"Man, you crazy Ty, how you just gone make the dude be light skin?" Jay asks still laughing loudly as they ride the elevator to the third floor.

"Trust me the man is light skin," Ty says with a disgusted look on his face, "because all Keldrick ever dated was red boned, and light skinned chicks in school."

The elevator stops.

"You right Ty," Jay replies as they step off the elevator with their bags, "But what you so mad about?"

"Man, Keldrick is like a brother to me," Ty says, "so I just don't know how I didn't know he was…"

"And Ty you still don't know," Jay says, "K.C. always had the prettiest females in school before he fell for Whitney's fine ass, so I'm gonna give him the benefit of the doubt."

"You right Jay," Ty replies, "plus you know my little

cousin from Tampa her name is Cameron too." "That is *not* a good example Ty." Jay tells him.

"Why, not…" Ty asks with his forehead wrinkled tightly. "Your cousin Cameron Ty…" Jay says. "Yeah, what you trying to say Jay?" he asks.

"Man, your cousin got a dark blue temp fade, a hundred tattoos," Jay reminds his friend, "and she dress harder than both of us. Your cousin is a stud Ty."

"Blood of Jesus don't speak that on my family Jay," Ty says, "she's just confused right now." Jay laughs hysterically again.

"You're a hypocrite Ty," Jay tells him, "but I'll deal with you later about that. That's K.C.'s room at the end of the hall." "Yeah, I can see where the room is," Ty says, "But you can deal with me now. How am I a hypocrite?"

"Later Ty… Just worry about all that later on." Jay insists. "Hell, no Jay," Ty contends, "Come on with it."

"Ok, bet," Jay agrees, "You always say all gay people are going to Hell, but when it comes to your own family they're not going to

Hell, they're just confused. I don't think that logic is fair." "Shut up," Ty says, "we here to see about Keldrick."

"Yeah, I thought you would see it my way and try to change the subject." Jay says as they approach K.C.'s room. "Whatever dude." Ty replies as he opens the door to Keldrick's room.

"Keldrick Jermaine Cole…" Ty says looking at his old friend for the first time in years. "Ty and Jay where the hell did you guys come from?" K.C. asks sitting up in his hospital bed with a genuine smile on his face.

"Atlanta. And you look terrible by the way." Jay says

sitting his Louis Vuitton duffle bag down beside him sporting a real smile of his own. "I still look better than you though." K.C. replies.

"Man, whatever bro you're tripping." Jay says sharing a good laugh with his old buddy. Ty walks towards Whitney who's sitting in the chair next to K.C.'s bed.

"What's up Whitney," Ty says, "How you doing, you still fine as hell I see?" Stepping forward as well Jay says, "How you let my boy get shot that's the question?"

"Hello to you too Jacody," Whit says sarcastically, "and thank you Ty I still look decent I guess." "No, Whit you still fine," Jay agrees, "but we're not talking about that right now? I want to know what went down."

"Baby," K.C. says to Whit careful not to expose the rift between them, "give me a minute alone with my boys please."

"Sure baby," she replies and kisses him on his forehead, "I'll be right down the hall in the snack area." "Ok baby." K.C. says.

As Whitney walks out K.C.'s smile fades. "So, what happened to you bro..." Ty asks.

"Why does it matter?" K.C. asks as he tries to get out of the bed.

"What are you talking about Keldrick," Ty says, "Of course it matters bro, why do you think we flew back home?"

"Yeah K.C.," Jay says, "What the hell are you talking about?"

"How did ya'll even know I was in here?" K.C. asks hobbling towards the bathroom. "Facebook," Jay says, "do you remember Jessica from school?"

104

K.C. looks at Ty and smiles mischievously. "Jessica Martin?" K.C. inquires.

"Yeah, Jessica Martin…" Ty says in acknowledgement.

"Hell, yeah I remember her freaky ass," K.C. teases Jay, "that was my baby."

"Oh, hell no K.C., not you too bro…" Jay protests. "What bro," K.C. says laughing with Ty at Jay's expense, "You know Jess was extra friendly, *especially* with the football players."

"Whatever bro," Jay says, "Anyway she posted on Facebook that you were dying, so we came…"

"To watch me die Jay," K.C. says, "So that's what it takes to get some love from my brothers huh? I gotta get shot. I don't see or hear from either one of you for five years. But now that I'm on my death bed ya'll show up to bury me!"

"Calm down Keldrick." Ty says. K.C. crosses his arms and looks at Ty in confusion. "Ty who the hell is Keldrick… And since when do you call me that?" K.C. asks.

"Since now," Ty says, "since we're grown ass men, and not little boys anymore. What's wrong with wanting to transition into true manhood?"

K.C. burst into hysterical laughter. "So, let me get this straight Ty," K.C. says, "calling me by my government name makes you feel like a man?"

"Maybe it does," Ty says, "I see everybody else we went to school with on Facebook and Instagram still doing what they were doing seven years ago. I swear they spend their entire lives on social networks flexing like everything's okay, but it's really not okay…"

"Man, what the hell are you talking about Ty?" Jay interjects. "Yeah dude," K.C. says, "you lost me. What the hell do you mean everybody from school is still doing the same thing they been doing? What exactly is it that they're doing?"

"Struggling," Ty says, "everybody's either stuck in one spot or they're moving backwards."

"Direct your comments and emotions Ty," Jay says, "don't just throw blank shots out. Who you speaking on my Ty? Because I know I'm constantly on every social networking site on the planet. But that's work to me, because I'm on those sites networking and pushing my music. So, if you're talking about me just be straight up."

"Jacody ain't nobody talking about you bruh," Ty says, "If I was I would direct my comments to you specifically. But if you are feeling some type of way about what I said, maybe you need to look inside yourself and figure out why."

"Look inside myself," Jay says looking towards K.C., "what the hell is he talking about K.C.?"

"Yeah Ty you're tripping homie," K.C. says, "you're not exactly on the Forbes list yourself my fam, so how are you going to flex on everybody else like we all just doing so damn bad?"

"You're missing my point." Ty replies. "Well make me get it Ty,"
K.C. says, "because I'm starting to feel real disrespected by the shit it
sounds like you're saying right now."

"Blood of Jesus… You know what," Ty says, "My mama always told me to never, ever cast my pearls before swine." K.C. gets up out of his bed slowly.

"Who you talking to Ty," K.C. says, "boy don't think just because I got shot I can't still beat your ass."

"Calm down K.C. and lay back down," Jay says, "you're not in any shape to be fighting right now." Jay helps K.C. get back in his bed.

"But I'm in perfect shape for it," Jay continues, "what you want to do Ty because you just called me a pig too?"

"Jay, sit down," Ty says, "we too grown for all that mess. All I'm saying is that I want more. I'm talking about myself too. Right now, I'm stuck, but at least I have a plan. In my mind if you're working for anybody other than yourself you're working backwards."

"Well I like my job," Jay says, "So, I'm glad I'm not inside your crazy ass mind. And by the way dude, you work for Six Flags, not yourself."

"You're right, "Ty agrees, "But unlike most people, I have a plan."

"Oh right," K.C. says, "You're talking about your little theme park dream, right?"

"It's not a dream anymore Keldrick," Ty tells him, "It's already in motion. I have the financial backing and most of the approvals and signatures I need to move forward."

"So then," Jay says, "What the hell are you waiting on Ty if you already have everything on point?"

"God," Ty replies, "Everything will happen for me in God's time. He's in control not me." "Man, you know what Ty," Jay says with his hands-on top of his head in surrender, "I don't even care anymore. You do whatever you have to do, but don't talk crap about the rest of us just because we don't see life the way you do. Now back to you K.C., who is Cam bruh?"

K.C. smiles unintentionally. Feeling both of his friend's eyes on him, he looks up and loses his smile quickly.

"A friend," he says, "my best friend."

"Like a homie?" Ty asks sitting down to brace himself for what he thinks his friend is going to say next."

"Yeah," K.C. says, "ever since ya'll both moved away it's been hard. After the injury, everybody started turning their backs on me. Ya'll know I dropped out, then after that I got locked up. I had nobody."

"What about Whit," Jay interjects, "I know Whitney didn't change on you, or leave you because she's still with you now."

"Yeah," Ty says walking towards Jay,

"It couldn't have been that bad for you to start messing around with... with this du... with Cameron."

K.C. gets out of his bed again and stands facing both men.

"Do not judge me," K.C. says, "neither one of you were there for me during or after prison. And yeah Whitney was there but it wasn't the same sometimes a man needs... another man he can talk too..."

"Blood of Jesus, I knew it," Ty screams, "A man *never* needs another man for any damn thing! It's a sin Keldrick. Damn it Jay I told you!"

K.C. crosses his arms tightly and tilts his head to the side. "So, it's a sin to be weak," he says, "it's a sin to know that you can't endure a difficult situation in your life by yourself. Or is the sin reaching out to your brother for help? Tell me Ty because I am *completely* lost."

"K.C. what are you saying bruh," Jay interjects again, "stop beating around the bush and just say what it is so we can all be clear."

K.C. sits back down on his bed. "Look," K.C. starts, "yes I still had Whitney, and I probably always will, but it wasn't the same anymore. We lost our connection back in high school after my injury. She went from my best friend and my number one fan to my caretaker. She started acting like she was my mom, and I hated that. So, I think once she started trying to control me, I decided then that I was going to find somebody to replace her."

"Somebody you could relate to like a homeboy." Ty says. "Exactly," K.C. replies, "and when I met Cam, I knew that our meeting wasn't an accident. The more we talked and got to know each other the harder I fell."

"You fell," Jay asks, "damn K.C. how you do that man?" "He fell," Ty says, "Yep I told you what it was... I knew it."

"Falling for Cam was easy," K.C. says, "when we started hanging out together everything was so natural. Cam did things for me over the past six months that Whit never even attempted to do for me or with me in seven years. Because of Cam I had a car I could drive, a G.E.D., and decent job options. And that's huge for an ex-felon. So, think about all of that before you judge me for cheating on Whitney." "What," Ty says, "man we don't give a damn about you cheating on Whit. It's just the whole Cam thing we don't agree with. It's disgusting Keldrick, and you should end it now."

"Wait," K.C. says, "what do you mean it's disgusting? What's wrong with Cameron Ty?"

The door opens and a beautiful dark-skinned woman walks in slowly, with her tear-filled eyes fixed on K.C.

"Who the hell is this?" Jay asks delighted by the woman's natural beauty.

"Baby," K.C. says, "You came back."

"Baby," Ty says in total confusion, "Blood of Jesus. What kind of freaky four-way love affair you got going on Keldrick?"

"Ty and Jay," K.C. says, "allow me to introduce you both to my Cam."

"What!" Ty says. "Wait this is Cam," Jay asks, "this is *the Cameron* that shot you?"

"Yeah," K.C. replies, "you thought she was going to be light skinned with a big booty, right?"

"No," Jay says, "I thought she was going to be 6'2 with a goatee and an Adam's apple." "What?" K.C. says smiling in confusion.

"Yeah," Ty says, "This guy thought you were gay Keldrick, but I told him you weren't."

"Man, please," Jay says, "You thought Cam was a sweet light skin dude with a light brown finger wave just like I did."

"Wait ya'll thought I was gay," K.C. asks, "What just because my little brother is a faggot I have to be one too?"

"Watch your mouth Kel," Cam says, "that's very disrespectful."

"I couldn't care less if it's disrespectful or not," K.C. says, "he's my little brother I can call that *fruit* whatever I want to."

"How come I never met your brother?" Cam asks.

"Wait a minute," K.C. says, "stop trying to small talk me. Why the hell did you try to kill me?"

"First of all," Cam begins, "I didn't try to kill you. You broke my heart Keldrick."

Cam sits close to K.C. on his bed.

"Stop calling me that," he says, "my name is K.C., it always has been and it always will be. Ya'll, can't just change my damn name." "You can't be that kid in high school forever Kel." Ty says.

"Ty, get out of my room right now before I hurt you real   bad."

K.C. says through clinched teeth. "Whatever bruh," Ty says as he walks towards the door, the truth hurts."

"Bring your ass back here Ty!" K.C. demands. Ty turns around before walking out of the door to look back at his angry friend.

"You keep throwing all these shots," K.C. continues, "you throwin' all these mother fuckin' shots, if you got something to get off your chest be a man and get it off!" Ty slams the door back closed and turns around to face K.C. completely.

"You know what Kel," Ty says, "We've been biting our tongues for so long…" "We," K.C. says, "Who is we, Oh you on his side Jay?" "Man, do not put me in this," Jay says, "Ty sit down and be quiet bruh."

"No, I been quiet too long," Ty replies, "you want the truth Kel…" "Yeah," K.C. replies, "Hell yeah give me the truth Ty. What have you been biting your tongue about?"

K.C. gets out of his bed again and stands up facing Ty. Ty hesitates before speaking again knowing full well what the consequences of his words could be.

"You're not that same dude you were in school," Ty tells him, "after the injury everything changed... *You* changed Kel. You used to be everybody's inspiration and hope. That's what you embodied to me and a whole lot of other people. On top of that, you were always my big brother. I never had to worry about anything because everybody knew if they had a problem with me they were going to have a problem with you. But after you got hurt, I guess a part of you died bruh. You were so negative and helpless. Whit had to step up and baby you because you acted like you couldn't do anything for yourself. You dropped out of school and ran to the streets. Yeah... *you left us* long before we ***ever*** left you. You destroy every good thing in your life because you're still trying to go back and be the young K.C.... What I'm saying is Kel, K.C. the kid, died a long time ago. He died so grown ass Keldrick could live. Let Keldrick live big bruh."

K.C. has never felt more vulnerable than he does at this very moment as he tries to control his quivering lip. He knows he can't deny a word of the truth his friend is speaking to him.

Falling down to his knees a single tear begins to stream down his strong black face. He looks at Cam, staring down at him with no emotion on her face.

"You too baby..." he says.

"K.C.," Cam says shaking her head at him, "I really just came to make sure that you know when you get out of here, things are going to be very different."

"What are you talking about?" K.C. asks making his way to his feet again. Cam stands up from his bed and

112

begins walking towards the door. "It's over Kel," she tells him, "I can't live like this anymore you…"

"It's not over Cam," he says, "baby, don't say that… and don't leave me like this. We can work it all out, Whitney means nothing to me."

Cam turns around as she opens the door and looks back at him with an angry scowl on her face. "Funny how you told Whitney the same thing about me," she says, "Goodbye Keldrick." Cam leaves, and K.C. and his friends are left sitting in the screaming silence.

(LOVE)

Love is walking through the Millennia mall with a tall brown skinned man named Corey. Love and Corey have known each other for almost two years now. They met at a bar one night, the same day Corey was released from prison after serving five years for a failed robbery attempt.

Love eventually took Corey in and helped him reestablish himself in society. They've been extremely close ever since. "Are you hungry Lance?" Corey asks. "No. Not really." Love replies.

"Well you're starting to look sick bro," Corey says, "so I'm buying you some food anyway. Now what do you have a taste for?"

"I told you I'm good C," Love insists, "I'm just not in the mood to eat right now." "I know," Corey replies, "you haven't been in the mood for anything lately. She really messed your head up Fam."

"Who Whitney," Love asks, "No I'm good I just don't

know what to do next."

Corey smiles knowingly. "It's called love, Love," Corey tells him, "funny how your nickname is something you know nothing about. When I was younger I fell for a couple of good women. The feeling was amazing while everything was good, but when it all went sour it hurt worse than death." "Really," Love says, "*you* were in love with
two *women?*"

"Hell yeah," Corey replies laughing lightly, "What am I super gay man? I wasn't born into this lifestyle I became accustomed to it. But before, yeah, I had some great experiences with quite a few women. That's how I know you need to explore whatever this is you have with Whit to see where it could go. Don't get stuck like me, if you have a chance to be normal take it."

"If she was anybody else maybe," Love says, "but this situation is too dangerous now, especially since I actually like her now."

"It's not your fault," Corey says, "You didn't try to fall for the lady, but somehow you did. So, you can either be a man and explore the situation, or be a little boy and hide from your true feelings. But I can promise you this, if you don't find out where you and Whitney could potentially go you'll regret it later on."

Love looks down at the ground. "All I wanted to do was destroy him," he says, "It was never supposed to be about her."

(Whit)

Whitney is just leaving class, walking down the same

114

side walk where she met Love. Her mind is everywhere but one thing she's able to focus on without any difficulty is Cameron Jiles. Whit is attaching a large video file to a multimedia message on her phone as she thinks randomly to herself. ***This is not over. I'm going to destroy that little black bitch. She's going to wish she never met K.C.***

Whitney's phone vibrates right before she can send the video out. It's a text from Love that reads, "We need to talk." Whit smiles at the text, and then finishes sending the video message to its unsuspecting recipient.

(K.C.)
(Hours later K.C. and his friends are still in his hospital room talking)

K.C. is up pacing back and forth in his hospital room talking to himself aloud. "She can't just leave me," he says, "She would never… really leave me. Would she? I'm the only man she's ever trusted, so she can't just let that go. Whatever, I'm done crying though."

"Man, I hope so," Jay says, "I've known you forever and I've only seen you cry twice and the other time you cried bones in your leg were broken severely. This is some real feminine junk right here though. Since when do you cry over chicks?"

"Wait a minute Jay," Ty says standing up, "Boy, I know you ain't talking about anybody crying over a female."

"What the hell are you talking about Ty?" Jay asks.

"Oh, so now you got amnesia right," K.C. asks him as

he chuckles loudly, "see you can pretend to be a hardcore pimp with no emotion, but see you already know that's how *I* really was in school. But you, you were a sucker for love. Everybody knows Jessica had you gone bruh. You were in love with the class jump off."

"Watch your mouth K.C." Jay says walking towards the window.

"He's right Jay," Ty agrees, "so you can't judge him."

"Ty what the hell are you talking about," K.C. interjects, "You and Brittany had like five abortions from tenth grade to graduation. Your sensitive ass did more crying back then, than *both* of us."

As all of the tension in the room slowly begins to fade away, the three of them share a much-needed laugh together.

"Enough about the past though K.C.," Jay says, "what do you plan on doing about Whit and Cam when you leave the hospital in the morning?"

"I know exactly what I'm going to do." he replies.

"Really, and what is that?" Jay asks. "I'm going back to hoeing."

K.C. says with a large smile on his face. "Blood of Jesus," Ty says, "that's my boy. Now you're talking with some sense Keldrick."

Jay looks at Ty with his mouth and eyes wide open. "Ty, what the hell are you listening too man," Jay says, "Did you hear what this fool just said?"

"Yeah," Ty says, "He said when he leaves he's going back home right?" "No fool," Jay says, "he said when he leaves he's going back to *hoeing*!"

"What," Ty says, "Keldrick… I mean K.C. I thought we were making progress here. How can you sit on the floor and cry over a woman you claim to love and then ten minutes later decide to run back to the streets?"

"You two fools wouldn't understand." he replies. "You're right," Jay says, "I don't understand. So, make me understand how you go through an almost death experience because you broke this woman's heart, and then you decide to turn around and do some more dumb dirt?"

"I'm getting married at the end of this year." K.C. says.

"To *who bro*," Jay says, "which one?"

"Yeah Kel which girl do you plan on wifin' up," Ty asks, "And more importantly when you gone tell Jay I'm going to be the best man?" Ty asks.

"What," Jay says looking at K.C., "You tripping Ty, you know I'm the best man. Right big bruh?"

"Both of ya'll are worried about the wrong things," K.C. says, "just know that at the end of this year I will be at the altar standing face to face with the true love of my life, and my best friend will be standing right by my side."

"I got you bro you already know I'm going to be standing *right beside* you Kel." Ty says walking towards K.C. to shake his hand for a sense of confirmation.

"Yeah we're all gonna be right there fam..." K.C. says.

"Yeah, I know we all gone be there," Ty says, "but I'm gonna be right beside you right bro..."

"Yeah whatever Ty," Jay says laughing loudly, "K.C. knows I'm his best friend, you gone be the ring bearer or something... I don't know yet but we'll find something for your ass to do." They all laugh.

"Nahh you got me fucked up Jay..." Ty says

laughing at himself.

"See the way I see it," K.C. says, "if I'm going to be the *best husband* I can possibly be, I need to get all the running and gunning out of my system now. Then when I say I do, I really will."

"I guess that makes sense bruh," Jay acknowledges, "whatever you do wrap it up though. Protect yourself from new babies, crazy ladies, and sexual rabies."

"Boy you stupid," Ty says bursting into laughter, "now let's go grab something to eat downstairs I'm starving."

"Yeah," K.C. says, "I know that was a long flight I'm good though, ya'll go head I'm just gonna take a power nap."

"A power nap," Ty says with an amused grin on his chocolate face, "boy you getting' old as hell."

"Na man," K.C. says with a smile of his own, "I'm not really physically tired bro. I'm more so emotionally tired. Everything is moving way too fast for me right now, and I can't control any of it. Not yet anyway."

"Oh, okay cool," Ty says, "Get all the rest you can because tomorrow night we're gonna to hit every strip club in the city, this is a homecoming fool. You know we gotta turn all the way up."

Ty and Jay execute their old secret hand shake with K.C. then they head out of the door towards the elevator at the end of the hall. "We gotta make things right with Kel bro." Jay tells Ty as they walk. "No, I agree," Ty says, "I just don't think we're the ones who should be doing the bulk of the apologizing."

"Yeah, but it's not about all that Ty," Jay explains to

his stubborn friend, "I just don't want to be petty you know?"

"Me either." Ty says as they ride the elevator down to the hospital lobby. "Good," Jay says, "My thing is Kel is a good dude bro, and we used to be so close... all three of us. He left us at a point but at the same time he was hurting in more ways than one and we didn't..."

"Oh, hell no," Ty interjects, "I can tell exactly where this conversation is going man. Look Jay I agree Keldrick is a really good dude, shit that's our brother. But at the same time, we didn't ask him to turn his back on us."

"Ty," Jay says, "at what point did we ever go out of our way to try to be there for him after he got hurt?" Ty hesitates to respond as they approach the eating area in the hospital lobby.

"We didn't." Ty says. "Right," Jay replies, "we didn't even try. So, I can't just completely blame him for everything that happened back then."

"Well we're here now Jay," Ty says, "let's just take it one day at a time and see how everything plays out."

"Sounds good to me..." Jay agrees.

"I uh," Ty starts, "wanted to talk to you about something else."

"I'm listening fam..." Jay tells his friend. "I'm kinda glad Keldrick decided to take a nap instead of coming down here with us."

"Oh yeah," Jay says, "Why is that?"

"I wanted to talk to you privately bro..." Ty says stepping closer to Jay as he looks deep in his eyes.

"Man Jay," Ty continues, "I'm about to tell you something that you can't tell anybody, especially not

Keldrick."

"Okay…" Jay says obviously unnerved at this point.
"Man, I'm serious Jacody," Ty says, "Take this to your
grave bro."

"Aw damn it." Jay says. "What?" Ty inquires. "Go
ahead and say it," Jay says, "We just dodged the bullet
with K.C., and now *you* wanna come out the closet and
shit. I ain't trippin fam, and I'm not gonna change up on
you. We're brothers for life. To be honest Ty I kinda
always knew you were gay. But your secret is safe with
me bro."

"Good," Ty says leaning in closer to Jay, "because I'm
in love with you."

"What the fuck?" Jay says pushing Ty back from him.

Ty bursts into jubilant laughter. "Bro, I'm not gay," Ty
tells him still laughing at his reaction, "You shoulda seen
yo face though bro. Na man, I was gonna tell you I like
Cameron."

"Oh shit," Jay says trying to steady his heart beat,
"Bro I was gone beat yo ass. I mean I was cool with you
being gay or whatever, I just wasn't gone let you bring that
shit to me. So, you like Cam? Man, K.C. is gonna kill
your stupid ass before this trip is over with, you gotta
stop playing with that man I'm telling you Ty…"

"Yeah whatever," Ty says with an amused smile, "And
what was all that crap about you always knew I was gay?"

"I was being honest," Jay says laughing, "Na, I was
just trying to make you feel comfortable in your own skin
dude."

They both laugh. "I appreciate that fool," Ty says,
"But no I'm definitely straight, but I do like Cam's fine

black ass foreal."

"I guess," Jay says paying attention to his friend's outfit, "nice boots by the way." "Yeah," Ty says, "Thanks bro."

(Cam at Bahama Breeze)

Cameron is standing outside of her job on break making an urgent phone call.

"Hello," she says with a hard grimace on her pretty dark chocolate face, "may I please speak to Dr. Sanchez? Ok well when he is no longer busy tell him to call Ms. Jiles back as soon as possible. Thank you."

She hangs up and then walks back inside to clock back in to work. As she walks in she notices in the back corner of the restaurant Whitney is sitting at a table with two handsome men.

One is light skinned with dreads the other is tall and brown skinned with a low hair cut full of waves. This shouldn't cause an immediate problem for Cam, except for the fact that the table Whit is sitting at is in her section. She is their waitress.

Cam keeps her cool, grabs three sets of silverware wrapped   in napkins, three menus, and approaches their table, trying to go through the normal motions of her job description. "Good evening and welcome to Bahama Breeze," Cam says, "my name is Cam and I'll be your waitress for the evening."

Her voice sounds just as unreal as it always does. Whit thinks to herself. "It's nice to meet you." Love says. Corey nods his head to Cam in salutation.

"Can I get the three of you something to drink to start off?" Cam asks through a painful smile. "Yes, I'll have water." Love says. "One long island iced tea with a splash of mango for me please." Corey says.

Whitney is taking her sweet time, pretending to still be looking over the drink selection in her menu to be difficult. Cam rolls her eyes at the only woman she has ever truly hated.

"And you ma'am," Cam says as politely as she possibly can, "what can I get you to drink?"

"Um… I think I'll just have a sex on the desk," Whit says purposely, "oops I mean sex on the beach *how silly of me*. I'm so embarrassed." Whitney's mock surprise is sickening to Cam. She holds her tongue and just pretends she didn't hear the comment.

"Ok I'll get those drink orders right out to you all," Cam says finally, "Here is your silverware."

It takes everything in Cam not to take one of the sharp knives and stab Whit in the top of her head with it repeatedly. Cam starts to leave the table to get their drinks.

"Oh, and Cameron," Whit says, "Hold the poison please. Thanks dear." Did I miss something," Love says, "where do you know the waitress from?"

"Nowhere," Whit says, "Now what did you need to speak with me about?" "Ooh I like her," Corey says, "bougie as hell." Whitney's lip curls up slightly in an evil smirk. "I am not bougie," she says, "I'm classy."

"At least you know there is a difference between the

two." Corey replies sarcastically. "Anyway," Whit says rolling her eyes at Corey, "What did you need to talk to me about Lance?" "A lot…" he replies.

"Don't beat around the bush Love," Corey prods, "give it to her raw. Let her know what the deal is fool."

"What are you his life coach," Whit says laughing snidely, "Why are you even here?"

"Don't do that Whit." Lance says. "Don't do what?" she asks.

"Don't talk to him like that," Love tells her, "now where should I start… First of all, I care about you a lot."

"Wait a minute," Whit interjects, "What do you mean don't talk to him like that," she asks pointing at Corey, "Lance, that is a grown ass man, he can speak for himself."

Cam returns to the table with their drinks on a small tray. After sitting each drink down, she pulls a small pad out of her apron.

"Are you all ready to order?" she asks. "Not yet," Love says, "give us a few more minutes please." "Yeah Cam I'll just snap my fingers when we need you," Whit says without even looking at her, "now run along."

Without a word Cam obediently walks away because she knows how badly she needs her job. "Now Lance what were you saying," Whit says, "Why are you taking up for this grown ass man?"

"Forgive me both of you," Love says, "I didn't formally introduce the two of you."

"Love what are you doing?" Corey asks with his eyes wide open.

"Nothing…" Love replies. "You're supposed to be

here to talk about you," Corey reminds him, "and where you're at emotionally. You are not here to talk about me or anything else, do not put your foot in your mouth boy."

Love looks at Corey and then at Whit. "Corey this is Whitney my girlfriend," he says confidently, "and Whit this is Corey… my partner."

"Damn." Corey mumbles under his breath. "Damn what," Whit says, "What are you saying Lance? What do you mean Corey is your partner? You mean like a friend, like an old homeboy, almost like a brother?"

"No Whitney," Love says, "Corey is my man. I'm on the DL."

"No fool, you were on the DL." Corey says shaking his head in disappointment." Whitney is speechless. She looks at both of them with real fear in her eyes.

"Are you serious?" she asks. "Yes." Love replies. "Boy we had unprotected sex multiple times, are you trying to kill me?" she asks. "Wait a minute Ms. Lady," Corey interjects, "Love shouldn't have told you anything in the first place, but what do you mean is he trying to kill you? What exactly are you trying to say?"

"I'm saying you two are disgusting," Whit says staring at him with venom in her eyes, "and AIDS is spread most commonly by gay men."

"Well that's your opinion," Corey says, "but at least Lance was man enough to tell you. I wouldn't have told you anything."

"Stop talking to me." Whit says. Whit slams her face down hard on the table as she feels light headed and dizzy.

"Are you okay?" Love says placing his yellow hand on her back. Whit pulls away from him quickly and slaps him hard in the face. Love's dreads sway violently as he reacts to the slap. "I knew it," she says, "I always knew there was something different about you! I just couldn't quite put my finger on it. But I knew it was something."

Corey stands up. "Whitney, I know you're upset, but don't put your hands on my boy again." Corey tells her. "Or what," she says, "You're going to fight a woman? I think not cupcake, now sit back down."

Whitney is more right than she knows. If Corey gets in any trouble while still on probation he's headed right back to prison.

"You better watch yourself." Corey threatens as he sits back down slowly. Love is silently staring off into space.

"So now what…" Love asks in a very light tone. Whitney laughs snidely. "What do you expect to happen next, Lance," she asks him, "This is where we end." "If that's what you want." Corey says.

"What's that supposed to mean Corey?" Whit inquires. "Who says the definition of a relationship has to be one man and one woman, or two men, or two women?" Corey asks. "Every normal person on the planet…" Whit says. "Whitney, people try new things every day." Corey explains.

"What are you getting at Corey," Whit asks, "because if you're trying to set up some kind of freaky threesome I'm not going for it, I got all of that out of my system back in my college days."

"That's sexy as hell Whitney, but that's not what I meant," Corey says, "well kind of but not exactly. It doesn't have to start out, or ever be sexual."

"It doesn't have to start out or ever be sexual?" Whit asks with her forehead wrinkled tightly.

"This," Corey says as he smiles, "whatever this is can be beautiful. It doesn't have to be ugly or disgusting unless you choose to look at it that way. Lance loves you, and you and I both love Lance. So, we can work this all out between the three of us as consenting adults, embarking on an innovative prototype of a hybrid relationship, between three people." Whitney cracks a genuine smile.

"That's kind of genius," she says, "as much as I hate to admit it that is an intriguing notion. And just how long have you been thinking about doing something like this Mr. Corey?"

"Just Corey is fine Whitney," he says returning her smile, "but I was locked up for quite a few years so I had time to do a lot of reading and research on the subject, and I believe it can work. But it will only work if we're all willing to try it and not be judgmental."

Cam approaches the table again. "Are you ready to order yet sir?" Cam says to Corey. Corey looks at Whit and Love for confirmation. They both nod in hesitant agreement, and then Corey focuses back on Cam. "Yes, ma'am I'll be ordering for the three of us."

Chapter 7

Lost

The rain that's falling on the windowsill

outside of K.C.'s window is landing in a pattern
that's very soothing to his ears. As
he lies in his hospital bed for the last time, he's thinking
about his life outside the hospital's walls.

Being in this room reminds me of prison, but not in a
bad way. I've had time alone to think and reevaluate the
direction I'm headed in. The truth is I'm not headed in any
direction. I'm just stuck like a lot of other young guys I
know.

Stuck with women we chose long ago, stuck with jobs we
don't like, and stuck in lives we wish we could change and
control. But it's too risky to leave or shake things up so the
majority of us just stay.

The sick part is we don't have to. We can leave
whenever we want to but we don't. Instead we treat
failing relationships like prison sentences, like they're just
something we have no choice but to endure.

That's wrong though, we shouldn't stay for the kids, the
money, or even security. We only live once, and I want to
live happy. If I end up marrying Whit, I want everything
to be right. If I marry Cam, I want Whit to respect the fact
and not interfere.

Most of all I want my daughter Jazemene to be happy.
In a perfect world, I could marry both women, move them

both into a huge house and enjoy separate but equal lives with each of them, or even allow all of our lives to harmoniously intertwine together. But I do realize stuff like that is only possible in movies, and romance novels. My life is neither of the two. "Rise and shine superstar." A familiar voice says as he walks in the room. K.C. looks up to see Ty dressed to the nines in white linen pants, a soft green short sleeve button down shirt, a white   cowboy hat, and white cowboy boots.

K.C. closes and rubs his eyes and then looks back at Ty again. "What?" Ty says with a proud smile on his face.

K.C. laughs heartily. "Ty what the hell do you have on," K.C. asks, "Is this some kind of joke?" Ty looks down at his attire with his brows wrinkled, then back at K.C.

"What do you mean... a joke?" he asks. K.C. sits up to get a better look at his friend's entire outfit. "Ty, you have cowboy boots on," K.C. says with real surprise in his voice, "Not just cowboy boots, boy you got pearly white cowboy boots on."

"So..." Ty says, "Why does it have to be a joke because I'm dressed nice? Do you know how much these boots cost?"

"No," K.C. replies, "but I bet you're going to tell me." "Damn right I am," Ty replies, "three hundred and fifty dollars."

"Right... and why did you spend that much on some cowboy boots Ty?" K.C. asks. "These are white leather Keldrick," Ty tells his old friend, "only classy white people wear these."

K.C. puts one arm across his chest, his opposite hand on his chin, tilts his head to the side, and squints, his tired eyes at Ty.

"So, which one do you want to be?" K.C. asks. "What do you mean?" Ty replies. "Well, you said only classy white people wear the boots you have on," K.C. reminds him, "So I'm asking you, do you want to be *classy* or do you actually want to be ***white***?"

"Come on K.C." Ty says flinging his arms wildly in protest. "Come on what," he replies, "answer the question Ty."

"Of course, I don't want to be white." Ty says. "Good," K.C. says, "because you're not, and you never will be. Do you remember what you said you were going to do after graduation Ty?"

"Yeah," Ty replies, "I said I wanted to be a policeman." "No before that." K.C. says. "Fire fighter…" Ty says. "Before that…" K.C. replies.

"Oh," Ty says, "I said I wanted to design and build a flying car." "Right," K.C. agrees, "and Jay and I told you, you would have to go to school to ever be able to do that. My point is this, you always have these amazing ideas and dreams but all you ever do is talk about them. You talk about everybody else around you, but you're no better off. Yes, you have a dream and a plan but that's all they are, is dreams and plans Tyrone. We all have those. You always look around, at people that you think are happy and successful. You try to emulate what they do, or at least what you think they're doing from the outside looking in, to create your own happiness. Just figure out what makes you happy Ty."

"The other night we were headed to a club in the A…" Ty says looking down at his hands as he allows them to massage each other so the fact that they're shaking won't be as noticeable.

"Okay," K.C. says, "and so what happened?"

"When…" Ty asks
looking up at his friend. "Ty," K.C. says, "you just said the other night you were headed to the club and you never finished your story bro…"

"Oh right," Ty mumbles, "We were headed to a club in Atlanta and Jay stopped at this gas station to get some cigarillos. This brand new, shiny, black on black, Mercedes Benz truck pulled up next to us. Two white guys got out wearing nice linen pants and cowboy boots. They had cowboy hats on their heads and Rolex watches on their wrists. When they walked, they looked like they were floating above the ground. Kel, I was like a happy little white lady at a bar no homo, but man I was really excited to see real cowboys. Their confidence and overall swagger was contagious and undeniable. As they were walking by the car, I stopped them and asked where they were from."

Ty smiles as he looks down at his expensive boots.

"What did they say Ty?" K.C. asks.

"We're from **Texas partner**." Ty says in his best country voice. "That's cool Ty," K.C. says, "that's really cool bro. But that's not
who *you* are or where *you're* from bro. You are a black man from Orlando Florida. Be proud of that. And if you decide you want to wear cowboy gear all year round that's fine too, but wear it because it's you, not because it's somebody you admire."

The door opens. "You still in the bed fool?" Jay asks. "I'm about to get up now." K.C. replies. "Good," Jay says, "Hurry up and get your stuff together, she's downstairs in the car waiting on you."

"Who is downstairs waiting on me, Whitney or Cameron," K.C. asks, "Hell it doesn't even matter I'm just ready to get the hell out of here."

Jay and Ty share a quick sneaky smirk. K.C. climbs out of bed, grabs his clothes, and makes his way to the bathroom.

Ty and Jay grab all of K.C.'s other belongings and wait out in the hallway for him. "K.C. ain't gone like this bruh." Jay says.

"I know," Ty replies, "but I don't feel like we had a choice."

"We had a choice Ty," Jay says, "we could have just gotten a rental car and picked him up ourselves."

"Oh, shit they got free rental cars now?" Ty asks with mock excitement. "Fuck you Ty," Jay whispers, "I'm serious bro. This shit will not end well fool."

"Man, I don't give a damn right now bro," Ty says, "My money is extremely tight right now bruh, I can't do anything extra and unnecessary."

"But that's your brother though right..." Jay says shaking his head. "Shut up fool," Ty says, "I hear him, he's bout to come out." "Yeah whatever..." Jay mumbles.

"Man, what the hell are ya'll out here arguing about now?" K.C. asks grabbing his belongings from his two friends.

"Uh," Ty mumbles, "we uh... I told Jay you scored four touchdowns in your first game as a freshman in high school, he said it was only three."

K.C. looks over at Jay with an intrigued smile. "It was three receiving touchdowns Jay," K.C. tells him, "and I also ran a kickoff return back on my first play ever on a high school football field. How did you forget that Jay, both of ya'll were down on the sideline with the team for the whole game?"

"Yeah, my bad..." Jay says as the three of them ride the elevator down to the lobby. As the elevator slides down the shaft K.C. looks at both of his friends and smiles.

"What you smiling at Kel?" Jay asks returning his infectious grin. "Nothing man," he replies, "I'm just glad ya'll are here bro." The elevator opens.

"Man, never think twice about it bro," Ty says, "you were hurt, and we came as soon as we heard."

After checking out at the front desk, the three guys head out of the front door. K.C. stops right outside the door to inhale deeply and enjoy the fresh air.

"Man, this is how I felt when I first got out of prison," K.C. admits, "But you two wouldn't know that because you weren't there when I got out."

"Don't start that again, let's get you home so you can take a good shower and change clothes." Ty says. "Cool," K.C. says as they continue towards the parking lot, "so where is our ride?"

K.C. stops in mid stride, and drops his bags as his heart stops beating. "Wait, what's going on?" he asks looking straight ahead in fear as if he's seen a ghost.

Parked at the curb just yards away from where they stand is an old blue Honda Accord, with a middle-aged heavy-set light-skinned woman behind the steering wheel. The woman steps out of the car slowly, almost as if it's painful for her to do so.

"Baby…" she says. "What's going on," K.C. asks again frantically, "Jay… Ty, one of you better start talking before I start swinging."

"Calm down Kel," Ty says approaching the car, "How you doing Mama Cole?" "I'm fine Tyboonie," she replies, "Now come give me a hug boy." Ty hugs the woman tightly and then kisses her on her chubby left cheek.

As she turns around she sees Jay standing right behind her and she smiles happily. "Jacody… oh I mean Mr. J' Milli," she corrects herself, "Boy I watched all your videos on YouTube about a hundred times." They hug.

"Well thank you Mama Cole that's what's up," Jay says, "I really appreciate the support." She turns again to look at Keldrick who hasn't moved an inch or taken his angry eyes off of her for even a second.

"Boy," she says, "Are you just going to stand there or are you gonna come give your mama a hug?" K.C. slowly looks back towards the hospital awkwardly. Then he looks back at her.

"Well…" she says. "No thank you," he replies, "I'm just going to stand here." She looks at him for a moment and then she smiles. "Is there something funny Mother?" he asks.

"Ty, get his bags and put them in my trunk please, so we can all get back to the house," she says, "I know you must all be hungry…"

K.C. grabs his bag and steps back refusing to let Ty

take his bags from him. K.C. looks intently at his mother. "I said did I miss the joke mother," he asks, "what was funny?"

She doesn't look at him or acknowledge his question. "Come on Kel," Jay says, "Let's get you to the crib so you can rest bro."

"Jay," K.C. says, "Don't try me bruh. I don't need any rest. Suddenly I have all the energy in the world. I feel like I could throw, catch, and run a football better than anybody on the planet. That's what you want to hear right Mom? The golden boy is ready again to make all *your* dreams come true."

"Blood of Jesus," Ty says, "Honor thy mother and thy father…" "Ty miss me with all that bull shit," K.C. says, "I don't have a mom, and I only had a dad when I was the kid who was ranked the number one high school recruit in the nation."

"That is not true," Mama Cole says with her hand over her mouth obviously holding back tears, "you have always had a mother and a father who love you very much Keldrick Jermaine Cole."

"To what end Mom," K.C. says, "Huh…a mother's love should be real, lasting… and unconditional. It shouldn't have died or faded away just because my NFL career did."

"Boy," Mama Cole says, "I am not about to…" "Man." K.C. interjects.

"Excuse me." she replies.

"You called me a boy," K.C. says through his teeth, "I was a boy, years ago when you turned your back on me, but now mother I'm a grown ass man. And I don't need or want you in my life ever again. After the injury, all I had was Whitney."

"And where is she now!" Mama Cole shouts. K.C. doesn't respond. "Where is she now Keldrick," his mother continues trying to keep her tone down, "If she loves you so damn much and she's always there for you… where is Whitney now? I can tell you exactly where she is if you want to know. Whitney is with her new man. Yeah, some young guy she said she met weeks ago, while the two of you were fighting."

"That's none of your business," K.C. says, "and I don't believe a word of what you're saying. Ty, where is Whitney, why isn't she here bro?"

Ty doesn't respond, instead he continues to look down at the ground near the car. "What the hell," K.C. says noticing Ty's reaction to him, "you know what, fuck you Ty! Jay, where is Whit bro? Can you call her for me?" Jay ignores the question as well.

Mama Cole steps around to the front of her car to be closer to K.C. She wants to make sure he hears her next words clearly. "Whitney is not coming son," she says, "It's finally over this time. The girl is trying to move on, and you should let her." K.C. drops his bags by his side, crosses his arms tightly, and wrinkles his forehead.

"How do you know?" K.C. asks.

"How do I know what?" she replies. He steps forward. "You said me and Whit are finally over," K.C. reminds her, "and I'm asking you how the hell, do you know that?"

"Because she brought all of your clothes and everything that you own and dropped it all off at my house," Mama Cole tells him, "She never did that before son. She also gave me that girl Cameron's number, the crazy one that shot you. I called her up, and she doesn't want you back over there either. So, I may not be what you want, but Mama's all you got right now son."

(Whit)

The champagne colored Expedition truck pulls into an empty parking space near the front of the movie theater. Corey is driving, Whitney is on the passenger side, and Love is riding in the middle part of the back seat leaning forward in between the two of them.

All three of them get out of the truck. Whit and Love immediately look down and check their outfits; Corey checks his watch and says, "Come on you two, we don't wanna be late. I hate missing the previews.

"Okay." Whitney replies sweetly as she grabs Love by his arm.

As the three of them approach the front of the theater, Whit secretly checks both men out and smiles happily as she's convinced that she's on a date with two of the most handsome men in Florida. Love looks down and notices her smile, but he dares not say anything, because he doesn't want to ruin her private moment whatever it may be. He's just happy that she's happy. The three of them carefully scan the movie titles flashing across the screen at the top of the box office.

"What are we seeing again?" Whitney asks. "It doesn't matter to me." Love replies.

"Man, I just want to see whatever the two of you

want to see." Corey says smiling warmly.

"Come on now boys," Whit says, "somebody has to pick something because we're next in line. And how does this work, who's buying the tickets?" Love rolls his neck, and looks at Whit like she's crazy for even asking that question.

"What…" Whit says noticing how completely feminine his mannerisms are when he's around Corey.

"I got it," Corey says, "See… Whitney, Lance is your man… but I'm both of ya'll's man." Corey laughs quietly at her confusion and then steps forward as the lady in the box office finishes with the customer in front of them.

"I'll have three for the *"Curtis Cringe"* at 8:30 please." he says. "Ok, that will be $28.50." the cashier replies.

Corey pays for all three tickets, thanks the cashier, and then leads Love and Whitney towards the door. "Thank you." Whitney says   as Love opens the door for her. After she walks in, the taller Corey holds the door open for Love to enter as well.

"Ok, so do both of ya'll want popcorn and soda?" Corey asks
heading toward the concessions.

"No," Whit says I'll just have a jumbo pretzel and some hot cheese please."

"Cool." Corey replies. "What about you, Lance?" Whitney asks him.

"Oh, you already know what I want, C." Love says looking towards his man. "Right," Corey says smiling to himself, "Blue Raspberry icee, and some Sour Patch Kids, right?"

"So… you think you know me huh…" Love replies smiling. "Yeah, I do," Corey says, "better than you know yourself. And with all this sugar you've been taking in, I hope you know a good dentist." Corey laughs teasingly.

"This line is way too long for all of us to wait," Corey continues, "so the two of you go find us three good seats. Our theater is down the hall on the left. I'll be in there in a minute."

"Ok… Thanks Corey," Whit says smiling as she grabs Love's hand, "Come on Lance, we need to talk alone anyway."

As they walk past a group of cute college girls, Whitney grabs Love's hand tighter when she notices how the girls seem to melt just from looking at him.

"What you wanna talk about baby?" he says completely ignoring the girls, and looking in her eyes as they walk.

"I wanna talk about this," she says, "this… relationship or whatever we're experimenting with."

"Well let's just wait for C," Love says, "then we can all talk about it together." "No," Whit says, "I said I want to talk to *you* alone."

Love looks at Whit again as they get closer to the theater. "But C said we should discuss any problems as a threesome." Love replies. "Look baby," Whit says, "C, or Corey or whoever he is… may be your man, but he's not mine yet. And frankly baby you act as if he's your damn father. Do you have daddy issues or something, because I seem to still be missing some huge pieces to the puzzle?"

Love opens the door for Whitney and they both step just inside the theater door together. "Where is all of this coming from babe?"

he asks with his brows wrinkled and his head slightly held to the side.

"Seriously," she says, "this is not normal, Lance. My boyfriend has a boyfriend. Maybe if all of our genders were switched, maybe this situation would be more common. But Lance, this is something I've never even imagined being possible, especially not in my own personal life. It's strange. Facing her completely, he grabs both of her soft yellow hands in his.

"Whitney," he says, "I think I'm falling... no, I know I'm falling in love with you. But I've been in love with Corey for over a year. The only reason we're standing right here together is because he loved me enough to talk me into trying to work things out with you. You have no idea how dangerous this whole situation could become because of certain people who are involved, and I pray you never do." "What are you talking about, Lance," she asks, "There's only me, you, and Corey, who else is involved?"

"I'm talking about K.C., Whit he's..." Love pauses, "never mind that when did you start calling me Lance?"

"After I realized that's what your man calls you," she admits, "Now what were you saying about Keldrick before?"

"Come on baby... let's find a seat before C gets back with the food." Love says grabbing her hand gently and ushering her towards the ramp that leads up to where the actual movie screen is.

As they sit down, with an empty seat on the other side of Love reserved for Corey, Whit is still looking at him in confusion.

"Do you realize how different you are when you're around him," she asks, "even right now you changed again because it's just us sitting here. You get so completely feminine around that man; you twist better than me. It is kind of cute when you do it, but you're my man so at the same time it sickens me."

"I'm sorry you feel that way," he says looking down towards his shoes, "I don't do it on purpose." "I know that," she says placing her right hand over his left hand gently, "The only reason I'm even here is because I do love you Lance... and I want to at least try to understand what this is. So, when did it all start?"

"What," he says," Oh, you mean C and me we..."

"No, Lance," she interjects, "I'm talking about liking men sexually. How long have you known you were gay?"

"Oh that," he says, "I guess I've always known." Whit sits back in her seat to take in everything Love is saying to her.

"How did it start?" she asks in a whisper. "Do you really want to know?" he asks. "I wouldn't ask If I didn't baby." she says while leaning close to him. "I know," he says, "but it's just weird." "What's weird Love?" she asks. "Nobody ever cared enough to ask before." he admits.

"I just asked," she says, "so tell me baby... I really wanna know." "Well for starters my brother is an asshole," Love says, "He's always been my mom's favorite. I never got half the attention he got growing up. That bothered me badly because I was the type of child that really needed attention. I was basically a mama's boy without a mom." Love laughs nervously to himself.

"At a very early age," he continues, "I found myself secretly, almost naturally mimicking my mother's mannerism, and speech tendencies. When she wasn't around which she never was, I used to sneak into her closet and model her clothes. I would even smother my face with her cheap make up and lipstick. When I was young my mother used to always have so many attractive young boyfriends who seemed to give her so much attention. I guess in my young mind to get as much attention as my mom was getting, I needed to be pretty like her. I was so confused."

"Oh my God…" Whit says leaning over to kiss Love softly on his cheek as he continues to talk.

"It's ok I'm dealing with it all now," he says, "I mean, I never had a dad. The closest thing I ever had was my brother's dad, Paul. He would come around about every other month. At first, he treated me like crap like everybody else, but in time everything changed."

"Why?" Whitney asks. "If I tell you this Whit, you will only be the second person I ever told this to." he tells her.

"Tell me Love." she says scooting even closer to him. "Maybe later," he replies, "it's extremely embarrassing." "No baby," Whit whines, "Please… tell me now. I wanna… you know share that pain *with* you baby."

Love hesitates to respond to her as the previews begin to play on the large screen in front of them. He looks down towards the bottom of the theater to see if Corey is coming, he doesn't see any sign of his man at all.

Love looks over in Whitney's eyes and has no doubt now that he's about to tell her the biggest, deepest, darkest secret he has. "It's okay Love…" she whispers.

"Well," he starts, "I told you how I used to dress up in my mother's clothes right?"

"Yeah…" she replies with her eyes wide open now.

"Well, one day when I was about nine years old, I had on one of my mother's Victoria's Secret bra and panty sets. And I thought I was home alone, but while I was in the mirror, I could feel somebody's watching me. I could feel it, but I guess I was too scared it was my mother so I waited a while before ever turning around to see who it was. Baby I still remember how hard my heart was beating during those terrifying few moments…"

"What happened, Love?" Whit asks eagerly.

"When I turned around," Love continues, "it was Paul, my brother's dad. He was drunk and high, and he kept touching himself while he was looking at me. He told me that I looked better in the underwear than my mom did, and I smiled because I wasn't used to being complimented at all. I was a very, very ugly little boy."

Whitney grabs his hand softly. "Don't say that baby," she tells him, "and I find that very hard to believe because you're so gorgeous now."

"Thanks Whitney," he replies, "But, I wasn't back then. I was however relieved that he didn't judge me or call me a little faggot or something like my brother would have. He promised me that he would never tell my mom as long as I agreed to play a game with him."

"A game," Whitney interjects, "what kind of game?"

"I was very scared," Love tells her, "so of course I agreed. I knew the way he touched me and the things he made me do were so wrong, but it felt so good just to be touched. Whit, do you have any idea how it feels to be a forgotten child that never gets hugs or kisses, or at least one kind word every now and then?"

Whitney's face is covered in tears now. "No, I don't know how that feels Love but I am very…"

"You're sorry right," Love interjects, "I don't want your sympathy babe but thanks just the same. But anyway, long story short, for the next ten years my brother's father raped and molested me, and eventually it just became a routine. I even began almost enjoying it, because it was the closest thing to compassionate interaction I ever got as a child. And I think I enjoyed the fact that this was our secret more than anything, it was something I could call my own. He bought me anything I wanted, took me places, and even defended me to my evil ass mother. He was my lover and the only friend I had."

"But Lance," Whit says, "Boy, you are drop dead gorgeous, and you're telling me you didn't have any friends growing up or even in high school?"

Love looks down at his feet. "I didn't look like this at all growing up," he says, "I started to change around the end of my senior year. At that point, a few girls at school had crushes on me or whatever but they almost always ended up hating me, or becoming my best friend. Something just wasn't right. It just wasn't real for me."

"Why," Whit asks, "What do you mean it wasn't real?" "I don't know," he replies,

"But for me it's never felt real being with any female until I met you. You… Whitney Michelle Powell, you made everything very real to me. And to be completely honest, the only reason we ever met is because I set it…"

"Man, it took me forever to get to the front of that

damn line." Corey says as he takes his seat next to Love. "Wait," Whit says, "What were you saying about us meeting, Love?"

"I'll tell you later babe, the movie is starting." Love says nervously looking at Corey out of the corner of his left eye.

(Cam)

Cameron storms in through the front of Dr. Sanchez's office, wearing her Bahama Breeze uniform.

"Where is he?" she barks at the receptionist. Completely frightened, the tiny Caucasian intern quickly turns around and points towards his door. Cam rushes past her desk and barges into his office with a vengeance.

"Listen Dr. Doolittle," Cam screams at him, "I don't know what you take me for, but that was very disrespectful!"

"What are you talking about my love?" Carlos asks. "You know exactly what I'm talking about." she replies.

Carlos smiles at Cam as he walks towards her. The smile is not to belittle her; he can't help it. She is just so sexy to him when she's angry.

"Oh, I do?" he says. "Yeah you do, so stop playing with me!" she demands.

"Ok," Carlos says, "Whatever I did… must have slipped my mind. So please refresh my memory, darling."

Cam quickly pulls her phone out of her tight work pants pocket, and begins scrolling through it to find the video that Whitney sent her.

"This!" Cam screams as she pushes the phone in his face forcing him to grab a hold of it as he stumbles back.

Looking at the video, instantly his face goes pale. "This is wrong." he mutters. "This is so wrong," he continues, "This isn't me Cameron."

"Carlos shut the fuck up," she screams, "that *is* you, that's *this* office, and that's Whitney Powell sitting on your damn face!"

"No, it's not!" he replies.

"Seriously Carlos," she says, "Are you really going to sit here and lie to me *to my face?*" "No darling," he says, "You don't understand. You can't possibly think I..."

"You're right Carlos," she interjects, "I don't understand. How could you do something so thoughtless? Why her? There are at least a thousand members of the female staff here; who I'm sure would love the chance to get some alone time with your smooth-talking ass in this office. So, why in the world would you choose her?"

"Cam," he says, "If you would just calm down..." "Boy," she interjects again, "Do not tell me to calm down." The graphic sexual sounds of the video are still playing loudly on her phone as he watches it.

"Ok," he says sitting down in his chair behind his desk, "I know what it looks like in this video but this is not me. Well it is me but not the real me."

Cam laughs snidely. "So now you have a body, double, right?" she says with her mouth twisted to the left side of her face as she is unconvinced by his explanation.

145

"No," he says, "What I'm saying is..." "Absolutely nothing..." she stops him mid-sentence once again. "She drugged me Cam," he says, "I didn't really want her, or I guess maybe subconsciously I did. But I don't love her, it was only physical."

"Yeah that makes it better." Cam says with mock appreciation.

"I tortured her for God sakes!" Carlos says standing up with some obvious authority finally in his voice.

"Torture..." Cam says as she laughs sarcastically, "Right, I saw how you unleashed your long tongue of death on her."

"Look," he says, "the phone fell on the floor so you didn't see what else happened. If you knew..."

Cam slaps him hard across the face. "Just stop it Carlos," she screams, "The part I did see was enough, and there's no way you can explain it. Why were you even talking to that devil?"

"Listen Cam..." he starts.

"No," she says, "I don't want to listen. Just answer my question." "If you would just shut up," he says, "I can try to make this make sense to you."

"I'm listening Carlos." she says as she sits down calmly in one of the chairs sitting in front of his desk.

"Cameron," he starts, "there are some things that you wouldn't understand." "Boy I am not stupid at all," she tells him, "I realize completely that I'm a damn fool. And I understand that you sir made me into that fool, but I'm glad your true character came out now before I invested any real time into... whatever this was."

"So, it's over?" he asks. Cam stands up and turns to leave. "It was that easy huh," Carlos says, "to just get up

146

and walk away right, Cameron? You turned back into that scared little black girl so easily that it's sickening."

Cam stops at the door. "She wins," he continues, "If you walk out of that door right now, Whitney wins." Cam turns around with her shiny face covered in warm salty tears. "She wins what… you," Cam asks, "If you're the prize then I don't want to win."

"She doesn't want me, Cameron," he explains to her, "she probably doesn't even want K.C. You both had Chlamydia and Gonorrhea by the way. But my nurses treated you when you first came in with a new experimental drug that knocked the diseases right out. I wasn't going to tell you at all because I figured that you would be embarrassed."

"What," she says, "Why are you telling me this now, because you got caught?" "No," he replies, "I'm telling you so you'll know more than you did before. Whitney just doesn't want you to be happy period, she wants to destroy you, and she'll use anybody to do it."

"But why," Cam says, "Why does she hate me so much?"

"Because Cameron," Carlos says, "you were sleeping with the only human being she's ever cared about in her life. Don't you understand that Whitney loves Keldrick more than she loves her damn self? And, it doesn't stop here. If you ever… ever go back to K.C. again, she will *end* you. You have no idea what that woman is capable of."

"Whatever." she says with finality as she storms out of his office door without looking back.

Chapter 8
Running

(It's a beautiful sunny day in Orlando)

"D addy…" Jazemene says with a
mouth full of pizza. "Don't talk with your
mouth full princess." K.C. tells his daughter.
She finishes chewing her food in a dramatic fashion.
Then she playfully opens her mouth wide to show her
daddy that her mouth is no longer full of food.

"Ok, now what were you going to say baby girl?" he
asks.

"Why did you leave me and my mommy?" Jazemene
asks her father.

K.C. looks down at his baby girl attentively. "I would
never leave you Jazemene." he says sitting his large pizza
slice down on his plate.

K.C. leans down and kisses her gently on the forehead.

"You did leave us Daddy," she says, "you don't live with
us anymore. You live with Mama Cole." Mama Cole
approaches their table with a large icee in one hand and a
well powdered funnel cake in the other.

"Oh lord," she says, "I love *Magical Midway*, and I
haven't been here since you were about ten, Keldrick.
This funnel cake looks so good, here both of ya'll have

some."

Mama Cole finally takes a second to notice that her son and granddaughter are not listening to her, something is wrong.

"Jazemene, baby what's wrong?" Mama Cole says attempting to pick her up. "Linda," K.C. says, "Don't do that."

"Don't do what baby?" she replies. "I am not a baby anymore," he says, "and I don't need you to baby *my baby*. I'm her father I can take care of her without your assistance."

"Well I'm sorry ba… I mean Keldrick," she says, "I was only trying to help. I haven't seen my grand baby in so long. I just…"

"Whose fault is that Linda?" K.C. asks. "Why do you keep calling me Linda, son?" Mama Cole asks him.

"That's your name." he replies coldly. "I'm your mother Keldrick," she tells him, "you can call me Mama or Mama Cole like everybody else."

"No," he replies, "I prefer Linda. I'm not everybody else. Your good mama routine doesn't impress me. I apologize but you scarred me way too badly when I was a kid to be able to believe in this friendly façade you parade around to people. I know the truth."

"You want to do this now?" Mama Cole asks. "Do what?" K.C. replies.

"You want to fight with me like this in front of your daughter?" Mama Cole asks sitting down to rest her tired feet. "What's wrong Daddy?" Jazemene asks her father.

"Nothing baby," K.C. says, "just finish your pizza so we can go." "Aww but Daddy we just got here." Jaze

says frowning her pretty
little yellow face up in protest.

"Do what I said," her father tells her, "We don't want
to occupy anymore of your grandma's time."

"I brought the two of you here because I want to
spend time with you," Mama Cole says inching closer to
her son, and granddaughter, "to try to make up for all the
lost time."

"Funny thing about time Linda…" K.C. says. "What's
that son?" Mama Cole replies. "It's not like an old sock,"
he says, "or a baseball glove, or even a love for that
matter. Once you lose time… you can't ever get it back."

Mama Cole sadly puts her head down momentarily.
Then she looks up at her son and forces a smile on her
face.

"Why didn't you ever go try out for the NFL
Keldrick…" she asks.

"Where did that come from?" he asks. After turning
her body towards him she comfortably crosses her legs
and arms.

"Almost two years after your injury I spoke with your
doctor's," Mama Cole says, "and they all said you made
a miraculous full recovery and you could start playing
again if you wanted to. They said they told you the same
thing."

K.C. squints, his eyes at her. "Oh, they said that
huh?" he asks.

"Yeah, they did," she replies, "So what was it? Why
didn't you try to play college ball or go pro? You were
still very highly recruited even after the injury."

"I didn't know they told you that." he says.

"They told you the same thing," she replies, "So why didn't you play?"

"I don't know why I didn't start back playing, I just didn't want to." he claims.

"Wrong," Mama Cole says, "You thought you couldn't. You thought after all those painful surgeries, and spending two long years away from the game you wouldn't be good enough anymore. You psyched yourself out son just like Derrick Rose did with the Chicago Bulls, after his first injury." "What are you talking about Linda?" he asks.

"Keldrick," Mama Cole says, "I've been watching you play football since the very first day you started learning how to throw one. You were four years old and it was Christmas Day. Your dad brought you a football. It was the only present he gave you that year. It wasn't new and it wasn't even wrapped up, but you loved that ball because it was given to you by your father. I remember you were really disappointed because he didn't stay long enough to play with you. So, I threw on some sweats and an old tee shirt and took you outside myself and played catch with you for hours. It was so strange that we played for that long because most four years olds don't possess an attention span long enough to do any one thing for four hours straight."

Keldrick laughs a little, as he and Jazemene listen closely to his mother's fond memory of his childhood.

"But I could see it in your eyes," she says, "even way back then. It was so natural for you baby. Whitney may have become your heart, but football was your first love son."

"You're right," he says looking down at his feet, "I

hate to say it, but you're right Linda. I wanted to... I want to go back to the game so bad I could taste it. I run every day, I hit the gym three times a week, and about a month ago the coach from the..."

"The coach from the Miami Dolphins wrote you a personal letter inviting you to come to one of their training camps," Mama Cole interjects, "I already know son."

"Wait how did you know that," he replies, "Did Whitney tell you?" Mama Cole smiles down at Jazemene. "What else did Whit tell you?" he asks.

"It's not important son." Mama Cole replies. "Yes, it is because I'm going to curse her ass out the first chance I get." he vows with pure conviction.

"For what Keldrick..." Mama Cole asks. "For telling you my personal business..." he says. "Well you should have started cursing Whitney out a long time ago then." Mama Cole says looking away from him shaking her head.

"And what is that supposed to mean Linda?" K.C. asks. "You really have no idea, do you boy," she asks him, "Jazemene, go play in the game room for a few minutes, you've heard more than enough baby girl." "No, Jazemene you stay right here with Daddy." K.C. says. "Really" Mama Cole says, "Fine have it your way son. The reason Whitney has such an open relationship with me is because *without me*, all three of you would have been homeless and hungry a long time ago."

K.C. quickly looks down at Jazemene with his shocked brown eyes wide open. "Jazemene baby you heard your grandmother," he says, "go play in the game room for a few minutes." Jazemene does as she's told.

152

K.C. and Mama Cole both watch Jazemene as she disappears inside the game room.

"What do you mean homeless and hungry?" K.C. asks.

"Seriously Keldrick," Mama Cole says, "are you really that blind? Whitney is not a lawyer son she's just in law school and working for a law firm as a secretary to support you and your child. God knows what else the woman has been doing to support the two of you."

K.C. stands up. "What the Hell does that mean?" he inquires. "It's not my business," Mama Cole says, "So I won't speak on that. But know that her love for you and her willingness to care for you knows no boundaries."

"Wait a minute Linda," K.C. says with a definite scowl on his face, "because I really don't like the way that sounds. Are you saying Whitney... sold her **body** to pay our bills?"

"Now son," Mama Cole starts, "I did not tell you that do not put words in my mouth. Whatever Whit has done..."

"I think I'm gonna be sick," he interjects, "how could she... be so reckless?"

"Reckless," Mama Cole says, "that girl came to my house crying her eyes out hundreds of times because all she wanted was for you and Jazemene to be okay. It hurt her to see either one of you go without. So yes, maybe she did do some things she's not exactly proud of, but know that they were all done for you!"

K.C. shakes his head. "What son," Mama Cole says, "what did you want her to do? You haven't been much help at all Keldrick since you got out of prison."

"So, let me get this straight," he says, "so you are the

one who pays our rent?"

"I have." she claims. "And our food..." he says. "Not so much anymore with the food," she replies, "Whit is on food stamps now, but she didn't want you to know." "Damn it!" he exclaims as he rushes towards the game room.

Mama Cole watches her angry son walk away as she remains in her seat shaking her head in silence. "My son," she mumbles, "that boy is never gonna forgive me for not being a perfect mom."

Now that he's been gone for several minutes, Mama Cole figures he must have taken Jazemene out through the exit on the other side of the building and left already.

"Mama..." K.C. exclaims. Mama Cole looks up immediately. She knows something is terribly wrong because her son hasn't called her mama in years.

"What son?" she says trying not to show any alarm on her face. "Mama," he says through panic and tears, "Jaze is gone..."

Mama Cole jumps up immediately and races past K.C. into the game room as fast as she can. "What do you mean she's gone," she asks, "She can't be gone. Hold up! Everybody in the building stop moving *now* Damn it! My granddaughter is missing, and I am going to find her before I leave here!"

"How does she look?" an older white lady asks. "What did she have on?" a young black guy covered in piercings and tattoos asks next.

"She's about this tall." Mama Cole says using her hand as an example by holding it down by the middle of her thigh. "She's light skinned," she continues, "and she's wearing pink shorts, a green shirt, and pink bows are in

154

her hair. My grand baby is very pretty and very hard to miss."

Keldrick is still standing outside the game room door in shock. After checking the women's bathroom thoroughly Mama Cole rushes in to the men's room with no regard for who might be in there only caring about finding her precious granddaughter.

Still nothing, there's absolutely no trace of five-year-old Jazemene anywhere. Mama Cole rushes back outside covered in sweat to find her son shaking and urinating on himself.

"She's gone K.C., she's really gone." Mama Cole says hugging her son tightly for the first time in over three years.

Mama Cole sits down at the table and pulls out her cell phone frantically. She quickly presses a couple buttons then places the phone to her right ear. After a few second, she closes her eyes tightly as tears begin to stream down her face.

"Whitney... baby," Mama Cole says, "Girl I don't know how to tell you..." Mama Cole pauses to listen.

"Calm down Whitney," Mama Cole says, "nothing happened to Keldrick. Are you sitting down? Ok well me and Keldrick brought Jaze to Magical Midway... well what happened was, Kel and I were talking and Jazemene went into the game room to play and now we can't find her."

From ten feet away Keldrick can hear Whitney on the other end of the phone, screaming at the top of her lungs.

(Cam)

It's been two days since Jazemene went missing. Cam is at home on the phone with Carlos and watching the news.

A special report takes over the regular scheduled news programming to ask everybody in the city to be on the lookout for a little five-year-old girl named Jazemene Cole. Cam's heart drops instantly. She closes her eyes quickly because she knows they're about to show a picture of the missing child.

And until they show that child's face it could be anybody's Jazemene Cole. Orlando is a pretty big city, so there could be a lot of little girls running around with that same name.

But in her mind, it can't be her Jazemene, the one she baby sat for K.C. countless times while he was out doing God knows what.

"This is a recent picture of the missing child, Jazemene Cole." the T.V. reporter says. Cam opens one eye then closes it back as both of her beautiful dark eyes begin to flood with new tears.

"Carlos… I have to call you back." she says as she's hangs up without waiting for a response. She jumps up, grabs her car keys, and rushes outside.

(Love)

"Hey C," Love says, "I'm about to run to the gym babe." "Wait look at this special report Lance." Corey says. "Little five-year-old, Jazemene Cole has been missing for over forty-eight hours at this point we haven't received any helpful information as to where she might be…" the reporter says.

"Baby isn't that so sad?" Corey says never taking his
eyes off the

T.V."Tragic,"Love replies dryly, "Well I'm leaving now,
see you later."

Corey cuts the T.V. off and jumps up. "Ok hold on,"
Corey says walking towards the bedroom, "give me a
second and I'll change clothes and go with you."

"Umm no… I mean you're watching T.V. boo just relax
and enjoy yourself." Love tells him. "I will," Corey
responds, "after I change clothes so I can go to the gym
with my boy."

"Corey," Love says with his hands on his hips and his
head tilted to the side, "you are not in prison anymore
and I told you about using your prison terminology when
referring to me. I am not anybody's *boy* I am a man."

"I'm sorry Lance," he says, "You know I don't mean it
in a bad way, but old habits die hard."

"Ok," Lance says, "Well you sit here and work on
breaking your old habits… alone. And I'll be back later."

"Wait a minute, have you figured out a way to pay the
twelve hundred dollars we owe in rent and the two
hundred and fifty-four we owe for the power bill yet?"
Corey asks. "I'll be back." Love repeats as he walks
out and closes the door
behind him. "You'll be back when?" Corey yells.

Love hears Corey through the door but doesn't respond. He
jumps in his car and speeds off with no intention of going
anywhere near the gym.

(Whitney's apartment)

K.C. is sitting in his La-Z-Boy chair. Jay and Ty are both sitting on opposite ends of the couch that sits across from K.C.'s chair. Whitney is up pacing back and forth; she's forgotten how to sit down.

She doesn't remember much of anything except for the conversation she had with her baby this morning when she woke her up and then got her dressed for her day with her father and her grandmother.

Whitney woke her five-year-old up around 7:30 a.m.

"Good morning to you," Whit sang from her daughter's bedroom door, *"Good morning to you, we're all in our places with sunshiny faces, and this is the way, to start a new day..."*

Jazemene rolled over in her twin bed and peaked out from under her *"Princess and the Frog"* bed sheets to see her beautiful twenty-five-year-old twin. "Good morning mommy." Jazemene said. "Good morning beautiful." Whitney replied to her adorable child.

"It's time to get up baby," Whitney said, "Your grandma and father will be here to get you soon."

Jaze sat up on the side of her bed with her feet dangling above the floor. Whit stood there for a minute in silence looking at Jazemene. Whit shook her head and smiled at how lovely her child was. Whit thought to herself that if she could, she would freeze time and keep Jaze at this age forever.

She wanted to stand right there and watch over and protect her daughter for the rest of her natural life. She wants the best for Jaze of course, but she knows that the older she gets the more independent Jaze will be of her love and protection.

"Come on baby," Whit said, "let's get you in the bathroom to brush your face and wash your teeth…"

Jazemene covered her mouth and immediately began giggling. Whit put her hands on her hips, cocked her head to the side, and smiled at her daughter curiously. "And what are you so tickled at little girl…" Whit asked Jaze.

"*Mommy*," Jaze said, "You said we had to get me to the bathroom to *brush* my face and *wash* my teeth…"
"Oh," Whit said walking towards her daughter joining in with her laughter, "So you're making fun of mommy huh?"

"Um," Jazemene smiled, "yeah…"

"Um yeah…" Whit mimicked Jaze playfully as she picked her up off her bed high in the air and swung her around in a little circle. Then she carried Jaze into the bathroom and put her down.

Jaze stood there staring up at her mommy as she put toothpaste on her little *Hello Kitty* tooth brush for her. Whit remembers clearly the look in her daughter's eyes as she handed her toothbrush to her. Jaze has almost the same look in her eyes every time she looks at Whitney.

She always appears to be awestruck by her mommy. Jaze loves her daddy very much but her mommy is her hero, and she wants to be just like her when she grows up. At five years old, she thinks she's already sure of this.

The rest of the morning is a blur now to Whitney as she finds herself still pacing back and forth from her kitchen to the front room where Kel and his friends are all sitting quietly.

"Whit…" K.C. says weakly. "What Keldrick!" she barks stopping in the doorway of the kitchen with her back turned to him.

"Come sit down baby…" he tells her. "No Keldrick," she says trying not to scream, "I don't want to sit down right now."

"Okay." he replies. Whitney continues to pace. K.C. watches Whit very closely as she paces back and forth. He's racking his tired brain trying to figure out what he could possibly say or do to fix what he's done.

The more he watches her though; he believes she has something else on her mind… like a secret. Kel knows if he keeps pushing her she'll tell on herself, she always has.

"Whitney baby," Kel says as she enters the front room again, "If you just sit down for a minute you might feel a little better."

"No Keldrick," Whit says, "I won't feel better if I sit down. Sitting down is not a soothing act for me or any *fucking body else* in history!"

"Then don't sit down," he replies, "I'm just trying to help you…" "You wanna help me," Whit screams walking back in the front room, "go get my five-year-old daughter and bring her home! No, in fact just rewind time for me before you and your incompetent mother ever came and picked my baby up, and tell me to decline you the privilege of taking her out of my sight… Go back in time and actually be honest with me Keldrick and tell me that neither one of you are smart enough or capable of taking care of small children on your own."

"Don't do that Whitney," Jay says, "that's not fair." "Yeah," Ty agrees, "Kel loves Jazemene and we're going to find her… trust me." "Oh, both of you just shut the hell up," Whit demands, "And no Kel I don't want to sit down!"

160

"I said okay Whit…" he concedes. "Damn it!" Whit screams out spinning around towards K.C with unforgettable pain and regret in her beautiful eyes.

"What baby," Kel asks, "What else is going on with you? I can tell there's more…"

"I don't deserve to sit down," Whit cries walking slowly towards Kel, "I'm no better than you. I don't pay nearly as much attention to my baby as I should. I'm always so busy with work, and other shit that doesn't even matter in a world without her. I'm guilty, I am so guilty… I'm a terrible mother…"

She falls into Kel's body. He catches her gladly, and holds her tight. "You are not a terrible mother," Kel tells her, "I don't want to ever hear you say that again. Now, we're going to continue to work with the Orlando P.D and we're going to find Jaze and bring her home safely together."

"No," Whit cries, "You don't understand I *am* a terrible mother.
I never really loved Jazemene…"

"What," Kel says with his face contorted harshly, "What the hell are you talking about Whitney?"

Whit continues to cry on his strong body. Kel looks at his two best friends for help. Ty looks down at the floor, and Jay just shakes his head.

"Whit," Kel barks, "What the hell are you talking about?" Whit doesn't respond she just continues to cry on his chest.

Kel stands up gently pushing Whitney off of him. Standing over her Kel looks down at Whitney with a scowl on his dark handsome face. Whit looks up at him through her painful tears.

"Damn it Whitney," he barks, "you better start talking, and you better start talking now! Did you have something to do with Jaze's disappearance?"

"No!" she screams. "Are you sure," he asks grabbing her firmly by her shoulders, "because if you did anything to…"

"No, Keldrick… God!" she screams. "Then what the hell are you talking about," he asks, "You said you never really loved her. How is that something you can say about your own daughter while she's missing?"

"Because damn it," she screams still in tears, "It's the truth! It's the fucking truth Keldrick… I only loved Jaze because she was an extension of *you*! I had your child Kel… Don't you see? The biggest thing to me was that I was having *your* child. I loved *you*… I was never able to actually transfer that love to our child. It wasn't until you started stepping out on me on a regular basis with that ugly black bitch Cameron, that I was able to start forming a real bond with Jazemene. The entire time you were in jail and prison, it was so hard to… care for and about her. Because… *you* weren't here…"

"Damn it Whitney…" Kel says unsure what else he can possibly say.

"You weren't here," Whit cries, "to love me for taking care of *your* child. I just wanted you to know and see that I could be a good mother and a great wife…"

"Honestly Whitney," Kel says, "That is… *so fuckin'* sick! This whole… thought process that you have adapted to, or I guess you were born with this natural lack of emotion. How can you create… or give birth to

162

something and not love it with everything you are?" "I'm sorry!" Whit cries reaching out for Keldrick. He quickly steps back out of her deceitful reach.

"I used to feel so bad," Kel says, "About cheating on you. I know how devastated I would have been if I found out you cheated on me. But this… this is much worse than being cheated on could ever feel. I believe you might one day try to hurt Jazemene to spite me…"

"No," Whit screams reaching out for him again, "Keldrick… I love you, and I would never hurt your daughter."

Kel gets down on his knees in front of her and looks deeply in her eyes. "She's *our* daughter Whitney," he says, "Jazemene is *our* daughter, not just mine. She loves you very much and so do I. And I'm sure you're just confused but I know you love her too."

"Okay…" Whit cries.

"Say it." Kel tells her as he stands up in front of her. "Say what?" Whitney cries.

"Say you love Jazemene," Kel tells her, "Say I love *my daughter* Jazemene Cole." Whit doesn't respond.

"Damn it, say it Whitney," Kel yells as he shakes her by her shoulders, "Say it! Tell me you love our daughter independently of me!"

There's a knock at the door.

"I got it." Ty says as he makes his way to the door. Keldrick sits down, and Whitney falls into his lap crying softly.

"It's the police…" Ty yells to everybody back in the front room. As Ty walks back in the room two white officers and a black man in a suit are following closely behind him.

"Whitney, Keldrick," Ty says, "This is Detective Ray and a couple of his men." "How are you folks holding up?" the detective asks Whitney and K.C.

Whit is still balled up in Keldrick's lap, so he reaches around her body to shake the detective's hand.

"We've been better Mr. Ray." Keldrick admits. "I understand of course," Detective Ray says, "Please, call me Carl."

Keldrick stares into Carl's eyes trying to detect whether or not the man is sincere or full of it.

"Really," Keldrick says, "You understand? What exactly do you understand Detective Ray?"

"Listen, Mr. Cole…" Carl says with his hands up in defense.

"I'm listening Mr. Ray." Kel interjects as Ty, Jay, and the two officers look on at their exchange.

"Mr. Cole," Carl says, "I'm here to help you…"

"You're here because my case ended up on your desk," K.C. corrects him; "You *are* being paid for this aren't you?"

"I am," Carl admits, "No one works for free Mr. Cole." "Keldrick is fine." K.C. tells him. "I'm sorry," Carl says, "no one works for free Keldrick."

"So then let's be clear," Keldrick says, "You did not come here on your own free will, and out of the kindness of your own heart to help us find our daughter."

"I apologize again, sir" Carl says, "I think we've gotten off on the wrong foot completely."

"Do you have any children Mr. Ray?" K.C. asks. "I do," Mr. Ray replies, "Four beautiful daughters, and one handsome son."

"What would you do," K.C. asks, "If you ever lost one of them?" "Well I would be devastated of course…" Carl tells   him. "I'm sure." K.C. replies void of emotion.

"Have you ever been arrested before Mr. Cole?" Carl asks taking out a small pad from a pocket in his long black trench coat.

"What the hell does that have to do with my daughter's disappearance detective?" K.C. asks picking Whitney up off his lap to sit her down and then stand up himself.

"I'm just trying to get some background information here," Carl says, "I'm also curious as to why you seem to be so agitated by my presence."

"Your presence is not agitating me," K.C. corrects him; "I just want to get things clear. We are not friends, and you did not come here to help us. You came to do your job Mr. Ray. And we expect you to do that job well. We love our daughter very much, and we expect you to get her back to us safely."

"I am very good at what I do Mr. Cole," Carl assures him, "But I need you to understand that though we may not know each other, and we may not be friends, job or not… I am here to help you. It just happens to be my job to help complete strangers."

Kel can see the sincerity in the older man's strong but gentle brown eyes. "Are we together on this?" Detective Carl Ray asks him. "I did three years in prison for robbery." Keldrick tells him.

"Fine," Carl says, "I'm very sorry to hear that son. Now tell me about your daughter Jazemene." With complete faith in Mr. Ray's ability to do his job well, K.C. sits back down near Whitney and begins to describe Jazemene to him.

(An hour later)

"Baby," Whitney says looking over at him, "Where are we going now?"

K.C. doesn't respond, he just continues to drive. Whitney continues to look at K.C. waiting on him to say something.

"Keldrick I know you hear me talking to you," Whit prods, "Where are we going?"

"We're looking for our daughter," he says, "You already know that Whitney." "Yeah," she replies, "But we have already refilled my gas tank twice and ridden around the entire city four times. So where else are possibly going to go now?"

"Anywhere and everywhere we have to," he yells,

"Damn it Whitney! Is your money, your gas, and this car really more important to you than your own child?"

"No K.C.," she cries, "I'm not that evil…"

"Then act like you care about finding our daughter," he screams, "I swear to God I feel like I'm in this all by my damn self!"

"I do care about finding her," Whitney claims, "I'm just tired…" "Tired," Kel laughs coldly, "Woman is your sleep more important than the well-being of our only child? Can you honestly go back home and lie down again in bed peacefully, knowing that our helpless five-year-old child is out there... out *here* somewhere... begging for us to please come find her..."

K.C. can no longer hold back his emotions as the tear flood down his face again.

"Never mind, Keldrick," Whitney sighs, "Just keep driving."

(Six hours later)

K.C., Ty, and Jay are all standing out on the balcony outside Whit's apartment talking. "Tell me again Keldrick," Ty says, "How did Jaze disappear?" "Linda and I were talking outside at Magical Midway," K.C. explains, "The conversation was... too old for her ears. So, I asked Jaze to go inside and play for a few minutes."

"By herself though?" Ty asks. "Yes, damn it Ty," Kel screams, "Obviously she was by herself! Do you think she could have been... taken while in my care?"

"Apparently so..." Ty replies.

"Shut the hell up Ty," Kel demands, "Jaze was not with me, by my side when she went missing!"

"Of course, not bro," Jay says, "Nobody is saying that. Ty shut the hell up!"

"I'm not the enemy here." Ty claims.

"Then act like it!" Kel demands.

"Look K.C.," Jay says, "We gotta take this to the streets fam. We gotta get out here and get dirty and come up with a lead to find Jaze."

"Jay, I appreciate that," Kel says looking at his old friend, "But Whit and I just rode around the entire city for four hours looking for her."

"That's not what I'm talking about Kel and you know it," Jay says, "We still got people in the streets we just gotta get out there and reconnect with them. They can find Jaze faster than any detective or law enforcement agent."

"You might be right Jay." Ty agrees. "You know I'm right," Jay says looking at Ty, "The streets talk K.C. but not to the police."

"What you got in mind Jay?" K.C. asks. "Well," Jay says, "I say we head over to Silver Star and talk to Loco Blue, and GQ. They know every move the streets make." "Yeah maybe…" Kel replies.

"We're going to find Jazemene bro." Jay says looking at his distraught friend. "It just doesn't make sense," K.C. says, "I swear to God she was only in there for a few minutes. And then she just, she just…"

K.C. chokes on his words with his left fist pressed tightly against his forehead trying to fight back the tears.

"Blood of Jesus," Ty says, "wherever my goddaughter is she's ok.
And no harm will come to her in the *precious* name of Jesus. Amen."

K.C. looks at Ty with tears in his eyes and a dark scowl on his face. "Ty," he says, "It ain't time for all that. This ain't got *nothing* to do with no Jesus. All your praying and wishing on stars ain't gone bring my baby back. So please don't go to catching the Holy Ghost and piss me off."

"Attacking my faith Keldrick," Ty replies, "is not

going to make you feel any better." "Yeah well all that praying ain't gone ease my pain either!" K.C. yells with a lot obvious pain in his voice.

"How do you know?" Ty asks. "How do I know what?" K.C. replies stepping towards Ty. "How do you know my prayers won't ease your pain?" Ty asks.

"Because I know Tyrone..." K.C. yells. "No, you don't know," Ty tells him, "You don't know a damn thing. You got your head stuck so far up your own ass you couldn't even see how much your own daughter needed you before she ever disappeared."

Jay quickly steps in between Ty and K.C. "He didn't mean that last part K.C., so just calm down." Jay says. "I meant every word." Ty says.

Jay turns around to face Ty. "Look nigga if he starts swinging I'm not gonna be standing right here, so I hope you know what the hell you're doing." Jay tells him.

"Yeah," Ty says, "I'm not worried about him beating me up... he ain't gone kill me." "I'm not even going to hit you Ty," K.C. says, "but you're going off the deep end just because I asked you not to pray for me."

"No, you continuously try to belittle my faith," Ty says, "I'm not perfect and I never will be but I *know* who my maker is and I'm perfect in *His* eyes."

"Hmm," K.C. grunts, "that nigga must have cataracts."

Ty quickly looks up at K.C. and loses his cool. He rushes at him full speed tackling him to the ground as K.C.'s head smacks hard against the concrete during the fall.

K.C. feels dangerously dizzy after the blow to the

back of his head. Caught completely off guard K.C. had no time to counter attack. Ty is too full of rage to realize his friend is nearly unconscious. Blow after blow Ty continues to punch a defenseless K.C. in the face and chest, as his eyes roll into the back of his head.

"*My entire life I lived and hid in your shadow*," Ty yells in between powerful punches, "*But I'm...so... tired...of...being...your...bitch made... invisible shadow.*" K.C.'s eyes close.

After the last punch Ty falls forward on his bloody faced friend's chest. Lying there he realizes K.C. is not breathing. Ty panics as he sits up quickly and begins grabbing and pulling K.C.'s shirt collar.

"Kel... Kel wake up bro," Ty yells, "Wake up bro, please don't do this to me fam! You're my big brother and my best friend. I need you bro!"

"Move back fool you've done enough," Jay says kneeling down close to his injured friend's chest, "he's not breathing Ty!"

"Ahhh!" the pain filled scream came from behind them.

Ty and Jay turn around to see who the loud scream came from. Standing there behind them in shock is Cam. "When did you get here?" Jay asks.

She ignores them both rushing to K.C.'s limp body. It's taking everything in her, to not pass out from the déjà vu of seeing K.C. lying lifeless before her covered in blood.

Pushing both men out of the way Cam focuses in on K.C. and begins to perform CPR on him. Whitney rushes out of the door to see what the commotion is.

"What happened!" she yells. Looking down at the ground she sees Cam kissing K.C. in a puddle of blood.

"Bitch… What are you doing to him?" Whit screams as she pushes Cameron to the side. Ty and Jay immediately snatch Whitney out of Cam's way so she can continue to try to revive their best friend.

Whitney continues to holler while Ty and Jay hold her back. "You bitch you tried to kill my husband again," Whit screeches, "You killed him…you finally got what you wanted you killed him!"

K.C. begins to choke spitting up unknown liquids all over himself. Cam turns to Whitney with her eyes squinted tightly, and her upper lip curled even tighter.

"Whitney, you can have Keldrick," Cam says, "But he's not your husband, hell he's not even your man. You handicap him, and threaten him to try to force him to be with you."

Cam laughs sarcastically. "Is that your definition of *true* love," she continues, "because if that's what true love is I can do without it."

Cam stands up. "Leave my house!" Whit screams.

K.C. rolls over and crawls inside the house.

"No," Cam says, "I'm not going anywhere. Don't you feel some type of way at night, lying next to a man that has no intentions of ever marrying you? He's in love with me Whitney. Damn it! He left your heart *way* back in high school girl… with all the childish games that you *still* play today. But I'm not here for you, and I'm not here for K.C.'s dumbass."

"Then why the hell are you here?" Whit asks snatching her arms loose from Jay and Ty's grasps. Cam looks down at her shoes, fighting back tears.

"I…I saw… I saw it." she mumbles.

"You saw what Cam?" Ty asks. "I saw the news. I saw… somebody took Jaze." Cam says unable to fight the tears any longer.

Whitney steps towards her. "Cam how do you know my daughter?" Whitney asks feeling completely numb from head to toe.

"K.C.…" Cam starts.

"K.C. what…" Whit inquires.

"After he started working and going to school for his G.E.D.," Cam says, "he didn't have time to watch her while you were working and going to school yourself. So, I sacrificed and rearranged my schedule so that I could watch Jazemene for him."

Ty and Jay look at each other and shake their heads. After a few moments of awkward silence both men walk inside the house to check on K.C.

Whitney and Cam are still completely focused on each other. "So," Whit says, "you mean to tell me you have been keeping *my* child without *my* permission?"

"Whitney, I had no idea she was your daughter," Cam claims wiping more tears away, "I didn't even know you existed until the morning I shot Keldrick's lying ass."

"How many times did you keep my daughter Cam?" Whitney asks.

"Whitney," Cam says, "I swear to you I had no idea she was your daughter, or his daughter either for that matter. *K.C.* told *me* Jazemene was his niece. He said he didn't have kids. He told me he wanted me to be the mother of his first child..."

"I see," Whit says, "And these tears...they're for *my child*?"

"I love that beautiful little girl," Cam says, "I didn't care who her parents were, in my mind she was my daughter too."

Whitney steps face to face with Cam and looks deep into her warm chocolate eyes. Whit can't help but see that this woman that she hates so much is a genuine human being. Whitney hugs Cam tightly.

"I can't continue to hate anybody who loves my daughter enough to cry for her." Whit tells her. Hearing this, Cam hugs Whitney back.

The door to the apartment opens.

"What the... are you two hugging and crying... together?" Ty asks. They don't respond.

"Blood of Jesus," Ty continues, "well this probably won't last long...because um Keldrick is lying in there on the kitchen floor in a puddle of blood, and he doesn't even remember his name."

"What!" the women exclaim in unison. "Yeah, he seems to have mild amnesia," Ty says "Well I'm guessing it's mild because he remembers you Whit."

"Me..." she replies.

"Yeah, he's asking for you. Come on." Ty says as he ushers both women inside the apartment. Cameron feels a slight chill as she enters Whitney's home for the very first time.

She notices how well put together everything seems to be. All the lights are dim and there's an enticing aroma of baked spaghetti and French toast in the air.

Cam carefully takes note of everything she sees. The short walk to the kitchen seems like the longest walk of her life. She looks carefully at every picture she sees on the wall of K.C. and his daughter and wonders why he lied and said she was his niece.

"Suga mama…" K.C. mumbles sprawled out on the bloody kitchen floor. "Did he just say…" Whit starts.

"*Suga Mama*…" Ty and Jay say in unison.

"Yeah," Ty says, "That's why I came to get you."

"Wait who is Suga Mama?" Cam asks with her brows tightly furrowed.

"Me," Whit says in a shocked daze, "but he hasn't called me that since high school." "Why did he call you that?" Cam asks.

"Baby," Whit says kneeling down close to K.C., "what's wrong?"

K.C. laughs. "I'm good Suga Mama," he says, "Where's Mama Cole?"

"Ty, why did K.C. used to call her Suga Mama?" Cam asks.

"It's a long story miss lady." Ty replies never taking his eyes off of his friend lying helpless on the ground.

"Not really," Jay says, "Whit always had a big butt, and back in school K.C. gave her the nickname Suga Mama because she used to walk like the old lady on that cartoon show *The Proud Family*."

"How cute," Cam says with no emotion, "So why is he calling her that now?"

"I think when he hit his head it messed with his brain or something." Ty says.

"How did he hit his head?" Whit asks from the floor.

"Ty helped him," Jay says, "he tackled him and when

K.C. hit the ground his head bounced on the concrete and Ty just kept punching him in the face."

"Don't blame this on me!" Ty exclaims.

"Then who the hell do we blame it on Ty?" Jay asks.

"Not me," Ty replies, "It's not my fault he just keeps... he always tries me and treats me like I'm still that little boy back in school..."

"Ty, you almost killed him, that is not okay." Cam says. "Wait a minute girlfriend number two," Ty says stepping back, "I still don't even understand why you're here. You're not even his girl... he doesn't want you. You can leave."

"You don't know me," Cam says, "and you obviously don't know Kel. You just beat him to a pulp, so you don't give a damn about him." "That's my big brother," Ty says stepping backwards in defense, "I would die for that dude."

"Yeah, you would also just as soon kill him." Whit says.

"Really Whit," Ty says, "You're taking this bitch's side? Forget it, how about everybody just team up against Ty. Blood of Jesus I can't win for losing!"

"Boy, do not you the Lord's name in vein in my house," Whit shouts, "Your religious little front doesn't fool anybody Ty. We can all see right through your stupid ass."

Ty steps towards Whitney full of anger. Whit ignores him turning her attention back to K.C.

"I never claimed to be religious," Ty corrects her, "I'm spiritual."

"It takes a whole lot more than just saying I'm

spiritual, to actually
be spiritual Ty," Jay says, "Damn even I know that."

"Forget all of ya'll I'm gone!" Ty turns to leave.

"Tyboonie is that you?" K.C. asks sounding almost
childish.

Ty stops cold in his tracks, and closes his eyes as they
fill with tears. He slowly turns around and walks back
towards his best friend.

Now down on his knees next to Whitney he looks deep
in K.C.'s lost eyes. "What did I do," Ty cries with his
face drenched in real tears, "What the hell did I do?"

(Jaze)

"Uncle L..." a tiny voice squeaks in the darkness. "Yes
Jazemene." the man responds. "If you're my Uncle how
come I never met you before?" Jaze asks.

"No sweetheart I'm not your real uncle but I am a
close friend of your family." the man replies.

"Uncle L..." Jaze says again. "Yes Jazemene?" the
man replies. "How come you hate my daddy?" she asks.

"I don't hate him darling," the man replies, "he just has
something very important that belongs to me."

"No," Jaze says, "You said you hate him, and you love
my mommy."

The man slams his fist down with a powerful thud.
"Stop asking so many damn questions little girl before I
hurt you really bad!" he yells.

"I'm sorry Uncle L," she says starting to cry, "Don't
be mad at me. I'm just ready to go home. You said my
daddy was coming to get me, where is he?"

"I'm sorry Jazemene," he says, "I didn't mean to raise

my voice, I'm just frustrated. And I'm calling your daddy now so he can come get you."

He dials a number on his cell phone then puts the phone to his ear.

"Hello... may I speak to Keldrick Cole please," the man asks, "It's none of your damn business who I am. If you must know, I have his daughter and unless I get fifteen hundred dollars by tonight..."

The man pauses in midsentence.

"Wait," he says, "Keldrick what? Are you serious? Wait when did, he... That can't be true." The man hangs up his cell phone quickly.

"Come on Jaze let's go," he says, "I'm taking you home." "Why are you crying Uncle L?" she asks.

"Your daddy is hurt really badly Jaze now come on let's go." he says wiping his face roughly.

"But I thought you hated him." she replies.

"I do," the man says, "I can't even punish him without him stealing all the attention for himself some kind of way. He's a very selfish man. Enough of that let's get you home your daddy needs you now."

(Carlos)

Carlos is an extremely intelligent man, who knows himself very well. So, when things change in him, be it physical, mental, or emotional it's not hard for him to detect the change.

He is fully aware of how he feels about Cameron Jiles, and what she now represents in his life. If he is not

177

able to reconcile with her and steal her heart away from Keldrick Cole she will always remain for Carlos the one who got away.

Carlos refuses to live out the rest of his life this way. He's ready and willing to do everything in his power to make Cameron his again. She hasn't been answering his calls or responding to his texts. Carlos called her job and they said they haven't heard from Cam in about three days. They also said she had been terminated because she didn't show up to work or attempt to call out two days in a row. After Carlos hung up the phone he jumped in one of his sports cars and raced down the street en route to Cam's house. His music is playing loud through his car speakers but all Carlos can hear is complete silence. The bright lights all around him are disturbing. They're all selfishly distracting him from focusing on her.

The only thing in Carlos Sanchez's world worth focusing on is Cameron Candice Jiles. His love for her was definitely nothing short of a freak accident, but it's here now and it's very real.

Carlos is a firm believer in the fact that we do not choose who we love. We can fight our feelings and even attempt to hide them. But doing so will never change how or what we truly feel.

Carlos knows from experience how dangerous and painful it can be to hide one's love and true sentiments. As he races down the street he's dodging every inconsiderate car that blatantly ends up in front of his.

Carlos slams his fist down on his expensive dashboard as he brings his car to a stop at yet another red light. Carlos is sure the entire world is against him, and he feels like he's stopped at every possible red light en route to Cam's house.

Five minutes later he finally pulls up to Cameron's house in a black on black drop top BMW coupe. After parking wildly on her lawn, he rushes full speed through her uncut grass to her front door. After looking inside, the front window expecting the worst, the doctor panics even more because he sees nothing. Beating loudly on the front door Carlos begins to yell her name.

"Cameron... Cam baby, are you here? Cam just let me know you're ok!"

The door opens slowly. Cam is wrapped tightly in an old blanket. Her face looks drained and lifeless. Without even looking at Carlos, she turns leaving the door wide open and walks away.

After a few steps, she drops the blanket revealing a silk pink bath robe. Carlos notices the ends of her robe's sleeves are drenched with blood.

He closes the door quickly and locks it. Cam sits on the couch in a daze. He races to her to check the source of the blood that's dripping from her sleeves.

"Cam what's wrong," he asks taking her left hand in his, "Why are you bleeding... Cam, you slit both of your wrists!"

Carlos immediately runs to her bathroom to get everything he needs to take expert medical care of her. Then he rushes back to the sofa in the front room where she's sitting quietly

"Why did you do this to yourself baby?" he asks.

Cameron doesn't respond, she continues to stare out into space like he's not even there.

"What's going on with you?" he continues.

"Cam," he says wiping excess blood from her freshly cleaned and wrapped wounds, "Baby, tell me what happened so bad that you would try to kill yourself?"

Cam falls helplessly into his chest like a baby, and begins to sob uncontrollably.

"Cam baby please tell me what's wrong." he pleads.

"It's Kel." she mumbles through her tears.

"What about him," Carlos asks removing her from his chest, "Is he here?" Carlos stands up to quickly survey his surroundings.

"No," she says, "he's dead."

"What do you mean he's dead?" Carlos asks.

"No, I don't mean actually dead, but his mind is gone." she explains through her tears.

"His mind has been gone for a long time." Carlos says playfully, trying to lighten the mood.

Cam stands up and storms away from him. After several steps, she turns around in a rage.

"I'm serious Carlos," Cam cries, "he got into a fight and his brain has reverted back to a childlike state."

"Seriously," Carlos inquires, "that could be severe, but it could also just be temporary. What happened to him?"

"It's a long story," she says sitting lazily on her grandmother's old ottoman, "but he doesn't remember anything except Suga Mama and his childhood homeboys. I left before he had a chance to *not* recognize me." Cam stands up dizzily and then begins to pace back and forth.

"Wait," Carlos says, "What? You left what, and who is Suga Mama?"

"Whitney," Cam tells him, "that was his childhood nickname for her. But it doesn't matter. The only thing that matters is whatever me and K.C. meant to each other no longer exists in his mind."

"So, what does that mean?" he asks. "You win. I guess..." Cam mumbles sadly. "What do you mean I win, Cameron," Carlos asks, "This isn't some childish game, or a race between me and him to your heart. Unless... you've made it into one, is that what this is to you, a competition?"

"No," she says blowing her nose before she speaks again, "I just thought that after he realized I was gone he would..."

"He would what," Carlos says, "oh, I get it. Once he thought that you had finally left him, you figured he would panic and then come running to save you from the evil, smooth-talking doctor, right?"

"I didn't say that, Carlos." she replies walking towards him.

"No," he says, "you didn't say it. You would never actually say anything like that, but that's what you were thinking."

Cam walks closer to him as he stands up to leave.

"Carlos," she cries, "Please don't..."

"Please, call me Dr. Sanchez," he says, "have a wonderful evening, I'll show myself out."

After he walks out Cam falls out in the middle of her den floor screeching in pain and reaching out towards the door.

The dark air is filled with *Jazmine Sullivan's* voice bleeding through her surround sound speakers singing, *"I'm in Love with Another Man"*.

(Cameron)

There is no way I can make it on my own. I know it would be much easier to just play that role and become Carlos' wifey or whatever he wants me to be. But I know where my heart is.

K.C. is everything I never thought I wanted in my future mate, but somehow, he became everything I need. God, that man is everything I will ever need.

Please fix this, just let him be okay. In my mind, I know my chances are not good at all, but you said you will never leave me or forsake me. And not being able to live the rest of my life with Keldrick Jermaine Cole is the most despicable punishment you could ever give me Lord. I only breathe to live him, he's not perfect but he's perfect for me.

I won't accept this, because I know it's not over. He's going to be okay, because if he doesn't come back to me... everything I am will cease to exist. If he's not coming back to me Lord, please take my breath away now

Chapter 9
Just the Three of Us

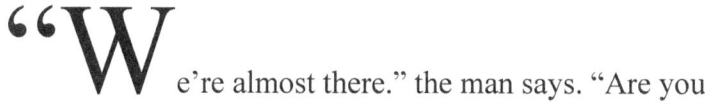

(Jazemene and her abductor are riding in his car)

"We're almost there." the man says. "Are you ready to see your daddy?" he continues. "Yes Uncle L." Jazemene says with an excited smile on her face.

As they turn the corner to the street where her mother's apartment is, she sits up on the edge of her seat to try to get a better view.

"That's it right there Uncle L." Jaze says pointing to her mother's apartment building.

"I know which one it is Jaze… Uh, I mean I know *you* know which one it is." the man nervously corrects himself.

He parks in front of the building next to the one Jazemene lives in and surveys the lot to make sure no member of local law enforcement is lurking around waiting to catch him.

"Well beautiful, it's been fun," the man says, "now give me a hug and you be good. Make sure you take care of your daddy as well, he needs you now."

"Uncle L…" Jaze says. "Yes darling…" the man

replies. "You remind me of my daddy," she tells him, "even though you don't even know him."

The man laughs. "Jazemene, I would pay to hear you tell your father that." he tells her.

"Why…" she asks. "It doesn't matter sweetheart," the man says, "but it was really good to see you my dear."

The man smiles a genuine smile. Jazemene opens her own door and then grabs her gift bag off the seat next to her.

"Give me one more hug Jaze," he says, "I don't know when I'll see you again. Hey and don't tell them you were with Uncle L; it will be our little secret."

"Okay." Jaze says looking at the strange man. "Can you keep a secret Jaze?" he asks.

"Uh huh…" Jaze replies nodding her tiny head up and down.

"Ok good," the man replies, "just tell mommy you were with a stranger."

They hug once more, and then in a flash Jaze gets out of the car and disappears into the next building quickly. The man wipes several tears off his face and then quickly drives away.

(Inside Whitney's apartment)

"Suga Mama…" K.C. belts at the top of his lungs. Whitney rushes into the den for the tenth time in the past hour.

"Yes Keldrick, what do you need now?" she asks.

"Change the channel on the T.V.," he says in a childish

tone, "I don't wanna watch football no more. I hate football."

Whitney snatches the remote from him and changes the channel again for the fifth time in the past hour.

"Keldrick I don't know what's wrong with you," Whit says, "and the doctors all say this is going to take time, but I can't let Jaze see you like this. I know she's going to come home any day now."

Whitney begins to cry. "My baby's going to be just fine," she continues, "because she's strong just like me... just like her daddy used to be. I love her now, because she's all I have left..."

Keldrick who doesn't seem to hear a word she's saying looks up at her searchingly and says, "Who is Jazemene?"

Suddenly Whitney feels numb from head to toe as her body quickly gives way to unconsciousness.

"Suga Mama..." K.C. says as he crawls next to her body and begins to shake her.

There's a knock at the door. "Suga mama, wake up," Keldrick says, "Somebody's knocking at the door."

The tiny knock is growing stronger by the second. Completely confused about what he should do next K.C. makes his way to the front door.

"Who is it?" he asks.

"Daddy it's me Jazemene!" she yells happily. "Who is Jazemene?" he asks trying to see her through the peep
hole.

"Daddy... it's me your baby," Jaze says, "Open the door Daddy I miss you."

185

"I don't know a Jazemene, little girl," he says placing his ear closely to the door to listen to her response, "I think you have the wrong apartment."

"No, I don't Daddy," she says, "You're my daddy. Your name is Keldrick Jermaine Cole, and your birthday is October 17th. Your favorite color is…"

The door opens slowly. K.C. looks down at the beautiful little girl who has his eyes, and Whitney's face and skin complexion.

"My favorite color is what little girl?" he asks kneeling down to be at eye level with her. Jazemene puts her head down, covers her eyes with her tiny hands and begins to cry.

"It's blue Daddy," she cries, "your *onliest* favorite color is blue." She looks up at him through her tears.

"Was I gone too long Daddy," she asks, "Did you and Mommy forget about me already?"

"I'm sorry little girl you do look familiar but I don't have any kids." K.C. says as he starts to close the door in her face and walk

back inside. Jazemene stops him from closing the door in her face and with all her might she pushes it open.

K.C. stands back as the small girl barges in. She walks directly into the den, where she finds her mother's limp body in the middle of the floor.

"Mommy…" she screams "Mommy, are you okay," Jaze cries, "Mommy, wake up now!" Jaze continues to scream and cry. Her words are no longer audible.

As K.C. looks on, Jazemene rushes to the kitchen and opens the fridge. On the bottom shelf, she sees a bottle of Dasani water. She hastily grabs the bottle and runs back to her mother. After several attempts, she realizes she can't open the bottle herself. She hands it to K.C.

"Daddy or whoever you are can you please open this for me…" Jazemene asks. K.C. opens the bottle and then hands it back to her. She quickly pours the contents onto her mother's head and body.

Whitney still doesn't move. Jazemene throws the bottle down and runs towards K.C. She wraps her arms around his legs as tight as she possibly can. "Daddy…" she says crying in full force now.

"I am not your daddy little girl." he tells her again trying to push her away from him. "Daddy please… please daddy help my mommy!" Jaze yells frantically.

"Jazemene is that you?" a weak voice says from the floor. Jaze turns around and sees her mother's eyes batting slowly as she tries to focus. "Jazemene baby… I must be dreaming." Whitney says trying to sit up to no avail.

"Yes, Mommy it's me." Jaze says rushing to her mother's side.

"What's wrong with my daddy Mama?" Jaze asks lying down next to her mother on the den floor.

"I don't know baby." Whitney replies.

"Well, is he going to be okay Mama?" Jazemene asks.

"I don't know." Whit replies honestly.

(Two days later Love and Corey are on the couch watching basketball on the television in their apartment)

"So, you're really going to do it huh?" Love says

smiling with his cell phone held tightly to his ear.

"Who," Corey asks, "Who's going to do what?" Love holds a hand up signaling Corey to be quiet.

"Really… no you can't be serious," Love says, "You just got your baby back."

"Who Love," Corey says, "Who can't be serious? And what baby came back?" Love holds the same hand up a second time.

"Well what's the plan Ms. Independent?" Love asks continuing his conversation as if Corey hasn't spoken a word. Corey stands up trying to hold his usual jealous rage at bay. "Lance," he says sternly, "who are you talking to, and what's going on?"

"Hold on boo…" Love says into the phone. Then he holds his hand over the phone so the person won't be able to hear him talking to Corey.

"Boo," Corey says with his arms folded tightly and his head slightly cocked, "Who the hell you calling boo…"

"This is Whitney fool," Love says, "now calm down. She's leaving
K.C. for good and she wants to move in with us."

"She's not serious Lance," Corey replies taking his seat back on the sofa, "she's just angry right now she's never going to leave him though. Here let me see the phone."

Love walks the phone to him. Corey takes the phone and walks towards the kitchen.

"Hello…hey baby," Corey says, "Yeah it's me boo."

"Oh, so now she's boo huh?" Love says in a very jealous feminine tone as he turns around on the couch completely to face Corey.

"Yeah, baby don't worry about it," Corey says into the phone, "he didn't say anything important. Yeah so what's going on, do you need me to come beat that dude up for you?"

"What," Love says turning around again this time much more masculine, "If she needs somebody to come protect her it'll be me not you, old man."

"It's so weird how you do that Lance." Corey says with a perplexed smile on his face.

"It's weird how I do what?" Love asks.

"How you go from boy to girl to boy again based on the situation," Corey says, "It blows my mind every time. Yeah, you sure did say he does that baby, but I never really noticed it until now."

After a moment Corey looks at Love and then burst into joyous laughter.

"What, what's so funny Corey?" Love asks.

"Nothing boy…" Love replies.

"No, tell me what she said." Love demands.

"She said you're afraid that once she moves in you won't be the prettiest girl in the house anymore." Corey says.

Love smiles and says, "Nope, I'll still be the prettiest mother fucker here…"

"Lance, watch your mouth," Corey says, "There's a lady on the phone."

"Mmmm, she wasn't a lady last night…" Love says with a coy smile on his face. "Baby you were kind of naughty last night." Corey croons into the phone.

"Yeah, I did like it baby," he continues, "you made all my fantasies a reality. Ok… yeah 7p.m. is fine. We'll be here all night so just come whenever you can. Ok bye baby."

Love leaves the room with an obvious attitude. Corey watches him leave and smirks to himself because he thoroughly enjoys making Love jealous.

(Inside Whit's Apartment)

Whitney is packing several bags full of clothes and other personal items. K.C. is sitting on the arm of the sofa with absolutely no idea what's going on. One by one Whit begins taking her bags outside to her car.

After she's done she takes a much-needed seat on the sofa next to K.C. After a few minutes she takes his hand, and then kisses it. "This is by far the hardest thing I've ever had to do," she says, "I'm leaving you Keldrick."

The door opens. "Knock, knock." Ty says. "Where you at Kel…" Jay says. As they make their way to the den they see Whitney breaking the news that they already heard to K.C.

"I still love you," Whitney tells K.C., "I will always love you. But baby, things are different… they're just not good right now. Things are not good for either one of us right now. But there are no mistakes, everything happens for a reason so we have to accept what's happening in our lives and allow the changes to happen."

"And…" Ty interjects. "And what Tyrone…" Whitney says looking at Ty with a scowl on her face. "And…tell the man the real reason why you're leaving him." Ty demands.

Whitney looks back at K.C. "Kel,' Whit says, "I um…I

190

don't know how to tell you this. I found…" She hesitates as tears begin to form in her eyes.

Ty agitatedly walks towards them and snatches Kel's hands away from Whitney. "It's over Kel," Ty tells his friend, "She found somebody else bro."

Ty turns to look at Whitney. "You didn't deserve my brother anyway." Ty tells her. "Okay…" Whitney says standing up to leave.

"And another thing," Ty says, "In high school my brother hit all your friends, and your cousin Cammie." "So, what," Whit says, "I've been sleeping with Dr. Sanchez for years."

"No surprise here," Ty says, "I knew you were a slut back in high school Whitney. Plus, I figured there was something going on between you and *Dr. Doolittle* anyway."

"And why is that Ty?" Whit asks.

"The money Whit…" he replies. "What money?" she asks. "Your car," Ty says, "the clothes, all the jewelry… In fact, Whit, how have you been paying for law school?"

"That's none of your business Tyrone." Whit tells him through clinched teeth.

"Right," Jay says, "I bet it was a private *medical scholarship*."

"Both of you bums can go to Hell." she says grabbing her expensive Michael Kors bag so that she can leave.

"Run Whit," Ty says, "That's what you do best. See Kel still doesn't know what happened between me and you back in high school…"

"What," Jay says looking at Ty, "You hit Whitney bro? Damn and you never told me."

"No," Ty replies, "you know how everybody loved Whit so much for staying by Kel's side after his injury."

"Yeah…" Jay says.

"*Shut the hell up Ty*," Whit screams, "Damn! Will you ever get a life? That was *eight years ago* let it go!"

"No, this is the perfect time to expose this," Ty smiles, "Whitney was planning on leaving Kel way back then bro."

"What…" Jay says looking over at Whitney's reddened face.

"Yeah," Ty replies, "It's true. I had to beg her to stay with him, because I was afraid he would commit suicide after losing his precious *Suga Mama.*"

"Do you have a point Ty?" Whit asks obviously aggravated.

"Yeah," Jay interjects, "*the point is Whit you went from sugar to shit*! And my boy has never loved anybody else like he loves you. And whenever he needs you the most you just leave…like he never meant a damn thing to you. You know what…"

"No, I don't Jay, but I bet you're going to tell me." Whit says with a hand on each hip.

"I swear to God," Jay starts, "I hope the man you chose, the man you're leaving my brother for is gay on the down low. I hope he cheats on you with a hundred different men, and I hope he gives your trifling ass AIDS!"

Whitney looks at K.C. still sitting in silent confusion. She smiles, as she slowly walks towards him. She sits her bag down and then kisses him softly holding his dark face delicately in her hands. Then looking in his eyes, she says, "I love you Keldrick Jermaine Cole, but this is the last time we will ever kiss."

There's a knock at the door. "Come in…" Ty yells. Detective Carl Ray walks in. He can immediately feel the bad vibe as he enters the main room of the small apartment. "If this is a bad time I can come back." Carl says. "You're fine," Jay says, "Hell if you leave, by the time you come back nobody here now, will still be living here sir."

"How do you mean?" Carl asks. "Whitney here…" Jay starts. "Shut the hell up Jay," Whit barks, "How may I help you detective?" "Well Ms. Powell," Carl says, "I received word that your little girl made it back home safely. So, I just wanted to stop back by and follow up with you and your husband, boyfriend… or whatever you two are."

"Yeah Whitney," Ty prods, "What are you and Keldrick?"

"Thanks for stopping back by Detective Ray," Whit says completely ignoring Ty's comment, "Jazemene is fine now, she's safe and sound."

"Glad to hear it," Carl responds stepping forward to get a better look at the blank face of K.C., "So where is little Jazemene, and what's wrong with Mr. Cole?"

"Jazemene is with my mother for a couple weeks," Whit says, "While I'm getting adjusted at my new place she'll be back and forth from Keldrick's mother's house to my mother's house."

"I see," Carl says, "And what about Mr. Cole?"

Whitney kisses K.C. once more, grabs her Michael Kors tote purse, and walks out of the door without another word to any of them. Ty looks at K.C. and then at

Jay. "I'll see myself out." Carl says heading towards the still open door.

"Let's go Kel." Jay says to his clueless friend. "Go where Jay?" K.C. asks.

"I don't know fam," Jay replies, "anywhere but here." "Where did Suga Mama go?" K.C. asks walking towards the still open door. "She's gone bro," Ty says, "Put these shoes on and let's go man."

K.C. does as he's told. The three friends slowly make their way to the rental car, without a clue what they should do next.

(Inside Dr. Sanchez's office)

Sitting at his expensive desk, wearing another luxurious suit, with one of his exquisite watches glistening on his bronze wrist, the good doctor has his head down as he's lost in deep thought.

(Carlos)

What is wrong with me? It's all so stupid. I was never supposed to give a damn about Cameron. It was supposed to just be a brief favor for Whitney. But not now...now there's absolutely no denying my feelings for her.

I wouldn't exactly call it love. It's something different, I usually have several hundred women on speed dial to use interchangeably at my disposal on any given night.

But Cam makes me want to be different, almost

faithful. No more going to the movies on Tuesday night's so none of my other women will see me with her. I want to step out with her on my arm in public. And not be afraid to lose other women, because she'll be my only woman.

Cameron Jiles makes me want to stand up and be a good man. I have to start holding myself accountable. Love is not a game, but it is undeniably painful when you allow someone to snatch it away from you...

There's a knock at the door. "Who is it?" Carlos asks almost in pain. "Maintenance," the lady responds as she opens the door and walks in, "this won't take long I'm just going to clean your windows and empty your trash cans Dr. Sanchez."

The woman looks to be about twenty-three years old. She has blue and blonde weave in her hair and several gold teeth in her mouth. She has a nice shape and a decent face, but it's smothered in cheap make up and looks clownish behind her huge fake eyelashes. "Alright," he says, "Just be quick about it and please don't bother me."

"Yes sir," the girl replies, "I'm not going to bother you. It's none of my business what you're going through Dr. Carlos."

"Dr. Sanchez will do fine." he says with his head still down. "Oh, excuse me," she says looking towards him, "Dr. Sanchez. It's not my place to say anything about what you do in your spare time but..."

"Then don't." he says. "But I'm just saying if you ask me..." she starts. "I didn't ask you." Carlos interjects. She puts her rag down in her bucket and approaches his desk.

"Look Doc," she says, "She ain't yo type... she just a

hood bitch like me. She can go to all the schools she wants to, and get all the degrees or whatever she can, but deep down she still hood. She ain't for you Doc. She is gone always feel like she ain't good enough for you and if you care about her feelings you shouldn't want her to live like that."

He looks up at the lady for the first time." What are you talking about lady?" he asks.

"That girl Cameron," she replies, "I know you green Doc, so I'm just trying to lace you up on some G shit." "Green…" he says, "what is that a racial slur? I'll have you fired for that…" "Na Doc…" she says laughing to herself.

"It ain't like that," she continues, "green just means you ain't hip to the streets. You're a square Doc. You ever heard of Meek Mills?"

"No, I can't say that I have," Carlos replies, "Did he study at Harvard?" "Na," she replies, "he studied in the streets of Philly. He's a rapper, and he's got a song called *"Levels"*. You should check it out. He's basically saying people on your level don't do the things that people on my broke ass baby daddy David's level do. Stay in your league Doc, if you want to mess around with somebody like us from time to time, cool but know what it is and what it ain't. You feel me?"

"Yes," he replies, "I think I'm starting to." "It's simple Doc," she says, "You're her only meal ticket, and she's just your cheap toy. So, let her be that. But if you're looking for a new toy I'm available…"

He turns his chair around to face her. She smiles a toothy smile, and then turns around backwards and slowly lifts her skirt up revealing her perfect butt sitting up just right in a pair of blue lace boy short panties.

Carlos sits back in his chair and spreads his legs. He can feel his blood boiling and his body getting tense. He can remember a time when having sex with new women is what he lived for, and this is a new conquest right in front of him.

Stepping out of her shoes she begins walking towards him. She steps right in between his legs and starts to undo her blouse. Once her blouse is half way unbuttoned, he reaches up to caress her large caramel breast.

The door opens, swinging wide open. Cam is dressed in an all-black rain coat and her long curly weave is soaking wet. She has a red umbrella clinched in her right hand that she obviously didn't use. "Who is that?" the maintenance lady asks."

"That's... my *cheap toy* that I fell in love with." he says looking at Cam. "So, what you wanna do Doc?" the maintenance lady asks stepping back to look at him, with her neck cocked and arms folded tightly.

"I think you should leave..." he says politely. "Lame," she says angrily fixing her clothes, "that's why I don't mess with square ass niggas."

She continues to mumble as she quickly gets her bucket and rags. She looks at him once more, and then walks out slamming the door behind her.

"Carlos..." Cam says with a blank look on her face.

"Cameron..." he replies awaiting her first move. "I have to move on," Cam says, "I realize that but I don't know how to. That man taught me how to love, so how do I love in a world without him?"

Carlos stands up. "Cam," he starts, "we've been here before. And like I told you last time the man is not dead."

"You're right he's not dead," she says, "it's much worse than that he's living… without me."

Carlos leans forward with his fist on his desk.

"If you're still so in love with K.C.," he says, "why are you standing here in my office, and not at Whitney's house with him trying to jog his *damn* memory?"

"Because I love you too Carlos," she says, "I realize that now."

"So, you love me… but you're in love with him?" Carlos asks.

"Yes… I think," Cam says, "I don't know Carlos, I'm just tired of… crying. And I'm tired of being alone and miserable."

"Do I make you happy," he asks, "Have I ever… made you happy at all?"

"What?" Cam asks.

"You heard me Cam," Carlos says, "I said do I make you happy?"

"I uh… Yes," Cam stutters, "When you're near me… I feel um…"

"You don't love me Cam," Carlos interjects, "Sometimes you don't even like me. It's obvious. If I ask if you're in love with K.C. you never hesitate to confirm that you are. When it comes to whether or not you love me, you have to rack your brain trying to make stuff up. You become a stuttering wordsmith in search of the perfect explanation for your feelings for me. But you don't love me, not at all Cameron. But I'm not even mad at you, because a heart breaker like me always ends up getting his heart broken the worst. I deserve this."

"No, you don't!" Cam screams throwing her umbrella down to the ground.

"You do not deserve this from anybody," she says, "especially not from me. I know how you feel right now and nobody deserves to feel that way. But I'm going to fix it… Love is a battlefield, and we can either choose to fight, or we can become casualties of war. We *choose* whether we're happy or unhappy. I know how corny all this sounds right now, but I'm old enough now to know it's the truth. You once told me… we control nothing. You said we think we're in control, but that thought is really just a false idea that's been printed on our brains since birth. We are now, and will always be controlled by our fears, and the things we love. Right…"

"Yeah… I may have said something like that." Carlos says sitting back in his chair obviously intrigued now.

"No that is exactly what you said Carlos," Cam assures him, "I know because it became my mantra. I recited those words… *your* words every night like a prayer since the day I heard you say it."

"Oh really…" Carlos says. "Yeah really," Cam replies, "and I looked at you and all your success, and wonderful worldly accomplishments, and believed all of what you said to be true." "As you should…" he says.

"No sir I shouldn't," she replies, "because it's not true. We all have choices, some more important and harder to make than others, but they are ours to make. Those choices are what shape our lives, not just our fears and the things we love. No sir, I am not in love with you, and

I may not even love you yet..."

Carlos sighs loudly.

"*Yet*," she repeats loudly, "*But...* I know in time I can, because Carlos Luis Sanchez you are a very loveable man, with endless loveable qualities that you exude quite naturally. Waiting for my dreams to come true with Keldrick is not a healthy path for me at all."

Carlos laughs out loud. "So basically," he says, "you're ready to be with me because, you feel like you can't be with K.C.... and in your *mind,* you're choosing to be happy because, since you can't have the man you're actually in love with, you're going to settle for a man you think you could possibly love one day... How is that supposed to make me feel Cameron?"

"I'm going to tell you exactly how to feel, and how not to feel." Cam says reaching behind her to lock the door. Next, she slowly walks towards his desk. As she gets closer to him she reaches into her right coat pocket and pulls out the all-black twenty-two caliber handgun, and sits it on his desk.

Then she reaches into her right pocket again and pulls out her cell phone. After a few clicks, on the keypad she sits her phone down on the desk right next to her gun.

Beyoncé's 2013 hit song "*Dance for You*" begins playing loudly through her phone's speakers. Cam wets her lips as she steps back away from his desk to give him a full view of her.

Slowly unbuckling both straps on the front of her black raincoat, Cam is methodically caressing herself as she rolls her hips to the smooth beat of the song.

Taking a couple of strategic steps backward she

opens her rain coat exposing her matching Victoria's Secret leopard print bra and panty set that Carlos bought her while they were in Paris.

With her hands across her chest she pushes the coat off her shoulders. Ciara's song "***Body Party***" starts to play on Cam's phone. As her coat hits the ground she gets down on all fours turning around so that her back is facing him.

With her hands outstretched in front of her she puts her face on the floor and her behind in the air slowly grinding to the beat.

She knows how turned on he must be because she has forced herself to a level of ecstasy she has never known. Now laying down flat on her stomach Cam crosses and flexes her legs to maximize the size of her ass.

Rolling over to face him she gets back on all fours and begins to crawls towards him. Carlos turns his chair sideways to face her as she crawls around his desk.

She pulls herself up to a squatting position with her hands on his knees. She feels mesmerized staring in to the eyes of the gold Medusa head that is his Versace belt buckle.

As she unfastens the belt she continues to look into the buckles eyes'. The luminous buckle is turning her on even more. "You're my king Carlos." she says in a trancelike state. "What…" he says smiling down at her.

"You're so unreal to me," Cam says, "You're like an American king. You have the cars, the clothes, the houses, the jets and everything."

Cam sits back on her heels with a strange look on her face.

"What's wrong baby…" he says in his thick accent.

"That's how I know I love him…" she replies.

"What are you talking about now Cameron?" Carlos asks.

"You gave me the world," she says, "and everything in it, and I was willing to give it all back to you just to be with him. That's real love Carlos."

"You know what Cameron," Carlos says fixing his expensive belt, "get the fuck out of my office now! If this is your idea of a painful joke, it worked you have succeeded in hurting me once again with your words, but the joke is not funny at all!"

Cam grabs his hands.

"No Carlos," she says, "I was just being honest with you… Don't punish me for that! Damn! You're the one I want Carlos; don't you see that…."

"Hell, no Cameron…" Carlos replies in his thick accent. Cam sighs in real frustration. "Keldrick," she says, "will always represent certain real things in my heart and my past, but you are my present and my whole future."

"Your perfect meal ticket right…" Carlos asks with a mean glare on his face. "No Carlos," she claims, "I don't want your money or anything from you. I just want to be yours for tonight… and every other night for the rest of my life. Because you make me feel so alive baby…" "What exactly are you saying Cam?" Carlos asks leaning back with his arms folded tightly.

"I don't know," Cam admits, "I guess I'm saying let's be together." "And what about Keldrick?" he asks.

Cam sighs again. "Before the accident," Cam says, "he and I could have been good together. But there are no mistakes, so maybe… maybe the accident happened so that I could be with you."

"I don't want to think about any of that right now," Carlos says, "weren't you in the middle of something?"

"Yes sir…" Cam says with a seductive smile on her face. She slowly unzips his pants with her teeth. Carlos palms the back of her head as she pulls his throbbing member out. He guides her perfectly for the next ten minutes until he's finished.

Then he kneels down to kiss her softly. She swallows before she speaks. "Do you forgive me baby?" a still confused Cam asks. "Yeah, I guess so." Carlos replies as he stands up and refastens his clothes.

"We're going out tonight." he tells her. "What… where are we going?" she asks sitting down in his chair behind him. He turns around towards her. Cam grabs his trim waist and pulls him towards her. He takes both of her elbows in his hands passionately as she holds him. "I don't know… how about we do dinner and a movie." he says.

Cam snatches her hands away from him quickly. "That's it," Cam pouts, "no surprise trips to Paris on a private jet, no fifty-thousand-dollar shopping sprees?" Carlos furrows his brows tightly trying to figure out what to say next. Cam's frown fades into a cute grin.

"I'm just kidding *Dr. Sanchez*." she says leaning gently on   his stomach. "You should see your face baby." Cam says as she stands up in his strong bronze arms.

"Dinner, and a movie sounds great," she continues, "but you have kind of spoiled me. You can't just get me that high on life, and then expect me to be satisfied with a normal relationship anymore. I'm just saying…"

"Everything we've done *is* normal to me Cameron."
he says looking down into her caramel eyes. Carlos
softly kisses the top of her forehead. "I know baby," she
says lazily, "that's what I love about you. You're my
absolute dream come true. I love your accent; your
style… everything about you just screams perfection to
me Carlos. And most of all I want your normal to
become my normal."

As she wraps her slender arms around his waist he
takes her pretty black face in his hands and explores her
eyes again.

"Well my dear," he says, "the life that you aspire to live,
is reserved for a very special lady."

"What's her name Carlos?" Cam whispers.

"Mrs. Sanchez." he replies.

"Oh," she says smiling to herself with her face
pressed gently against his chest, "I think I could go for a
Mrs. Sanchez one day, I could be Hispanic, right?"
Carlos steps back to look at her.

"No baby… I don't think you could ever pass as a
Hispanic." he tells her laughing to himself. Cam gasps as
she playfully hits him across his left arm.

"So, what do I look like a fuckin' Nigerian?" she asks
with her arms folded across her chest.

"I don't know about that baby," he says, "but I'm
only kidding with you my love. You would make an
absolutely stunning Mrs. Sanchez. There's one thing I have
to tell you though my love." Cam looks up into his serious
eyes.

"What Carlos?" she asks. "This is the last time I will

ever accept you back into my life like this," he says, "I cannot **stand** the thought of losing you again, so if you ever even think about leaving me again, just know that you're dead to me... I love you that much Cameron."

With her head back safely on Carlos' chiseled chest Cam gazes at the stars outside of his large office window. There has never been a more perfect and serene night in Cam's entire life. These are the moments she's always dreamed about. She realizes one day she has to find a way to put herself in position to live inside of these moments on a more consistent basis. She still loves Keldrick Jermaine Cole very, very much, but she's also tired of being alone. Cam knows that K.C. can no longer or ever again be a serious factor in her love life. The man is damn near a vegetable; he's no good to himself or anybody else for that matter.

Life goes on. With all the obvious positives that come along with dating Carlos, the only comforting thought in Cam's mind is the fact that she'll never have to work again once they get married. Poor Keldrick she thinks to herself.

(Ty, Jay, and K.C. are on the way to the mall)

"So, what's the plan Jay?" Ty asks. "Yeah what's the plan Jay?"
K.C. mimics laughing to himself. "Shut up K.C." Jay says looking over his shoulder at his friend laying in the backseat like a big kid.

"Now look Ty," Jay says, "Whit said the doctors told her anything significant from his past could possibly jog his memory and return him to his normal mind state."

"Ok." Ty replies with his forehead wrinkled. Jay looks at Ty. "You get it bro…" Jay asks.

"No," Ty replies, "why of all places are we going to the mall to jog this fool's memory?"

"Are you serious Jay asks," looking at Ty with a smile on his face as they wait at a red light, "when we were kids all the way until graduation we spent every Friday night at Millennia mall trying to get girls. Bro this is the perfect place to jog K.C.'s memory."

"You know what Jay, you're right bro." Ty agrees. "I know I'm right," Jay says, "but if this doesn't work I give up bro."

"Blood of Jesus," Ty says, "I wish it was that simple for me. This
is my fault so I can't give up until my boy is back to normal. I don't have much money left in the bank and if I take off any more time from work they're going to fire my ass. But I'm here bro… until this is over, I'm right here." Ty looks over the seat at his damaged friend.

"So, you're going to risk everything you've worked for, to see K.C. back to good health?" Jay asks.

"Hell yeah," Ty says without hesitation, "that's my brother… and I would do the same for you man." Jay looks at Ty again as he parks the car in the mall parking lot.

"That's love bro," Jay says, "that's real brotherly love my nigga. I'm proud of you." They shake hands before stepping out of the car.

"Where's Suga Mama?" K.C. asks from the backseat.

"K.C. shut up!" Ty and Jay say in unison.

"And get out of the car bro…" Jay says.

The three friends head towards the entrance of the mall side by side. As they get closer to the front doors of the mall they all feel a strange chill, as if they're stepping back into their youth.

"Man…do ya'll feel that?" Ty asks.

"Yeah bro, it's been a long time since the three of us stepped through these doors together. Right Kel…" Jay says looking at his tall friend as they all walk inside the huge mall.

"Where's Suga Mama at Ty?" K.C. says. "Man, forget Whitney," Ty says, "We're going to find you a new *Suga Mama*, tonight bro."

"There's only one Suga Mama Ty," Kel says, "What is he talking about Jay?"

"Nothing Kel," Jay tells him, "just have fun tonight bro… do that for me." Ty stops walking and looks at Jay. "What," Ty says, "You know what… *no*. Tell the man the truth Jay. She left you Keldrick. Whitney left you for some other guy. She left you… and she moved in with him. She's gone bro, just like your freaking mind, and if I can't fix you soon I'm going to lose my entire life!"

"That's enough Ty," Jay says, "you're going too hard on him. He can't handle all that right now bro." "Damn it," Ty says, "Yeah man I know. Look Kel… bro I need you to try real hard to remember. I need you to be okay so I can be okay too."

"I'm not a child," K.C. says, "I may have my moments and I may not remember some things but I'm still a man." "You're a man huh…" Ty says. "Yeah I'm a man Ty." K.C. replies.

"Then show me," Ty says waving his arm in the direction of the huge mall crowd in front of them, "go get a woman." K.C. turns around and begins surveying the crowd.

"Wait, slow down," Jay says, "let's go, find us a table in the food court and chill first. Then when Kel sees a cute breezy he wants to holla at, then he can call her over to the table and talk to her."

"Cool, look there's an open table right there." Ty says pointing to a nearby table, where a young Asian family is standing up to leave.

As they sit down Ty begins to shake his head.

"Man, this is hopeless," Ty says, "How is this fool supposed to pull a grown woman with the mind of a child? Did you see how he was when Whit left him? That shit was sad bro."

"Be positive bro anything is possible." Jay says. "Wait," K.C. says, "Suga Mama left me? Where did she go?"

"You see this shit," Ty says looking at Jay, "like I said... *hopeless*."

Jay laughs lightly. "Shut up Ty," Jay says, "you stupid bro. Look Kel there's a bad red bone right there." K.C. turns to see who Jay's pointing at.

"Where..." Kel asks.

"Nigga you see her," Ty says, "right there in the red skirt. Don't get nervous now bro you're the *Chocolate God*, the *Black Beast*. Kel "K.C." Cole you never get turned down fool. Go ahead bro..."

Ty ushers K.C. towards the attractive young lady who could easily pass for Rhianna's younger sister. K.C. gets up and approaches her. He taps her on her slender yellow shoulder. She turns around with an attitude, but immediately starts smiling as soon as she sees K.C.'s face.

"Hi." he says.

"Hello…" she replies.

"Um… yeah so did you… I mean are you from here?" K.C. says pointing down at the ground.

She giggles. "Um," she says, "are you asking me am I from the mall?"

K.C. laughs nervously at himself. "No ma'am," he says, "I mean are you from the city?"

"Well I was born in Miami," she explains, "but my dad moved me and my sisters here when I was like four. So yeah, I've been in Orlando most of my life. Are you from here?"

K.C. looks back at Ty and Jay quickly, as they both watch him very closely. Then he turns back around towards the pretty lady.

"Did you hear me," she says still smiling at him, "I asked are you from here?"

"Um, yeah… I think so." he tells her.

"Wait… what?" she says, laughing to herself as she leans comfortably on his shoulder.

"How do you not know where you're from?" she asks.

"No, I mean I fell and hit my head…" K.C. stops in the middle of his sentence as something behind the young lady catches his eye. His heart stops, his entire body goes numb, and he can hardly breathe. The young lady is talking to him but all he can hear is his own heart starting to beat again wildly.

The lady K.C. has his eyes on has the face of an

angel. To him, she looks like a perfect black china doll.

"Is she real... she can't be." he mumbles aloud. He squints, his dark caramel eyes to get a better view. The young lady in front of him grabs his shoulder and begins to shake him.

"Are you even listening to me?" she asks.

"Um... No, actually I'm not. Excuse me, but I gotta go..." he says as he walks past her in the direction of the beautiful girl in the distance.

"What is this fool doing now?" Ty asks.

"I don't know," Jay says," but man he had that chick, did you see how hard she was smiling?"

The lady in K.C.'s sights is standing next to a handsome man who is dressed very nicely. The man is obviously with her, but K.C. doesn't even notice him.

As K.C. walks up face to face with her, his heart stops again as he gazes into the depths of her dark eyes. K.C. tries to regain what little composure he had, before he attempts to speak.

"Hello," K.C. says, "my name is...um Keldrick, Jer... Jermaine... Cole." He swallows hard. His mouth is extremely dry now.

The lady tries to speak, but Keldrick puts a finger on her lips so she can't speak. He licks his lips.

"I'm not the smartest man on the planet," Keldrick tells her, "or the richest, but you make me want to become everything you've ever dreamed of. And I don't know if love at first sight really exists, but I do know when I saw you... you altered something inside of me."

"Don't you see me standing here?" the man standing beside the lady says. K.C. looks at the man and notices his face is almost familiar. "Yeah, I see you standing there bro," K.C. says, "but now we're both standing here." K.C. gently moves the lady to the side, and steps into the man's face.

"So," K.C. says, "What you got a problem or something Chico?"

Ty and Jay see what's going on from the table. They both jump up and rush to K.C.'s side.

"Cuz if you got a problem," Kel says, "we can…"

"You good Kel…" Ty says stepping up in front of him.

"Yeah," he replies, "I'm straight." Ty and Jay look at the girl, and then at each other.

Ty immediately grabs K.C.'s arm and tries to lead him back to the table. K.C. doesn't budge, and he never takes his eyes of the man with the girl.

"K.C. let's go bro, these people are obviously on a date and we're disturbing them." Ty says.

K.C. looks at Ty with his brows wrinkled, and then he looks at the lady. "Am I bothering you Ms. Lady…" he asks.

She looks at the man she's with, as he stares back at her with a cynical look on his bronze face. Then she looks back at K.C. with tears in her eyes. She steps closer to him and looks as deeply as she can into his lost dark caramel eyes.

"You really don't know me, do you?" she says wiping a few tears away and forces a smile. She pauses before she speaks again. She puts her tiny hand over her mouth as she ponders what to say next.

"Is it possible… to fall in love at first sight twice," she says, "with the same person? In one lifetime…"

K.C. raises his left brow as he turns around to look at his two friends standing behind him. Jay stares back at him, as Ty looks down at the floor and shakes his head. K.C. looks back at the beautiful dark-skinned angel.

"Am I supposed to know you," Kel asks, "see I had an accident and they tell me I…"

"You don't have to explain Keldrick. It's okay," she says, "I'm just so…" She starts to cry again. He takes her hand in his and kisses it softly.

"Don't cry pretty lady," he says, "what were you trying to say? You're so what…"

"I'm, I'm so… happy." she mumbles through a host of tears.

"Why?" Keldrick asks. "Because," the lady replies, "I never thought you would ever look at me this way again."

"Seriously," the man with her says, "I don't have time for this. Are you ready to go Cameron?"

She turns around towards the man and says, "I can't just leave him like this Carlos. I hope you understand."

"So, what are you saying Cam?" Carlos asks. "I'm saying I have to make sure he's okay." Cam replies.

"So how are you getting home, you rode with me?" Carlos asks crossing his arms tightly.

"Ty, and Jay can you guys drop me and Kel off at my place," Cam asks, "I'll take care of him, I know what to do."

"I bet you do," Carlos says snidely, "just give him the same treatment you gave me an hour ago, on your knees, in my office. That should fix him right up. Whatever Cameron you already made your choice, so like I told you in my office you're dead to me. I don't give a damn what happens, you better not ever need me for anything   in life again!"

Carlos walks off angrily. After he's gone the four of them leave the mall together with new found hope for Kel's recovery.

Chapter 10
Addiction

(Ty and Jay are dropping Cam and K.C. off)

"Cam..." Ty says. "Yes Ty." she replies. He turns around to look at her in the back seat. "I know you didn't ask me what I think, but I'm going to tell you anyway." Ty says.

"Okay." she replies.

"Before we drop you guys off," Ty says "I just want to make sure you realize when he gets better, he's going to end up going back to Whitney at some point." Cam smiles at Ty.

"You're exactly right Ty," she says, "I didn't ask you. But to be honest, I don't really care what happens after he's healthy again. Kel is worth my time. If we don't end up together that's something, I'll just have to deal with."

Cam looks out of her window, with her smile still in place. The ominous glow from the street lights on her street, have never been as beautiful as they are right now.

"Turn into the cul de sac on the left," Cam says, "and that's my house up there on the right." K.C. looks out the window at Cam's house.

"I know this house..." he mumbles. "Yeah, you do Kel..." Cam replies.

"I think... I used to live here." he says.

214

"Damn," Jay says, "She's like medicine to this nigga. You hear this shit Ty?"

"Yeah, nigga," Ty mumbles as he parks in front of Cam's house, "I ain't deaf I hear em'."

"Are ya'll getting out or…" Ty starts. "Ty shut the hell up!" Cam yells.

"What is wrong with you," she asks, "Is it that hard to believe that a dark skin chick could possibly be good for Keldrick?"

"What," Jay says, "We never said anything like that. Your color has nothing to do with anything Cam."

"Then why do ya'll always have an attitude when I'm around..," Cam asks, "and I don't even know ya'll. I mean… I feel like I will never know either one of you guys, because you won't allow me to."

"Blood of Jesus girl," Ty says, "we don't have a clue what you're talking about." "Are you serious Ty," Cam says, "You two have been giving me the business since the first time I met ya'll. I don't get it though, because ya'll don't like Whitney, and ya'll don't like me. Do ya'll just want Kel to be single like ya'll so the three of you can just run wild? Like… what is it? Please explain…"

"I got this Ty," Jay says holding his hand up, "when we first met you, you had just shot our best friend. Yeah, the dude who looked out for us and protected us our entire lives was lying on his death bed because of you. You also were causing static between him and his fiancé. Whitney is the only chick we've ever known him to love."

"Well damn it there's a new chick in town," she says, "and he loves me too. Either way, I'm tired. Kel and I will see you both tomorrow."

"You might see Ty but I'ma be back in the A boo." Jay says.

"Why are you going back so soon?" Cam asks. "I have a show tomorrow night." Jay replies.

"A show," she says, "what kind of show?" "I rap." Jay replies. "Oh, is that what you do," Cam says, "does that pay well, or at all for that matter?" Jay's face is turning red with rage.

"What he means is," Ty interjects, "he's going to a few Atlanta strip clubs to pay several DJ's to spin a few of his songs in the clubs to let people hear his music."

Cam laughs. "So, what you're saying is," Cam asks, "he doesn't actually have a show..."

"Really Ty..." Jay says. "Now don't get it twisted now Cam," Ty says, "my boy has plenty of talent, he just lacks focus sometimes."

"I believe you," she says, "so after your show, are you coming back sir?"

"You don't give a damn if I come back or not, so why ask?" Jay says with pure venom in his voice.

"No...I really do care. I care about both of you, because you're a part of him." Cam says pointing at K.C.

"I just want ya'll to understand that your boy fell in love with me, like legit love," Cam continues, "and I feel the same way about him. It's weird but I felt like I knew you both before I ever even met you."
Cam says.

"And how is that?" Ty asks.

"Kel talks about ya'll all the time," she says smiling at him,

"I feel like I went to school with ya'll and everything."

"What did that fool say about when we were back in school?" Ty asks.

"Oh god," Cam smiles, "I feel like he told me *everything*."

"Like what." Jay asks. "Okay," Cam says leaning up in the front seat between the two of them, "Like the time Kel had to save you both from getting your asses kicked in the cafeteria…"

"Which time," Ty laughs, "that was like every other week." "The time he had a football game out of town," she says, "and he jumped off the team bus in front of the school after Whitney texted him and told him what was going on."

"Aw hell yeah," Jay says, "I remember that day…"

"Yeah," Cam laughs, "he said he ran all the way from the bus to the lunchroom and ended up fighting three dudes, who you two owed money to." "Three," Ty says looking at Jay and then at Cam, "no it was like five of them niggas. Kel faded every last one of them chumps, and made it back to the team bus before it drove off."

Ty, Jay, and Cam laugh. "But why did ya'll owe them money?" Cam asks. Jay and Ty look at each other and start laughing all over again. "We uh," Jay says, "We used to bet on Kel's game stats. We would tell him before the game what we bet, and this nigga was so raw he used to damn near match whatever we bet."

"Yep," Ty says, "Me and Jay were making a killing." "Until," Jay says, "One of Ty's side hoes told the guys we were betting that K.C. was our homeboy."

"They found out we were hustling they're asses," Ty says, "So naturally they wanted us dead. But after *the*

Big Black Beast put them paws on them niggas in front of the whole cafeteria they paid us what we owed them."

"The big black beast…" Cam says. "Aw yeah," Jay says, "That was one of K.C.'s many nicknames back in school. Ya boy was… Hell still is a legend in the city."

"He didn't tell you about all the hype he used to get back in school?" Ty asks.

"Nope," Cam admits, "honestly every story Kel ever told me about high school involved the two of you. He may have been a big deal back then, and the big man on campus, but what he misses most of all from his younger days was hanging out with his two brothers that left him when he got hurt."

"Damn," Jay says, "you know Cam… You alright with me home girl…" "Yeah," Ty agrees, "you cool, but you know if you had gone to school with us you would have been ***my*** girl. Because these two shallow ass niggas only dated red bones back then."

"That's true." Jay agrees.

"Awe that's sweet Ty I guess," Cam laughs, "and ya'll are both cool with me. See we can be friends if ya'll just let your guard down. And I promise… I won't shoot your boy ever again." They all share another laugh.

"Well guys it's been my pleasure," Cam says, "but I need to get my man inside and get to work on putting him back together again." "Break a leg K.C.!" Jay says smiling.

"Be careful Cam," Ty says, "I'm praying for both of ya'll." Cam smiles back at both of them, and then she leads the only man she's ever truly loved to her front door.

"Here Kel, hold my purse while I unlock the door."

Cam says.

"Yes ma'am…" Kel replies in a childlike tone. Cam looks at him.

"You don't have to call me ma'am Kel," she says as she uses her key to unlock her front door, "you're older than me. Now come on baby let's go inside."

As they walk inside Cam watches Kel carefully. After a few steps, he stops and looks down at his feet.

"What's wrong K.C.?" she asks him.

"Suga Mama… she's gone." K.C. says. Cam sits on her sofa and pats the cushion next to the one she's sitting on, signaling Kel to come sit down.

"Yeah," Cam says, "Come sit down so I can take your shoes off for you." He does as he's told. Cam kneels down in front of him and unties each of his shoes, and then takes them off. Cam sits comfortably on the floor Indian style in front of him.

Placing his left foot in her lap, she begins gently massaging it from the bottom to the top. Kel lays his head all the way back against the top of the sofa.

The ex-football star sighs gently as he closes his tired eyes. "How does that feel baby…" Cam asks. Kel sighs again with a faint smile on his smooth dark chocolate face. Cam smiles to as well because she thought she would never see him smile again.

(Ty and Jay)

As Ty and Jay ride down International Drive, they're both lost in a silent walk down memory lane. The beautiful ghosts of their past are stuck here on these streets forever remembering and reliving the good and bad times that made them who they are.

"I wanna move back home." Jay admits.

"With your parents," Ty asks, "I don't blame you bro that movie theater, they have is nice as hell."

"No fool," Jay says, "I mean I wanna move back to Orlando."

"Yeah," Ty replies, "I feel you bro maybe we should."
"Maybe..." Jay says.

"It's definitely been on both of our minds for a reason bro." Ty tells him as he pulls into their hotel parking lot. "Yeah," Jay says, "I mean we both left home right, but now that, we're a little older and it's time, that we start trying to build something... real with our adult lives."

"That's deep bro," Ty admits as he pulls into a parking space near their upstairs room, "I like it. I mean in a few months I might be able to transfer here and start working at Disney World."

"Yeah," Jay agrees, "And I could ask my dad for a loan to open my own studio here." "Now you're talking little bro," Ty replies, "Turn your talent into some definite cash."

Ty parks the car. "Let's get upstairs," Jay says, "I'm tired as hell and my plane leaves at 6:45 a.m."

"Cool." Ty says as they both get out of the car and head towards the stairs.

After walking in the room Jay heads to his bag and starts looking through it for clothes so he can jump in the shower. "You mind if I shower first bro?" Jay asks. "Na," Ty replies, "Go head bro. I'm gonna run to the drink machine and grab a couple cokes, you want anything?" "Grab me a Dr. Pepper fam." Jay replies. "Bet," Ty says grabbing his hotel key off the table by his bed, "I got you bro."

Ty walks out of the hotel door. After closing the door behind him he steps close to the rail overlooking the parking lot. Down below he sees a sexy white woman getting out of a yellow drop top mustang. He wants to say something to her, but he decides not to.

Ty shakes his head and then heads towards the stairs to go down to the drink machine. So many things are running through his busy brain. His favorite thought is Cameron Jiles, and her gorgeous smile and perfect body. Ty smiles.

"Keldrick is gonna kill my ass," he whispers to himself with a satisfied smile, "Yeah he's gonna definitely kill me. But I think Ms. Jiles just might be worth it."

Ty approaches the drink machine. He pulls out four single dollar bills. He hears footsteps behind him. He turns around but he sees nobody. It's very dark outside, and Orlando's crime rate has seen a significant rise as of late, or at least that's what Ty heard on the radio earlier. Hell, Ty only has seven bucks on him so he's not really too worried about getting robbed, but still nobody likes to be violated period.

"Hey…" a sweet voice says. Ty turns around to see the pretty white lady peeking around the corner at him.

"Hello…" Ty says with a big smile pushing the cash back in his pocket forgetting about the drinks completely.

"What's your name beautiful?" Ty asks.

"Nicole…" she replies. "Nicole what…" Ty asks stepping closer to her.

"Nicole Bourgeois," she says stepping from around the corner,

"What's yours?"

"Tyrone Carter," he says, "But you can call me Tyboonie."

Nicole giggles.

"Tyboonie…" she repeats.

"Yeah Tyboonie." he tells her. She giggles again trying to keep her balance in her high heels.

"You'll have to excuse me," Nicole says, "I'm a little drunk. My husband is asleep and I don't have my key to get back in the room." "Husband…" Ty asks. "Yeah, his name is Kurt," Nicole admits, "So, I'm stuck out here all alone now."

Ty smiles at her. "Now how can you be alone," he asks, "If I'm standing right here with you?"

Nicole giggles again flashing her beautiful smile. "I guess you're right Tyboonie," she slurs every word, "You know what?"

"What?" Ty asks as he steps even closer to her. "I've, never been with a man like you before." Nicole admits. "A man, like me…" Ty says. "A brother…" Nicole says licking her full pink lips.

Ty looks her up and down. Her shape is exquisite. Nicole is wearing a short hot pink and white club dress, and white six-inch heels.

"Well," Ty says, "There's a first time for everything. And honestly I've never been with a white girl before."

222

"Oh," Nicole says stepping close to him, "Maybe we owe it to ourselves to… explore with each other."

"I agree…" Ty says. Nicole grabs Ty and begins kissing him. As she kisses him she pulls him back around the corner near the maintenance closet. Ty looks up and sees the door to the closet. He reaches behind her and opens the door.

Once inside the closet he quickly closes the door behind them. Nicole pushes him back gently. Then she squats down in front of his and tries to open his pants. She's having trouble so Ty reaches down and does it for her.

As Nicole gives Ty the best sample of oral sex he's ever had in his life he reaches into his back pocket where he finds a lifestyle condom. Ty looks down at Nicole through wide eyes. He's absolutely amazed by her dynamic technique and concentration.

"Oh God…" Ty whispers in pure ecstasy. Nicole slurps the tip of him several times before swallowing him whole once again.

Ty can't handle anymore.

"Stand up Nicole…" he moans. She does as she's told. Nicole turns around and knocks several boxes of the top of the dryer that was behind her. Then she turns back to Ty. He opens the condom, throws the wrapper on the floor, and then slides it on himself.

Ty can't help himself he's so lost in Nicole's beautiful blue eyes and lustful passion. He steps forward and lifts her up to sit her on top of the warm rumbling dryer. Nicole leans back and spreads her legs for him.

"One night only Tyboonie," she moans, "I belong to

you…" "Blood of Jesus…" Ty growls as he steps up and pulls her soaking wet panties to the side. Ty slides in her warm body with ease. He can feel her vagina gripping his penis as he strokes in and out of her.

He's in heaven inside of Nicole's body for the most part, but the small condom he has on is uncomfortable to say the least.'

"Damn it," Ty says pulling out of her, "This ain't gone work."

"What baby…" Nicole whines.

"Hold on." Ty says reaching in his back pocket for his almost empty wallet. Inside his wallet he sees the edge of a gold wrapper.

"Hell yes!" Ty says snatching the magnum condom out of his old wallet. Nicole smiles at him and then she climbs down off the dryer.

"What's wrong Nicole?" Ty asks as he removes one condom and slides the new one on.

"Hit me from the back…" Nicole moans as she bends over the dryer.

"Blood of Jesus…" Ty growls.

(Inside Love, Corey, and Whitney's apt.)

Whitney is lying in bed naked, between Love and Corey who are both sleeping.

(Whitney)

This can't be real. I have two gorgeous men who adore me, and cater to me. No woman deserves to be treated this good... No, I take that back I deserve it. I'm a queen and I should be treated as such. Who says a woman can only have one king? The more the merrier.

Just when I thought happiness was unobtainable for me, this happened. Love and his peaceful intimacy fell into my life at the perfect time, and with him came Corey in all of his strong, reliable masculinity.

Together they're both showing me what happiness can be. And I
really don't know if I'm happy yet, but for once in my life I can't think of anything to complain about. The house is always clean; all three of us share in doing all of the household duties, we enjoy spending time together, and the sex is everything I needed in life!

Whitney silently giggles to herself.

But I can honestly say it's not the sex, because the time we spend together is more satisfying than anything else. These two men are changing me for the better, and I love it. Together Love and Corey are the perfect man for me.

I thought the two of them were sexually active with each other at first. But they're not. Love and Corey have never had sex with each other once. Strange, but it's not my place to question their sex lives with each other.

I find it hard to believe that they never did anything but I'll probably never know the whole truth. Oh well. I really hope K.C. is okay, but I don't regret leaving him. I had to do what's best for me.

Whitney senses some movement on her right side. As she looks towards him, she sees that Corey is silently watching her through lazy eyes.

225

"What you over there smiling about beautiful?" he asks. "Life…" she replies. "Life has you smiling like that," he asks now smiling himself, "that's a blessing girl. *This* is what everybody truly wants. Sure, people claim they want money, fame, and fortune. But most of all, really deep down we all just want stability and pure happiness."

Whit rolls over to face him completely.

"Boy, where did you come from," she asks in genuine awe, "you just wake up thinking like that?" Corey laughs.

"Why not," he says, "don't I go to sleep thinking like this?"

"Yeah," she replies, "but I mean a lot of people talk like they believe the things you do, but I mean I've yet to see you falter."

"God willing you never will." he says confidently.

"Corey, do you ever think about how our lives would be if it was just you and me?"
she asks.

"All the time actually," he whispers, "but don't say that too loud because Lance already feels like you and I are getting too close, and leaving him out."

Corey looks over Whitney's nude body to see if Love is still asleep. "Is he still sleeping?" he asks her.

Whitney rolls over close to Love to make sure, and then she rolls back over to face Corey.

"Yeah, he is." she confirms.

"Good…" Corey says sliding deep down under the covers, making his way towards her perfect yellow body.

First, he kisses her left ankle. Her body begins to tingle perfectly. Corey takes her left foot in his hands, and begins tasting each of her delicate toes one by one, while gently massaging the bottom of her foot.

Paying close attention to the places on her foot, that are the most sensitive Corey relentlessly uses his tongue and lips to drive her crazy. Just when she feels like she can't take anymore he places her left foot down and picks up the right foot.

While sucking the toes on her right foot, and massaging the ball of her foot with his right hand, Corey reaches up in between her legs with his left hand to see how wet she is. As he gently touches her soft wet center she jumps in pleasant surprise.

Placing her other foot back down on the bed he begins to slowly make his way up between her legs, massaging and sucking her thighs along the way. With a hand on each one of her inner thighs, he pushes her legs as far apart as he possibly can. She moans quietly.

With his exceptionally big tongue Corey opens her soft wet center as she grinds on his moist hungry face. Reaching up under her, he grabs her round behind to pull her closer to him. Love rolls over and sees what's going on. He immediately pulls his member out through the slit in the front of his boxers, and begins to stroke himself as he watches them.

Corey's strong silhouette frame that Love can barely see through the thin white sheet is very intriguing to him, but Whitney looks so gorgeous lost in the passion Corey is blessing her with. She is the main cause of Love's arousal.

Whitney can feel him watching her. Scared to look at him Whitney closes her eyes, and continues to accept

Corey's perfect gift he's blessing her with. With her eyes still closed tightly Whit can feel Love's lips tenderly tasting hers. As she opens her eyes, her pleasure is heightened as she loses herself in his gorgeous green eyes.

She can't breathe, and she doesn't want to. Whitney Michelle Powell never wants to breathe again. She's silently and greedily praying that these two men take her breath away like this consistently until her life ends.

Their passion is almost too much for her but she welcomes it openly. Love starts eagerly kissing and sucking her neck, while Corey continues to devour her. Never taking his mouth away from her neck Love climbs on top of Whit and sits up on her stomach staring down at her in complete ecstasy.

Looking down towards her stomach she can see how ready Love is for her. For the first time Love notices how big Whitney's stomach has gotten, but he knows now is not the time to discuss it.

He begins tasting her nipples while grinding on her stomach. Sliding up closer to her face, he begins to slide his throbbing penis between her supple breasts. Still looking in his eyes Whit squeezes both of her tender breasts together, as he continues to slide between them.

Corey reaches up and pushes Love forward. Love grabs the back of Whit's head pulling it up towards her breasts. She instinctively opens her wet mouth, still holding her breast tightly together with her hands. Love continues to slide between them and now into her mouth. Corey, now at full attention sits up and takes his boxers off. After throwing his socks and his boxers on the floor near the bed Corey scoots up close to her to get in a good position to make love to her. As he enters her body, Love sees Whitney's eyes begin to bulge.

This moment is too much for him. Love's eyes begin to roll in the back of his head as he arches backwards towards Corey. Love feels like a sexy cowboy riding a beautiful horse as he follows the up and down motions of Whitney's body as she reacts to Corey's stroke pattern.

I love you Whitney…" Love whispers close to her ear. "I love you too Lance," she cries, "Perfect… this is just perfect…"

Corey continues to penetrate her in the same strong pattern. She can feel him in her stomach now. Her eyes begin to water. This feeling is so amazing she hopes it never ends.

Whit lets go of her left breast as she reaches up to wipe the passion induced tears from her beautiful yellow face. "Deeper…" she moans.

"Seriously," Corey growls, "Okay." Whitney gasps for air as Corey dives deeper inside of her warm wet center.

Gripping her waist Corey tries to pull her even closer as he continues to give her all of him.

"I'm about to cum…" Whitney moans loudly.

"Me too…" Love says. "Me too…" Corey says with one strong final stroke, going as deep into her body as he can possibly go. The energy and warmth between their three bodies is so intense, the entire bed is soaking with sweat.

Whitney shouts loudly as she finishes first. After hearing the pleasure in her screams Love falls forward on her after releasing his seed down her greedy throat. Corey continues to stroke with new found stamina. Reaching forward he begins to massage Love's back vigorously as he continues to make love to Whitney. Thirty minutes later Corey falls forward on Love's back totally exhausted.

(Carlos)

"Hello," Carlos says answering his cell phone at his desk, "what Whitney?" "Don't baby me Whitney," he continues, "No I don't want to talk about her, what do you want?"

Carlos slams his head down on his desk. Completely numb to the pain he slams his head down one more time. Then he stands up in a rage with the phone still up to his ear, and begins to pace back and forth in his dark office.

"Whitney what do you me to do," Carlos asks, "She left me, to go back to K.C. And now because of you I got my heart broken twice. I have never been an emotional man... but this time your games *went too damn far!*"

"I really don't care what you want any more Whitney," Carlos yells into the phone, "No, I am not going to call her or go see her. I don't want to talk about her. We have more important things to discuss anyway. Are you really pregnant, and if so when would you like me to schedule your abortion consultation?"

Carlos listens to her. "No," he says, "my money is *my* money. You have spent enough of it already. I paid for your school, your car, and plenty of other stupid things I shouldn't have! What the hell does my money have to do with your pregnancy? You are not having this baby Whitney, and that's final!"

Carlos hangs his phone up and solemnly sits back down at his desk. He lays his head down and closes his tired eyes. He hears his door open but he doesn't move. He hears soft footsteps entering, and now approaching him.

She runs her warm fingers through his tight curly hair. Gently massaging his scalp, with her palms and fingertips she's unknowingly guiding his mind to another place, a happier place. With one hand still massaging his tender scalp, she takes her other hand and begins firmly rubbing his tense neck. He still doesn't move or open his eyes. The massage feels so good. At this point he doesn't care who it is, he just doesn't want it to end. Masterfully she uses both of her supple hands to rub and kneed his neck and shoulders. Carlos can actually feel all the stress draining from his pain filled body. She pushes him forward, so that he's lying further on his desk.

Now that more of his back is accessible, she pulls his shirt up and begins to run her sharp blue fingernails up and down the length of him. He moans deeply in surrender. Reaching around in front of the good doctor she gently undoes his tie. Pulling it off of him she holds it out tight in her hands to examine it. Then she forces him to sit up straight as she wraps his Versace tie around his head blind folding him.

"Stand up baby…" she whispers with her wet lips on his left ear. He does as he's told, ready and willing to endure whatever will come next. Standing behind him, she reaches around in front of him caressing his chest, and wash-board abs. One by one she undoes each one of his shirt buttons.

Once the shirt is completely open he takes it off himself. Then she walks around to the side of him and greedily runs her bright fingernails up and down his delicious looking stomach. With her free hand, she reaches inside her panties and caresses herself, she can't believe how wet Carlos is making her without even touching her.

After sending her own arousal to an even higher plateau of brilliant lustful excellence, she walks back behind Carlos. She never once takes her hungry eyes off of him. Once she is positioned behind the gorgeous doctor again she pushes his body forward against his desk again.

Bracing himself with his hands on the edge of his desk Carlos stands firm. Down on her knees, she reaches around in front of him and undoes his belt, and his pants. Carlos lets his pants fall to the ground without hesitation.

She presses her nails gently into the sides of his stomach and then slides them down to the sides of his thighs. Noticing from his body language and moans that he likes the way her nails feel she presses them into his thighs just a bit deeper.

Scooting closer to him she begins to kiss the back of his thighs.
As she gently kisses the back of his strong bronze thighs she continues to press her blue nails even into the sides of them.

Carlos feels himself growing weak as she pays special attention to parts of his body that have never been catered to before. In his mind, he would try almost anything with her. He's more aroused than he ever remembers being. He quickly turns around and stands her up.

With both of his hands he begins to feel her face, trying to figure out who she might be. Working his way down to her large breast and perfect behind Carlos wrinkles his brows. He's almost frustrated due to the fact that he still doesn't have a clue who this mystery woman could be.

"Spread your legs..." he commands. "Make me…" she whispers defiantly. With his hand, firmly around her neck Carlos spins her around, so that her back is now to his desk. They have switched positions completely. Then he forces her to lie back on his desk. Both of her big beautiful breasts pop out as he snatches her blouse open.

Still blindfolded he can't see her breast but he begins sucking them non-the-less. Squeezing them and caressing them softly at first, then as his libido goes into hyper drive he finds himself helplessly wanting to hurt her.

He wants to make her feel real pain, while simultaneously wanting to push her to multiple orgasms. His body feels so cold, but warm at the same time. The fact that he has no idea who this mystery woman is has heightened his pleasure to an extreme level. Whoever this mystery woman is, she has unknowingly brought one of the good doctor's oldest fantasies to life.

Picking her up off the desk with ease he turns her around so that she is facing his desk and places her back down on it. He pushes her upper body forward so that it is lying flat on his desk top.

Then he reaches down and pushes her knees back to straighten her legs completely so that he can have the easiest access. With two
large fingers pressed deeply inside of her, he begins

smacking her firm behind as hard as he possibly can.

He doesn't have to move his hand much, as she is voluntarily grinding back and forth on his two wet fingers. Between moans she can hear the good doctor behind her opening a condom. He takes his fingers out, and steps back to put his condom on. Feeling around blindly on the left side of his desk he finds his cup of ice water. Reaching inside he grabs one cube and places it on his tongue.

With it hanging slightly out of his mouth he runs the ice cube up and down her unsuspecting back. While leaning all the way forward on her, placing the cube on her neck he finally enters her body. She screams loudly as she rolls up on the tips of her toes. He continues to grind inside of her slowly while rubbing the small cube on the back of her neck. Reaching back, she begins digging her nails
in the sides of his thighs again.

"Harder." she moans. Carlos stands up straight, spits the cube out on the floor, and begins stroking dangerously. He's so deep inside her now she can't breathe. Both of her legs are now shaking uncontrollably.

Gripping her slim waist tightly he continues to force himself deeper still. Trying to steady herself she lifts her left leg up on the table. After several more powerful strokes she pulls him out and squats down to finish him off orally.

He gasps as she swallows him whole and then pulls him back out. She swallows him whole again. She pulls Carlos out of her mouth again. She begins to gently lick the tip of him.

She takes him back deep in throat once more, as she feels his body growing obviously tense. She sucks him slowly at first, and then waits as his precious juices begin to flow down her wet throat.

Wiping the edges of her moist mouth she swallows everything he gave her. Standing up in front of him she reaches up and removes the Doctors' blindfold.

"You…" he says. "Yeah who were you expecting, "she asks," one of them rat ass nurses, or maybe your ugly ghetto sex toy Cam…"

"Watch your mouth," Carlos demands, "Cam is not ugly." "She's not me either." The lady responds.

"You've been cleaning my office for months now," Carlos says, "and I don't even know your name." "Chastity…" she says through a satisfied smile. "Chastity," he repeats, "so what now, Ms. Chastity? You got a hidden camera set up somewhere?"

"A hidden camera," she asks with her neck cocked to the side, and her left hand defiantly on her hip, "a hidden camera set up for what?" "Come on lady," Carlos begins, "we're both adults. Just be honest with me how much do you want? Just name your price, I'll write the check right now. I've been through this all before."

Carlos reaches in his desk and pulls out his Louis Vuitton check book. She looks at him as if he just slapped her or spit in her face.

"What's that look about lady," he asks, "I'm a very busy man just tell me how much you want so we can get this over with."

Taking a step back never taking her eyes off of him Chastity flips her long blue and blonde hair and places a hand on each of her hips.

"Five thousand dollars she says still looking at him very intently.

"Five thousand dollars…" he scoffs, "is that all? No, I'll triple that how's fifteen thousand sound?" He begins writing the check. "You really think that's what this is?" she asks.

"Save me the heartfelt lie about how you would never take advantage of anybody," Carlos tells her, "because you don't need the money. I know how much you make lady. We both know exactly what this is."

"First of all, my name is Chastity not lady," she tells him, "And I don't want your damn money. Not everybody is out to get you Dr. Sanchez."

"Please call me Carlos," he says snidely, "we're much better acquainted than we were before."

"Carlos, I don't want your money," she begins putting her clothes back on, "and I'm not trying to blackmail you. You must be married without a prenuptial agreement?"

"No," he says, "I haven't been married for quite some time now. But that's none of your business. Just take the check and leave lady." Carlos throws the check on his desk in front of her.

"That's sad…" she says.

"What's sad Ms. Chastity?" he asks.

"The fact that I could possibly be the one for you," she says, "but you're too blinded by your past and all the rat ass women who hurt you to see that."

"You keep saying that, what is a rat ass woman?" Carlos asks.

"A crumb ass bitch," Chastity explains to him, "a leech, or a gold digger… whatever you want to call them.

I'm not one of them. I peaked in here earlier and saw you had your head down *again,* so I did my best to try to brighten up your day Dr. Sanchez. That's all this was... this was for you, not me Dr. Sanchez."

"Carlos..." he reminds her, "I don't get where this is coming from. Weren't you the same one who was in here just days ago preaching to me about how men like me don't belong with women like you and Cameron?"

She looks away, and then puts her head down. "I mean isn't that what you told me Chastity?" he asks.

"Yeah," she agrees, "but that was before..."

"Before what..." he inquires.

"Nothing Dr. Sanchez," she says grabbing the last of her things, "I'll just excuse myself I've embarrassed myself enough for one evening."

She turns towards the door to leave. He grabs her arm before she can ever take a step. "Wait. Don't leave..." he says.

(At Cam's house)

Completely nude Keldrick is laying down flat on his stomach in the center of Cam's new California king sized bed that Carlos bought for her weeks ago. He told her she needed a much bigger bed if he was going to stay the night with her from time to time.

Cam is laying down on top of his strong dark frame completely naked herself. She smiles to herself as she thinks about the day Carlos had the bed delivered to her house. He told her, she needed a bed that was fit for a king and his beautiful *black* queen.

The man called her black, and made it sound like a compliment. For the first time in her life she felt like her skin tone was one of the defining factors that made her beautiful. Carlos' words and the look in his eyes rendered Cameron feeling nothing short of exceptionally lovely.

She can smell Kel's manliness, among the sweet aroma of the love they just made. She can feel and hear his heart beating calmly. Staring out of her large bedroom window the stars are finally smiling back at her. Running her finger tips up and down the sides of his stomach Cam has never been closer to Heaven.

"Keldrick…" she whispers through a lazy smile. "Yes ma'am…" he replies. "What do you remember about me?" Cam asks.

"Your smile," he replies, "I think I used to make you smile… a lot." "Yes, you did Keldrick," she admits, "all the time."

A calm rain starts to fall. "Make love to me again Keldrick." Cam pleads as she rolls over off of his body on to her back. Kel climbs on top of her and begins to make soft passionate love to her all over again. *The Big Black Beast* may not remember everything, but pleasing Cameron Jiles' body seems to come natural to him.

"It's like riding a bike…" he moans.

"What is?" Cameron moans back. "Making love to your body…" he growls deep in her precious left ear.

The more intense their sex gets the harder the rain seems to fall. Cam is staring intently out of the window at the apparent storm that's beginning to brew. Holding on to his strong back she willingly accepts every bit of

him. The storm and Keldrick are both growing

stronger by the minute. As he strokes, the top of Cam's head is beating softly against her light brown mahogany headboard.

Her cell phone begins vibrating. She doesn't want to check who it is, because she's almost sure it's Carlos. After about twenty seconds of continued vibration Cam realizes it's not a phone call or a text message.

Now she grabs her phone quickly. She gasps. "Kel..." she says. "Yes..." he replies continuing to stroke.

"That's not just rain... it's a tornado." she tells him. The whole house begins to shake violently. Cam grabs Keldrick harder than she ever has before.

Above their heads she can see a large picture frame about to fall off the wall. Cam is so startled by the movement of her house she can't compose herself enough to warn K.C.

There's a huge crash outside of her window like a lightning bolt struck a tree. Cam screams. The shaky picture finally falls off the wall and lands right smack on the back of K.C.'s already damaged head.

His body goes limp. Cam screams again.

"Kel," she says, "Kel baby please... please wake up. Keldrick I can't lose you again."

He doesn't move, or respond to her voice. She can feel the warm blood from the back of his head trickling down on to her body. She can't find his heart beat. Trying to find some kind of balance Cam slides from under K.C.

"Wake up damn it!" she screams. The house shakes again knocking Cam to the floor. On the floor she finds an old water bottle. Without hesitation, she grabs the bottle and makes her way back to the bed.

She frantically rolls his body over. Then she takes the top off of the bottle and pours every last drop on his head and face. He still doesn't react. Cam screams again long and hard.

She kisses him hard on the lips blowing into his mouth. She's hoping she can somehow breathe life back into his body one more time. With her fingers, she forces his eyes open. He appears to be looking back at her.

Then both of his eyes roll back into his head.

"Wake up Keldrick!" she screams. Then she slaps him as hard as she can. His head turns hard to the left from the impact, but he doesn't move.

"Wake up!" she screams again. She turns his head back so that it's facing her. Reaching back as far as she can, she swings again. He coughs several times, and then rolls over throwing Cam off of him. At the edge of the bed unable to stop coughing Kel falls helplessly to the floor. Cam climbs out of her huge bed and crawls up next to him. "Calm down," she tells him, "you're okay." He continues to panic.

"Take a deep breath," she continues, "Just do it Keldrick, damn!"

He inhales deeply, and then exhales. He does this several times as the cough disappears completely.

"Are you okay now?" she asks.

"Yeah baby," he says, "but why were you slapping me?"

"Baby," she says with her forehead furrowed tightly, "Who am I, Keldrick?" she asks him.

"What are you talking about girl?" he asks through a confused smile.

"What's my name, my whole name?" she asks.

"Cameron **Candice** Jiles." Kel says with no hesitation.

"Baby... Are you back?" she says sitting back to get a good look at him.

"Back..." he says, "where did I go boo?" She leans down towards him and kisses him hard on the lips.

"It doesn't even matter," Cam claims, "I'm just glad you're here now."

"Wait, what happened though Cam," he asks, "What are you talking about?"

"Apparently you were at Whitney's house," Cam tells him, "and you and Ty got into it and..." "And what..." Kel asks. "He messed you up bad baby..." she tells him. Kel laughs hard.

"Get the hell out of here baby," he says still laughing, "Ty messed me up? Nigga was I asleep?"

"No, I don't think so... Why you say that?" Cam asks.

"Baby do you see me?" he asks. She doesn't respond. "I'm too big
for that little dude to mess me up," he tells her, "Ty and Jay can't handle me together so Ty damn sure didn't beat me up all by himself."

"Well I don't know what actually happened because you were already on your back bleeding by the time I got over there." she explains.

"Wait you came to Whitney's apartment?" Kel asks. "Yeah..." Cam replies. "Why though..." he asks.

"I was at home on the couch and the news was on..."

Cam says looking at him with hesitation in her eyes.

"What... is that the end of your story?" K.C. asks.

"I asked you... Why were you at Whit's place?" he continues.

"You don't remember?" she asks.

"Obviously not if I'm asking you Cameron... Damn it," he exclaims, "Just answer my question and stop playing with me!"

"It's Jazemene," Cam says, "she got..."

"She got what Cam," Kel asks, "What happened to my baby?" He pushes her off of himself and stands up.

"Jazemene got kidnapped Keldrick," Cam tells him, "she was gone for days and nobody could find her."

"What," he says, "Where the hell is my cell phone?"

"I don't know," Cam replies, "My guess is Whitney has it..."

"Where's your phone Cameron?" he asks.

"Why," she asks, "I know you're not trying to call her on my phone..." "Cam...Give me your damn phone!" he demands. "No!" she screams. "I *am not losing you again*... Not to her." Cam tells him with finality.

"Wait, wait, wait," Kel shouts, "You just said that my daughter got abducted, and you have the audacity to be coming at me on some jealousy type shit? Right now though, really Cam? Just give me your damn phone."

"I am not giving you my phone," Cam contends, "I almost killed myself over you, while you were gone. I refuse to ever feel like that again."

"You almost what?" he asks.

"Before I let you kill me," Cam says, "I will let you die. And I really don't care how that sounds."

"I'm not dealing with all that right now," Kel tells her, "I'm going to act like I didn't even hear that crazy shit. I just want to check on my child is that okay with you?"

Cam hesitates looking down at her small black feet. She looks back at him and notices the legit concern on his face. She nods her head and then points at her phone lying in the middle of the bed. Kel grabs the phone, disconnects it from the charger, and takes it in the bathroom to make his call.

Cam's heart is beating rapidly. She can move but she's afraid to. She'd much rather just sit here on the floor lost in the moment when he came back to her in the middle of the mall.

She hears the bathroom door opening. Kel walks out slowly with a blank look on his face. "She doesn't love me anymore..." he says.

"I know," Cam says, "but I do baby, forget about that bitch." "Don't do that..." he says. "Don't do what?" she asks. "Don't call my daughter's mother a bitch, it's disrespectful." K.C. tells her.

"So, when I do it it's disrespectful," Cam says, "but when she does it to me it's cool because, I'm just the little dark-skinned side hoe from the ghetto right... I'll never be good enough to have your children or be your wife. I'm way too black right Keldrick!"

"Not right now Cam." he says. "I know Keldrick not now," Cam says, "not ever. It's not you Kel, it's me. I will never really matter to you. I'm just your get away, and your safety net. I'll never fit into your vision of the perfect family. *God,* I am so stupid! I have a guy, a damn good guy who lives and breathes *me*, just like you live and breathe

243

Whitney. But I keep breaking his heart for your dumbass."

"Don't..." he says.

"Don't what Keldrick?" she asks.

"Don't break his heart for me."

K.C. replies. "Really Keldrick," Cam cries, "that's all you have to say?"

"Yeah," he grabs her car keys, "I'm going to get my baby I'll bring the car back later. By the look of these foreign car keys, you and the doctor are more serious than I thought. It's not my business though. I'ma take the old car though, I know how to stay in my own lane. I'm gone I gotta go get my daughter."

"Your baby, what about my babies," Cam screams, "you made me get an abortion twice!"

"Plan B is not the same as an abortion Cameron." he replies.

"So, did you ever want kids with me?" she asks trying desperately to stop her tears.

"Children are... a wonderful thing," he says, "when built inside of a designed plan. But accidental children change the course of unwilling lives and cause distraction, and ultimately destruction. Cam, I'd love to talk more about this but I really have to go."

"No," she says with venom in her voice, "and what the hell was that an infomercial for Planned Parenthood?"

"I know it was deep right..." he says with a satisfied grin.

"Hell, no nigga, it was dumb as hell," she tells him, "people have unplanned babies all the time. And it may not be easy but they make it."

"Yeah well I gotta go so..." he says as he turns to

leave.

"You're not going to leave me like this, not again," she demands, "Now sit your black ass down and shut up!"

"No, I'd rather stand," he replies snidely, "You know you really are prettier when you're angry." "Fuck you Keldrick!" she screams.

"Damn it!" Cam says sitting down on her bed looking at him through new tears.

"How can you be so cold…to me?" Cam asks.

"Girl what did you do…give birth to me?" he says. "In a sense…" she replies.

"That's the problem Cam," K.C. tells her, "You think just because you came into my life and did some good… no I'll admit you did some amazing things to change my life, you made yourself believe
that nothing good can come to me unless it's through you. You don't want me to be good unless I'm with you Cameron…"

"That's not true baby," she claims, "I just know you would be better with me…"

"Right," he says with a smirk on his dark face, "and how do you know that *Cameron?*"

"Because *Keldrick*," she says, "that's my only hope."

"Why is that?" he asks.

"Boy you already know there ain't no me without you." she says.

Cam stands up and walks towards him. She takes the keys out of his hand and lays them softly on her bed. They look deep in each other's eyes, both searching for something totally different.

Keldrick leans down towards her face and kisses her,

never closing his eyes. He pulls his lips back and then kisses her again. This time Cam closes her eyes, enjoying his kiss with everything she is.

"Do you feel that?" he whispers to her. "Feel what?" she responds. "Exactly…" he says. Then he grabs her keys and leaves.

(Pastor Jackson)

K.C. pulls up to one of his old pastor's homes. The aging pastor is sitting on the front porch reading his bible when Keldrick arrives.
K.C. remembers vividly how Pastor Jackson was by his head pastor, Pastor White's side every Sunday in the pulpit at church when he was a child. He hesitates and then hops out of Cam's car and starts up the driveway to talk to Pastor Jackson.

"How are you K.C.?" Pastor Jackson asks hugging him tightly. "Doing much better pastor," he replies, "I'm doing much better." "Fine son," Pastor Jackson smiles a genuine smile, "I'm more than glad to hear that. Here sit down with me Keldrick."

"Yes sir." Keldrick says sitting in the rocking chair next to the one the pastor was sitting in when he pulled up.

"What's on your mind superstar?" Pastor Jackson asks. "A lot,
Pastor Jackson…" K.C. admits. "Well start from the top son," the pastor tells him, "You gotta start somewhere."

"How old are you now Pastor?" Kel asks him.

"I am Fifty-three next month." he says proudly.

"And how long have you been married Pastor?" Kel asks.

"Well, now," the pastor sighs happily, "Mrs. Jackson and I have been married for thirty-four years and together for thirty-six."

"Wow," Keldrick replies, "Excuse my French Pastor White, but how the hell is that possible?" "Well," Pastor White replies with a comforting smile, "I don't speak French, but I do speak the word of God, and that helps a lot more than you might think when it comes to matters of love."

"So, the bible," Keldrick says, "Pastor, you're telling me that the bible and or prayer kept your marriage together for that long?"

"There are many components that go into building and sustaining anything son." the pastor explains.

"Yes sir..." Kel replies listening closely to his pastor's every word.

"To build any relationship worth having," Pastor Jackson explains, "You must have understanding, effective communication, and love... but most of all you have to have understanding."

"But Pastor you said understanding twice." Kel tells him.

"That wasn't a mistake, Keldrick," the pastor says, "understanding is the key to everything."

"I see." Keldrick says. "But do you son," the pastor asks, "My spirit tells me that you're thinking of getting married soon. Have you already proposed to her?"

"No sir," Kel replies, "Not yet. But, do you think I'm ready pastor?"

"Son," he replies, "That's not for me to judge or decide. But, if you're not sure that doesn't necessarily mean that you're not ready it just means you may need to do a little more soul searching."

"Yes sir," Kel says, "I just don't wanna mess up and cheat, or be cheated on and then lose everything I invest in my marriage. I mean I'm a man so I'm gonna mess up sooner or later, but if my wife cheats that's something I won't be able to handle. Pastor, I guess my biggest concern is the fact that just about every black woman I come in contact with is so bitter and damaged. I want my relationship to last and flourish. But man to man, you know how men are sir." K.C laughs nervously as he awaits the pastor's response.

"Man to man," Pastor Jackson says, "I have never stepped out on my wife Keldrick." "Never," Keldrick says, "In thirty-four years?" "Not once," Pastor Jackson replies, "It's hard… it was hard, almost every single day, but it does get easier with time."

"I believe you pastor." Kel says.

"Son," Pastor Jackson starts, "Listen to me, and listen to me good. For a man to live and breathe and so believe that he is right, and can do no wrong when it comes to opposite sex is wrong. That thought process is *so* wrong son. I truly believe that if the roles of males and females were massively reversed, from the way they are now, there would be a lot of bitter men walking around harping about all the evil two timing women in their pasts. So, it's not at all right for us men to talk down to these so-called bitter women because most of them, not all of them… but ***most*** of them were made bitter by us. If we as men truly wanted change we could implement it, and enforce it as soon we got ready. Just imagine if men… strong men in every

248

neighborhood in every city in America made it their business to ensure that every other married man they knew was faithful to his wife and also took the time to mentor other men and guide them when they need guidance. If we as men made it cool so to speak, and acceptable to be faithful and committed… well then, the notion would no longer be the exception it would become the rule and the new standard. The world could run and so flow and flourish much easier with such a mold and diagram to follow and sustain. Don't you agree son?"

"Well amen pastor," Kel says laughing happily, "My god that was amazing sir. It's a stretch in today's society, but definitely a beautiful thought."

"If you want to propose," Pastor Jackson says, "Propose. If you want to be married, then be married son. But promise me one thing. If you do decide to tie the knot with the woman you claim to love… promise me, you will join me and be one of the bold exceptions to today's society and not the standard."

"Yes sir," Kel says looking deep in his pastor's eyes, "Yes sir, Pastor Jackson I promise."

(Ty, Jay, and Kel are in Cam's car headed to the mall)

"What's going on Kel," Ty asks, "Are you sure you're okay?"

"Never better… Thanks for that bump on the head bro, I needed that." he replies. "Don't do that bro," Ty says, "I told you it was an accident."

"Yeah," Kel says, "then after I was out cold, why did you continue to hit me?"

"I blacked out Kel…damn it!" Ty yells.

"Lower your voice now Ty," Kel says, "I'm trying to be cool about the whole situation. I'm in a good mood right now let me stay like that."

"Kel, why are we going to the mall?" Jay asks trying desperately to change the conversation.

"We're going shopping bro." he says. "For…" Jay replies. "A ring of course…" Keldrick says. "What…You really gonna do it this time bro?" Jay asks.

"Yes sir." Kel replies happily. "Does she know?" Ty says. "Nobody knows anything," Kel says, "and I want to keep it that way."

He looks at both of his friends intently. "We got you bro." Ty and Jay say in unison. "Okay I'm, trusting both of you," Kel says, "Now come on let's go in here and find my baby a ring."

Inside the mall Kel leads his friend towards the *Mayor's* jewelry store.

"And how are you three handsome gentlemen doing today?" a tall brown skin woman says as they approach one of the luxurious jewelry counters.

"We're fine," Kel says, "I'm just trying to find a ring for someone special."

"Ok," she says happily, "this is exciting. So is this a promise ring, an I'm sorry ring, or is this the big bang…"

"Yes ma'am, this is definitely the big bang." Kel says returning her smile.

"Sounds awesome big guy," she says nudging him with her shoulder, "so is this your first time, or have you been through this before?" "Nope, it's my first and hopefully last time," Kel says, "it's been a long time coming."

"Yes, it has." Jay agrees with a coy smirk on his face.

"Blood of Jesus," Ty says, "I'll believe it, when we get to the altar."

"The altar," Kel says, "dang can I get a ring, and pop the question first?" Ty and Jay laugh heartily.

"Yeah bro take your time we're just messing with you." Ty says.

"My name is Jamie by the way guys," the tall lady tells them, "now is there a particular ring you had in mind sir?"

"Yes, ma'am I want small blue stones, surrounding a large chocolate diamond, set in a yellow gold ring." he tells her.

"Follow me," she says, "I have the perfect ring for you."

As they walk K.C. notices the pleasant sounds of the Christmas music smoothly playing through the mall speakers. It's only November but he knows they always start early with the Christmas celebration here in Orlando.

For once he knows what he's doing and he feels completely at peace with his decision. As they approach a glass case full of engagement rings Kel feels his heart pounding steadily, and then rapidly.

"That's it." he says. "You don't even have to show me Jamie," he says, "I already see it. I don't care how much it costs I'll take it."

Jamie retrieves the ring for K.C. and hands it to him so he can get a closer look.

"Whoa, whoa, whoa," Jay says laughing nervously taking the ring out of Keldrick's hand,

"Of course, he cares how much it costs ma'am. How much

is it?"

Kel snatches the ring back.

"Box it, and bag it," he says, "like I said I don't care how much it costs. My girl is worth every penny I'll ever have."

"Yes sir," Jamie says, "follow me one more time and I'll get you all set." K.C. follows Jamie to the register and waits to pay for the ring. "Ok so with the insurance on the ring," Jamie says, "the   bottle of cleaner, and the ring itself your total comes out to $108,000.23."

"Hell no," Ty says, "put it back."

"Perfect…" Kel says pulling out a credit card his friends have never seen before.

Jamie swipes the card, and hands it back to him. A long receipt prints out. After its finished printing, she hands it to him.

"Ok Mr. Cole," Jamie says, "just sign here and here and you're ready to go." Keldrick signs the receipt, takes his bag, and heads back towards the car.

His two best friends hesitate, and then follow him in complete confusion. Once inside the car, Kel pulls out his cell phone.

"What you doing now *Keldrick Trump*…" Jay asks.

"I'm texting Whitney." he replies. "Right… so where did you get the money from to make a purchase like that Kel?" Ty asks.

"I'll worry about all that later on," K.C. replies, "this is just one moment, and a few meaningless dollars, but love lasts forever."

"Now you're the black Shakespeare," Jay says, "whatever man I just hope you know what you're doing."

Keldrick puts the car in reverse while holding the

beautiful ring in his right hand. "I know one young lady who's going to have a very happy holiday season this year." he says.

Jay laughs. "Yep," Jay agrees, "and I know another young lady that's not. Damn bro… she probably gone kill herself, or you."

(Hospital parking lot)

She's been waiting outside for hours parked adjacent to his car in the corner of the employee parking lot. It's raining again, but that's not bothering her. She's angry because she can't remember what he had for lunch today. Was it McDonald's or Burger King? And his shirt is it baby blue or light green? It's so hard to tell in the distance. Every time he goes to his car she wants to get out and approach him, but she doesn't know how. So, she just continues to watch him closely, never making herself known. He leaves the hospital every day at precisely 5:45.

When he pulls out of the parking lot, she waits long enough and then secretly follows him. He always stops at the *Crisper's* restaurant on Kirkland for a healthy snack before heading home alone to his quiet mansion.

Most nights he stops at the corner store that sits about three blocks away from the street that leads to his home to get a late evening copy of the newspaper.

That's where she parks her car and sleeps every night, until her alarm wakes her up at seven A.M. to follow him to work once again.

This has gone on for days now and she can't remember the last time she's bathed or even eaten for

253

that matter.

She knows this pattern isn't healthy or sane but she can't break the cycle alone. Secretly the thing she wants the most is for him to catch her following him.

(Cameron)

Is this what crazy feels like? I mean not just simple insanity but actual psychosis. Have I lost my grip on reality that badly, to the point of stalking him? I do love him but if he no longer loves me back I think I might hurt him eternally, whatever that means.

I feel like he knows somebody is watching him, he just doesn't know it's me. Wait... is that him? Yes, it's 5:45, he's leaving for the day.

Carlos walks out with a distant grin on his face. He's dressed in khakis and a teal polo dress shirt. He's on his cell phone chatting happily with someone.

As he reaches his new black on black Lexus truck he opens the back door and places his briefcase and laptop in the backseat.

Then he jumps in the front seat and cranks up. After he pulls out she starts to follow him. She notices he's taking a different route today.

As he turns onto Conroy street from Kirkland Boulevard, she's completely confused now as to where he's going. She follows him into the south end of the Serrano apartments. He parks close to the entrance, so she parks a few spaces down from him.

Emerging from one of the apartment buildings is a woman she's seen before. It's the maintenance lady from his office who was trying to seduce him that day. With her head tilted strangely to the side Cam reaches under her seat and pulls it out.

She checks it to make sure it's loaded. Then she opens the door and begins making her way towards his car. Her new gun is a beautiful all black glock pistol. She's ducking and dodging through the cars like some deranged top-secret agent on a desperate mission.

She's close now, close enough that she can smell the custodian's cheap perfume floating through the air. She's one car away, his window is down, and his back is turned.

"Wait Carlos," the custodian says, "I left my overnight bag upstairs I'll be right back."

The custodian places her purse down, closes the door, and rushes back upstairs. Now that she's gone, it's the perfect time to do it, and get it over with. When the custodian comes back she'll find the good doctor's brains all over her knock off MK bag, sitting in the passenger seat.

Kneeling down Cam makes her way to the front door of his truck. She stands up slowly, positioning herself just right so that he won't be able to see her in his side view mirror. She cocks the gun.

He can't hear her because his radio is way too loud. Cam aims it right at the back of his beautiful curly head. Her sweaty itchy finger is resting on and off the trigger from second to second.

"Lord, forgive me." she whispers. She's ready now. She positions her steady finger on the trigger. All of a sudden, her cell phone starts vibrating violently in her pocket. She kneels back down and pulls it out.

It's a text from Ty, telling her to meet him for a drink at 7p.m. Just like that the custodian is back, she throws her overnight bag in the backseat, jumps in the front seat and they speed off.

They never even noticed Cam crouching down right there between the cars. Cam closes her eyes tightly shielding her face from the confusing tears. She holds the cold gun plush to her right temple.

"Bang…" she whispers. She begins to panic. The pain and frustration are too much for her, she needs an immediate release. She looks around quickly, and then she pulls the trigger as hard as she possibly can.

Lights in apartments all around the complex begin to turn on, as people stare out of their windows in horror as they see a crazy lady pointing a recently fired gun straight up into the air.

Cam swears she hears sirens in the distance. She tucks the gun and makes a run for her car. Once safely inside she speeds away out of the complex, and then down Conroy street towards the mall to meet Ty.

(Ty and Cam are at the cheesecake factory restaurant in the mall)

Cam has never been inside of the Cheesecake Factory Restaurant before. Looking around at the exquisite décor, Cam can't help but to get lost in the beauty of everything.

"All I want for Christmas," by Mariah Carey is floating through the speakers. Cam closes her beautiful eyes and lip syncs a few of the lyrics. Ty can tell something's not right, she's seems lost in her own world.

He touches her shoulder gently. Eyes still closed she continues to sway to the music. He looks at her through squinted eyes.

"Cam…" he says gently touching her shoulder once more. She stops, and stares back at him. Her usually vibrant face looks drained to him and almost void of color.

"What are you staring at Tyrone?" she asks. "You Cam," he replies, "Are you okay? You seem…distant. You seem like maybe you finally…"

"Cracked…" she says. She smiles a creepy smile at him. "What do men think is going to happen after they break a woman's heart repeatedly," she asks him, "hmm…and not just any woman, a woman they know would die for them without any hesitation? You men are so sweet, and you build a poor girl up, and fill our heads with unobtainable dreams… Just to continue to get what you want. Money, stability, the booty, whatever the case may be. But the games take a dangerous toll on us. Some women can roll with the punches, and continue to be mistreated. Some women just settle for less, and end up with a man they would have never chosen. But some women, women like me, we evolve. Women like me Tyrone…we get even."

With that said she starts back lip syncing as if she never stopped. Ty stands up to excuse himself from the table. Cam grabs his hand.

"Please don't leave…" she tells him.

"I'm not crazy," she continues, "but I am hurting Tyrone, and you know that better than anybody."

"Why do you keep calling me Tyrone," he asks, "and

what do you mean *I* know better than anybody that you're hurting?"

Caressing his hand softly, she smiles up at him with those magical eyes. He sits back down, but he pulls his hand away from her in the process.

He quickly looks around to see if he's somewhere watching them. Ty doesn't see him anywhere.

"I'm probably going to leave soon," he tells her, "but your intrigue, is slightly outweighing your crazy right now. So, I'm all ears for the moment."

Cam slides her chair closer to him. "What is it you want to hear sir," she asks, "Any requests?"

The closer she gets, the more he can smell her. "No, I don't want a song Cam." Ty says trying to cover his nose and mouth in the politest way possible.

"So, what is it you want Tyrone?" she asks through a pretty but creepy smile.

"I want to know why you said I of all people know your pain." he replies trying hard not to vomit.

"A woman's intuition," she tells him, "I notice you noticing me, even when you think I'm not taking note."

Ty laughs. "Wait, so that's what you think," he says, "You think I like you?" "Yes," she replies confidently, "you don't realize it yet, but that's why you hated me so much at first. You didn't want me to be with Keldrick because secretly you wanted me to be with you."

Cam slides closer again, her stench becoming almost unbearable now. "You are really going through it, aren't you?" he says trying not to cringe.

Ty wonders why it took him so long to notice her foul body odor. Could it be that she's right, that subconsciously he does have feelings for her?

"Tell me I'm wrong Tyrone," she says playfully, "to be honest with you, I think deep down I felt the same way about you."

"Cameron... you're really going through a lot," he tells her, "so your judgment is definitely impaired. But right now, at this moment, trust me... none of what you're saying even matters anymore."

"It matters Ty," Cam assures him, "It's never too late to try anything unless you're dead... or in prison with a life sentence. But we're not Ty, you and I... are as free as the birds." She smiles at him as she awaits his dignified response.

"What the hell are you talking about Cameron?" Ty asks.

"See it felt wonderful walking the streets of Paris France, and shopping endlessly with Dr. Carlos Sanchez." Cam explains to Ty. "I'm sure," Ty replies attempting to stand up from the table, "That's great Cameron, but I must be going now."

"But," Cam says grabbing his arm preventing him from standing up, "That's not really me. And that world... could never be real, or become commonplace to me. I know better." Ty remains seated and intrigued.

"Do you?" Ty asks checking his watch anxiously and trying to continue to hold his breath.

"Hell, yes I know better," Cam tells him, "I'm just a regular girl Tyboonie. I'm the little black girl next door. Never was it in the stars for me to live like Carlos' queen... I know full well where I belong." Ty checks his watch again. "And where is that Cameron," Ty asks curiously leaning closer to her no longer able to smell her obvious body odor, "Where exactly do you belong?"

The lights in the restaurant flicker, and then they shut off entirely. The restaurant is completely dark.

Other customers in the restaurant begin to panic, and gasp. The music stops, and then the lights come back on. Ty glances at Cam. She looks frightened. He smiles and then holds his head down.

The lady at the table next to them walks up to their table and begins to sing Whitney Houston's song, *"I Will Always Love You"*.

Two ladies from a table on the opposite side of them join her as they all sing together in beautiful harmony. After the last gorgeous note of *"I will always love you,"* they transition smoothly into Monica's, *"Angel of Mine"*.

The lead singer takes Cam by the hand and leads her out of the restaurant still in full song. At the door, the singer looks at Cam and says, "You're a very lucky girl." A beautiful man's tenor voice begins crooning from behind her.

Cam quickly turns around to find a tall brown skinned man smiling at her through every note he's blessing her with.

"Lately you've been," he sings, *"questioning if I still see you the same way, Cause through these trying years, we gonna both physically change, now don't you know you'll always be the most beautiful woman I know, so let me reassure you darling that my feelings are truly unconditional…"*

He takes her by the hand and leads her towards the center of the mall. All around her Cam sees huge grandiose Christmas ornaments and happy smiling people looking at her seemingly in awe.

The music stops again. Cam looks around desperately to find Ty. He's still watching her, but she doesn't see him. Chris Brown's song, *"Love More"* comes on.

With military precision, random people of all ages come out of the crowd and begin dancing together doing flawless choreography. The dancers circle around Cam and continue to dance passionately. Her heart is fluttering uncontrollably.

Cam notices there are several police officers on hand as well. She figures they were hired to protect her in case something goes wrong. But she knows nothing can go wrong tonight. This is her long awaited shining moment and the glory she deserves will manifest in this moment.

Two strong men come from the rear of the surrounding crowd carrying a large, gold encrusted, throne-like chair with blue padding on it. They sit the chair behind Cam.

Then a small girl walks up to Cam, takes her hand and makes her sit down on the beautiful chair.

"Please sit down, Ms. Jiles." the adorable little girl said before disappearing back into the crowd she emerged from. "All of this for me…" Cam whispers to herself as she basks in the unreal joy of the moment. All around her strangers are smiling and clapping just for her. Cam can feel their energy.

Looking around her Cam can't help but put both hands over her mouth as the current song playing through the speakers comes to an end softly. Suddenly the lights go dim, as a bold spotlight shines down on a rugged and musty Cameron Jiles.

"Let's slow it down now…" a familiar baritone voice says over the mall's loud speaker system. Right on cue Jagged Edge's old hit song, *"Let's Get Married,"* begins to play.

All of the dancers are down on one knee in front of Cam now, and they've made an obvious path for someone to walk through the center of where they're strategically positioned.

Another spotlight shines down the middle of the path between the happy dancers. As he approaches Ty hands him the ring near the back of the crowd.

He begins to walk through the crowd with purpose and control, beside him is an angel holding his hand every step of the way. *Jagged Edge* is taking Cameron to another planet mentally and emotionally. It's hard for her to focus now.

Her body is itching from head to toe, but she can't focus on that right now. All of the attention she's getting right now is everything she's been missing in life.

This moment feels better than her deepest fantasy ever could. Cameron is the beautiful queen and no one can steal this moment from her. There he is. Cam can finally see him approaching her.

He's dressed in all white from head to toe, in a three-piece suit. His hair is cut perfectly, and his mustache is trimmed just right. His smile is almost nervous, but it's perfect just the same.

The beautiful little angel who's escorting him has on a cute white dress adorned with multiple bows, and her long dark hair is flowing all around her adorable silly face. The angel approaches Cam first. Cam begins to cry.

"Hey Ms. Cam," she says, "Me and my Daddy wanna ask you something." He steps forward next to the angel and takes a knee as the mall lights come back on. The angel takes a knee right beside him. With a wireless microphone close to his mouth he speaks.

"Cameron Jiles…" he says in the sexiest voice she has ever known.

The chill that has overcome her body is undeniable.

"Since the moment I laid eyes on you," he continues, "something about you changed *everything* about me. I fell in love with you at first sight, not once but twice in *one lifetime*. Girl, you broke me way down, and then built me into a man. Not a boy… but a *real man*. Baby I am eternally indebted to you. I know I put you through a lot but I had to make sure you were strong enough for *both of us.* I need a soldier, and I choose you. So right here today in front of all these beautiful smiling people, I Keldrick Jermaine Cole, am asking you Cameron Candice Jiles, to do me this honor and make my dream come true. Will you marry me?"

Cam wipes her tears, as she scans the crowd. She sees Ty towards the back. He smiles, and then puts his head down.

She leans forward to the microphone and says, "K.C…. I never want to see your face ever again in my life."

She kisses Jaze on the cheek, and then walks towards Ty. Ty's eyes are bucked, and his mouth is gaping open.

"Cam…what did you just do?" he whispers. "I ended it…for good," she says, "now take me home…please."

Ty looks over at his best friend who's still down on

one knee with his head down. He knows he should run to his best friend and console him, but for once in his life Ty has the chance to get the girl. He won't let that chance pass him by.

Looking back at Cam he says, "Blood of Jesus Cam, are you sure?"

"Yeah Tyrone," Cam tells him, "Now let's go." "Come on then," he says, "because, damn you do need a bath girl."

Chapter 11
Full Blown

As Jacody Miller walks through the Florida Mall on Orange Blossom Trail he's thankful to have a few minutes alone. Life has been crazy lately for the twenty-six-year-old rapper.

Four years ago, he dove into his music so deeply he wasn't able to see or care about anything else. He was on Facebook one day uploading a new song he had just recorded at a local studio in Atlanta when he saw the post. When he saw that Keldrick had been shot something in Jay snapped, and he came spiraling back into reality.

The only current friends Jay had in his life up until that point was Ty, and countless nameless strippers at random night clubs he frequented in the A. And the dancers were never his real friends, but as long as he had money for them, they had time for him.

From the outside looking in so many people from Jacody's past and present think his life is easy, and perfect. His parents have both worked overtly hard and have afforded him and his baby sister a life that they will forever be thankful for.

His father told him about a year ago that if he and Jay's mother were to pass away, Jay and his little sister would get their mansion, all of their expensive cars, and a million dollars.

Jay is proud of his parents, but he would be prouder of himself if he could be as successful as them on his own. Jacody wants this more than anything. He also wants his bond back with his friend Keldrick. It just doesn't feel the same yet. He's hopeful that it will get better. Jacody and K.C. used to be so influential in each other's lives but time, disappointments, and life have a way of distorting relationships beyond repair.

People always forgot or never paid attention to the fact that Jay was the one who stayed up late with K.C. back in high school playing catch with him. Jay helped K.C. memorize plays, and his receiving routes.

Tyrone was their brother too, there's no doubt about that, but Jay put in just as much work helping Kel become and All-State receiver as Kel did himself. Jay also was there any time Kel ever needed advice about Whitney or any other girl back in school.

K.C. never forgot that, and he still feels indebted to his old friend to this day.

(Jay)

I'm twenty-six years old now. I'm dangerously close to thirty and I still don't have a real career. Sure, I can hit the military. That's always a viable option. But is that what I want? Hell no. That's what my dad did, and I'm very proud of my old man he did exceptionally well. His rank and pay grade at this stage in his career alone are more than enviable. Not to mention his countless successful business ventures outside of the military.

But that's not who I am, it's not what I want. I'm

tired of being single, but I'm more tired of fielding dumbass questions about why I don't have a real job. I'm like, "I do have a job bitch. I'm a rapper!" So, I deal with females on a nightly basis only. Like, we lovin' for tonight, but in the morning, you gotta go...see you in a couple months maybe.

Honestly, I think I'm just gonna move back here to Orlando with my boy Kel. Ty's dumbass is gonna get himself killed sooner or later. I'm tired of protecting him, because he honestly doesn't want to be protected. He's always searching for excuses for the things he does, and the things he should do but refuses to do. And now he's in love with Kel's girl Cam, this is a nuclear bomb just waiting to explode and destroy everything. Lord, please fix it. You know I can't.

(YMCA)

Corey and Love are both sitting on a workout bench as they watch Whitney as she makes her way to one of the water fountains near the middle of the weight room at the YMCA on International Drive.

"She is fine as hell son." Corey admits. "Yeah, I know," Love agrees, "If we can get her to start working out on a regular basis she'll get even better than she is now."

"Its sad man," Corey says, "a lot of women I went to school with back in the day that used to be just as fine as Whitney, are all way out of shape now." "Why is that?" Love asks.

"I don't know, but I don't think it's because they're

lazy," Corey explains, "Being fine for years as a young lady can kinda lull a woman into a false sense of security."

"How do you mean?" Love asks.

"Think about it Love," Corey says as Whitney sits down next to him, "For most of these women, they never worked out on a regular basis in their lives, unless they cheered, or played some kind of sport, ran track or that sort of thing. So, in their minds they were always effortlessly beautiful, with beautiful bodies, so they believed they would just stay that way… and some do."

"Right," Love agrees, "That makes a whole lot of sense." "But of course," Corey explains, "As time goes on all of our bodies change. With women, their bodies change more rapidly than ours. It all starts with the slowing down of their metabolism, and then some have children, body parts may begin to sag… so they have to start putting some sort of emphasis on keeping themselves toned up. If they care that is."

Whitney clears her throat. "Um," she says with a smile, "Why do I get the feeling this conversation started about my fat ass."

"Baby," Love says with a sweet smile reaching out to put a comforting hand on her knee, "You are nowhere near fat. And the conversation did start off about you but we were complementing you for taking an interest in your health and your body." "It's true." Corey confirms.

"I guess," Whit smiles, "Well right now I'm interested in taking a hot shower. Can we go home please sirs?"

"Yep, let's hit it." Corey says as he reaches down to grab his car keys and his workout bag.

(Love, Corey, and Whit pull back up to their home)

Whitney is lying on her back across the backseat. Love and Corey are in the front lost in an awkward silence. Corey received a phone call shortly after they walked out of the gym. The news he received obviously wasn't good.

As they pull up to their home Love notices a strange look on Corey's face. He's obviously unnerved and maybe even angry. Love pretends not to notice. Corey parks the truck and they all jump out and head to the door.

"Now that was a workout." Whitney says walking in first. "Yeah my whole body hurts." Love agrees following her inside.

"It's good for both of you," Corey says, "the more we workout the easier it will get. Well… not really but at least you'll see results." "Boy, you got us doing these ole prison yard workout routines," Love says, "that stuff was meant for people who have nothing to live for."

"Is that what we did," Whit asks, "a prison workout?"

"Girl, hell yeah," Love says, "this fool been trying to get me to workout with him since we met. Now I know why I never did."

"Stop crying Lance!" Corey demands.

"You know Corey," Love says, "ever since you got that mysterious phone call yesterday, and then the one you got when we were leaving the gym today you been acting mean as hell."

"Lance, mind your own business boy," Corey says, "in

fact just go get yo weak ass in the shower."

Love snaps his neck. He looks at Corey, then over at Whitney. "What you gone do Love…" Whitney says looking at him intently. Love looks down at his feet, shakes his head, and then looks back up at Corey.

"Corey, nigga you better stop talking to me like I'm a bitch or a kid." Love says with bass in his voice. Corey stands up.

"So, what you saying boy…" Corey says to Love. Love stays seated. "I'm saying, stop disrespecting me, especially in front of my girl." Love tells him.

Corey approaches Love. With his brows wrinkled tightly Corey stares down at the much smaller Love in silence. Love looks up.

"Why are you standing over me like that C," Love asks, "What are you going to do? You gone beat me up…"

"Corey, please go sit back down." Whitney says.

Corey points directly at her. "Bitch, stay out of our business," Corey tells her, "You speak when spoken too." Love quickly stands up nose to chin with the taller Corey.

"Take that back C…" Love says. Corey laughs snidely. "So, what you a man now…" Corey says.

"I've always been a man." Love replies.

Corey pushes Love back down to the sofa. "You ain't a man," Corey says with an evil smirk on his face, "you're my bitch, and so are you Ms. Lady."

"Ms. Lady," Whit says, "yeah I'm leaving. Love, call me later so I can come back and get all my stuff."

Whitney stands up and turns around to get her purse.

Corey grabs her by the back of her neck and pushes her back down in the chair face first.

"Bitch, you not going anywhere, you belong to me!" Corey barks at her. Whitney has never felt this much pain in her life. The force in which he pushed her with was unreal.

Her left shoulder is throbbing and it feels like it's out of socket. Her face is burning, as her tears begin to flow instantly. "Oh, what you over here crying…" Corey asks her.

"Na, you wanna cry," Corey continues, "I'm gon give you something to cry about." With a closed hand Corey punches Whit hard in the face.

She screams out as she falls to the floor holding her jaw. He swings hard again, this time striking her swiftly in her rib cage.

"Love, help me!" she yells. Love rushes Corey as hard as he can, knocking the large man to the ground. "Just leave Whit, I'll call you later!" Love yells.

Whit quickly grabs her purse and her keys and stumbles out of the front door. Once in the car she cranks up and speeds off, with no clue where to go.

She grabs several tissues out of her purse to dry her face. Pulling the rear-view mirror down so she can see herself, Whitney can see her face is already beginning to bruise.

"I wish K.C. was there, he would have beat Corey's ass for me," she mumbles to herself, "Love did fight for me but he's just not strong enough to truly protect me. It's the thought that counts but I need to feel safe and secure at all times."

Whit pulls out her cell phone. She calls K.C.'s

phone, after it rings twice she hangs up. Her pride is way too strong to just go crawling back to him.

She quickly throws the phone away from herself in the passenger seat so she won't attempt to call him again. She turns the music up loud in the car to try to clear her mind. Out of the corner of her eye she can see her phone lighting up, she grabs it. It's K.C. returning her call. She doesn't know what to do. She can't just ignore his call, but if she answers what can she say. The way she left him was so cold, almost inhuman. The man couldn't even remember his own daughter, and she just left him there to figure everything out for himself. She throws the phone back down. She knows he has his memory back now, because his mother called and told her. Whitney just hopes he can't remember how she left him.

Whit knows where she has to go. It hurts her deeply to have to move backwards but when life takes an unexpected turn like hers just did sometimes your parents are the best option to help you cope and find stability.

She looks up at her face in the rearview mirror again. She shakes her head in disgust.

Ten minutes later she pulls up to her parent's home. After parking, and climbing out of the car on wobbly legs, Whit makes her way to her parent's front door.

Whit tries to use her key to open her parent's door. Her key no longer works. Whitney immediately starts ringing the doorbell repeatedly filled with obvious frustration.

Her mother finally opens the door. "Mom," Whit says, "My key didn't work." "We changed the locks Whitney." her mother Annette replies.

"You what," Whit says, "But why Mom? Why would you change the locks on the doors and not tell me?"

"You don't live here Whitney," Annette says, "You do realize that don't you?" "I know Mama," Whit says, "But I've always had a key to the house."

"Well not anymore." her mother tells her.

"What did I do?" Whit asks. "What happened to your face Whitney," her mother inquires dodging her question, "Were you in a fight?"

"I'll be fine," Whit says, "But what's going on Mama? What did I do that was so bad?"

"Your father…" Annette starts. "My father what," Whit asks walking around her mother despite her mother's attempt to stop her, "Daddy… Daddy where are you?"

"Daddy…" she continues to call out to him. "Whitney!" her mother screams. "What Mom?" Whit replies.

"Your father's in his study," Annette says, "And he doesn't want to see you right now Whitney."

Whit's heart skips several beats. "He, doesn't what," Whit mumbles, "Why does my daddy not want to see me Mama?"

"You're not making good decisions Whitney," Annette tells her, "Your father has tried time and time again to keep you on the right track to getting your law degree. But you… you always find a way to mess it up."

"Are you serious," Whit laughs nervously, "This is about law school? Look I am not that far behind; I can handle my own business in respect to law school. I'll be fine."

"Fine," her mother says, "So what about handling your business in respect to your child?" "My daughter is fine," Whit says pushing past her mother again, "Jazemene... where is she?"

"She's not here Whitney." Annette tells her daughter. "Where is she," Whit asks, "Where is my daughter Mom? I know damn well you didn't call child services on me old woman..."

"You left your daughter's father," Annette says, "When he needed you the most, to move in with two strange men."

"Mom," Whit gasps in disgusts, "I told you that in confidence.
Did you tell Daddy... and child services?"

"Whitney," Annette says, "Your father spoke to a close friend of Dr. Sanchez. We know everything you've been doing. You're wrong Whitney, and I want you to leave my house now."

"Fine," Whitney screams, "***Give me my daughter**!* Where the hell is my daughter?"

"She's not here Whitney." Annette assures her only child.

"Then where the hell is she," Whitney screams, "I left her here with you, in your care!"

A door opens around the corner and down the hallway. Strong footsteps are approaching Annette and Whitney.

Whitney's father Josh walks around the corner to see his wife and daughter standing nose to nose. "Daddy..." Whitney cries as she runs to him. Whitney wraps her arms around her tall father and cries on his strong chest.

"Listen to your mother Whitney Michelle." her father

tells her. Whit looks up into her father's stern eyes. "What do you mean," she asks, "She's telling me to leave Daddy…"

"And I'm telling you to obey her," he replies, "Jazemene is with Mama Cole for now. You can find her over there, but you have to leave our house now."

Whitney pushes away from her father, and storms past her mother all the way outside to her car.

She grabs her phone out of the passenger seat as she drives off.

Whit quickly dials a number, and then puts her phone to her ear. "Mama Cole," she says seconds

later, "hey it's Whit. Yes, ma'am, can I stay with you for a few days? I uh… had a fight with my… boyfriend. Okay, thank you Mama Cole I'm on the way."

Twenty minutes later Whit pulls up to K.C.'s childhood home, Mama Cole's house. Mama Cole is already standing in the front yard waiting for her. Whitney parks the car, and then slowly steps out. Her usually confident legs feel like jelly.

She doesn't know if it's the workout that has her body this way or the beating Corey gave her. "Hey Mama Cole…" Whit says.

"Hey baby," she responds, "what happened to your face Whitney?"

"He…" Mama Cole covers her mouth.

"Enough said baby," she says, "now look, your baby is in here sleeping let's try not to wake her up, I don't want her to see you like this."

"Yes ma'am." Whit agrees. "Come on let's get you cleaned up," Mama Cole says, "a little makeup will hide that with no problem baby." As they step inside the house,

Whitney feels safe again.

The tears begin to flow again because now she's worried about Love. She left him there to get man handled. "What's wrong baby?" Mama Cole asks noticing the new tears.

"Nothing Mama Cole," she says, "I'm fine. Where's Jaze?" "She's in her daddy's old room, asleep in his old bed." Mama Cole says smiling faintly.

"She insists on sleeping in there," Mama Cole continues, "she says her daddy's bed is the only place in the world she feels safe."

"Yeah I know the feeling..." Whit mumbles.

"What you say baby..." Mama Cole asks.

"Nothing Mama Cole..." she replies. Whitney, peeps her head in K.C.'s old room before they pass by it. Her princess is fast asleep on top of the covers.

She's wearing one of his old practice jerseys as a night gown, clutching tightly to one of his old football's he was awarded after winning some huge game. Stepping into his old room, looking around Whit realizes how much she misses high school.

Not so much high school but the dreams and possibilities that were at their fingertips back then. K.C. was guaranteed to go to the NFL after two years of college ball, and Whitney was going to be this powerful attorney.

All four walls of K.C.'s room are adorned with trophies, plaques, and other various athletic accolades. Whit smiles back at Mama Cole who's watching her from the doorway.

"That boy was good Mama." Whit says. Mama Cole,

smiles. "You know what baby…" Mama Cole says. "What…" Whit replies. "He still is," she says, "Now come on before we wake my grandbaby up." Walking down the hall to Mama Cole's room Whitney can't stop thinking about Love. So, when am I going to meet this mystery man of yours Whitney?" Mama Cole asks.

"I don't know," she says, "I know you would like him though. He's smart and very sweet. He's so young though Mama, that boy gives me new life."

"How old is he?" Mama Cole asks.

"Twenty-one…" Whit says smiling bashfully.

"Whitney girl… you robbin' the cradle ain't ya?" Mama Cole teases.

They both laugh.

"He's very mature," Whit says, "and he's beautiful."

"That's nice baby…where is he from?"

"He was born and raised in Orlando." she replies.

"Is he tall, or short, how does he look?" Mama Cole asks.

"Where do I start," Whit says smiling giddily, "he's average height, light skin, and he's covered with tattoos."

Mama Cole looks disturbed.

"Does he have hair?" she asks.

"Yes, Mama he has long dreads with blonde tips." Whit says.

Mama Cole looks at Whitney through squinted eyes.

"What's his name baby?" Mama Cole asks with a look of horror on her face.

"Lance Orlandis Vinson…" Whit replies.

Mama Cole holds her head down.

"Whitney, you are to never talk to that man again,"

277

Mama Cole says, "Do you hear me? Never…" "Why not Mama do you know him?" Whit asks.

"No…I uh, he beat you up so he's not good enough for you," Mama Cole replies, "Just leave him alone for good."

Whitney's phone vibrates. She looks at it, Corey's calling. "Is that him?" Mama Cole asks. "No, it's his…" Whit catches herself.   "His what?" she asks.

"Never mind," Whit says, "how is Keldrick?" Her phone vibrates again. It's Corey calling back.

"Excuse me Mama Cole," Whit says leaving the room, "hello, Lance? Why are you calling from Corey's phone? He broke your phone? Where is he now? Did you call the police? Why not? No, Love I'm not going to calm down. He hurt us both and criminal charges should be filed. What do you mean something worse… something worse like what? No, I'm not sitting down, and I'm not going to sit down. Now tell me what's going on? Boy, you better stop playing with me and tell me what he did?"

Whitney sits down with her hand tightly over her mouth. She looks at her phone in tears, and then she throws it against the wall as hard as she can.

Screaming at the top her lungs she jumps up and starts stomping on the phone trying to destroy it as much as possible.

"Damn it," Whit screams, "God damn it! How could I be this damn stupid? Now… now I'm going to lose my life all for the instant gratification of a temporary fantasy."

Mama Cole walks in slowly. "Whitney…baby what happened?" Mama Cole asks.

Whit shakes her head several times trying to fight back more tears but she can't. Too weak to stand she falls back on a nearby love seat. Mama Cole heads to the bathroom. Moments later she emerges with a warm wet towel.

She sits next to Whitney, pulls her head into her chest, and begins to wipe her salty tears away with the warm towel. "Baby what happened," Mama Cole asks, "Crying about it won't help it love."

"No! Don't ever call me that name, ever." Whit says.

"What love?" Mama Cole asks.

"Yes." "Okay baby, but why not?" she asks.

"Because," Whit says, "that's his name. Lance Orlandis Vinson a.k.a., Love."

"So that's what he calls himself now," Mama Cole asks, "I'm sorry. I will never call you that again darling. So, what did he say that was so bad?"

"Lance, his boyfriend Corey and I all lived together," Whit explains, "And Lance just found out Corey has full blown A.I.D.S."

"Oh my God," Mama Cole says, "baby did you sleep with him too?"

Whit puts her hand over her mouth again and nods her head solemnly. "Yes ma'am." she whispers.

"Unprotected?" she asks. Whit nods again.

"Yes ma'am…" she says. "Why Whitney, you obviously knew their lifestyle?" Mama Cole says. "I'm in love with Love Mama," Whit says, "And I'm three months pregnant."

"By him?" she asks. "I don't know yet Mama Cole."

"What do you mean Whitney, who all were you with

around that time?" she asks.

"I was with K.C., Love, and Dr. Sanchez," Whitney admits, "I think it's Dr. Sanchez's baby though, but I'm not sure."

"Okay, so now what?" Mama Cole asks.

"I don't know Mama Cole," Whit says, "I'm done with Lance. Dr. Sanchez and K.C. are both in love with Cam. So, I guess now I'm just left with me."

Mama Cole shakes her head and points at the room behind them. "No, you're left with you and Jazemene," Mama Cole reminds her, "But that's not what I'm talking about. You need to go get tested today, I'm going to go call a friend of mine who works down at the clinic and tell her it's an emergency."

Mama Cole gets up to go make her call. Whit grabs her arm. "No Mama Cole," she says, "please don't do that I don't want anybody to know about this."

"Girl this is life or death; you need to know now." Mama Cole says snatching her arm away from Whitney. A week later, Whitney and Jaze are watching T.V. in the den, at Mama Cole's house. Mama Cole walks in from the back, taking rollers out of her hair. Whitney's new phone vibrates.

She looks at it and sits it back down. "That boy calling again..." Mama Cole asks. Whit doesn't respond.

"Whitney," Mama Cole says, "It's been a week now. I don't want you dealing with that sissy anymore but you should at least answer the phone, and let him know how you feel. Let him know you have moved on, and he should do the same."

The phone vibrates again, and Whit ignores it again.

Mama Cole shakes her head.

"Well, you two put your shoes on we're gonna head out as soon as I'm finished with my head." Mama Cole says. "Where are we going Mama Cole?" Jaze asks.

"Your mother has grown people business to handle little girl," Mama Cole tells her, "so, don't worry your pretty little head about a thing."

Ten minutes later Mama Cole emerges from her room dressed and ready to go.

"Let's ride ladies." she says. As they back out of the driveway Whit says, "Mama, you know what's crazy …" "What baby?" she replies.

"The night I left Keldrick," Whit says, "Jay said he hoped whoever I left his brother for would turn out to be gay, and give me AIDS." Her phone vibrates.

"Answer the phone baby." Mama Cole says. Whitney looks at it. "It's a text not a call," Whit says,

"Love says his test came back negative. How is that possible?"

"I don't know baby, but he's still a sissy so it's gonna get him sooner or later." Mama Cole says.

"Love always told me he and Corey never slept together," Whit tells Mama Cole, "Maybe he was telling the truth. Maybe he got tested because of the possibility that Corey could have given it to me, and then I might have given it to Love…"

"Hell no…" Mama Cole says.

"How do you know, Mama," Whit asks, "He may be telling the truth."

"Just erase that sissy's number and never speak to him again." Mama Cole demands.

281

"Mama Cole, don't call him that." Whit says.

"Don't call him what," she asks, "a sissy? That's what he is baby.

He's a faggot."

"No, he is not," Whit says, "also don't talk like that in front of my daughter. Lance is a very good man, who went through some tragic things in his childhood."

Mama Cole turns around to look at Jaze. "Grandma is sorry for cursing in front of you baby." she says.

"I do apologize for speaking like that in front of the baby," Mama Cole continues, "but nobody forced that boy to be like that, it was *his* choice."

Whitney's entire face is red. "No," Whit screams, "It was not his fault or his choice Mama Cole! He was molested and raped repeatedly as a child!"

"And you believe that bullshit, do you?" Mama Cole scoffs at the idea.

"Why do you have such a problem with Lance?" Whitney asks.

"Uncle L's name is Lance." Jaze says from the back seat.

"Who is Uncle L baby?" her mother asks.

"Oops…" Jaze says.

"Oops, what do you mean oops," Whit exclaims, "Who the Hell is Uncle L?"

"Stop yelling at the baby," Mama Cole says, "you know children have wild imaginations. Now, we're here at the clinic go get your results Whitney, we'll wait in the car for you."

Whitney turns around to look at her daughter. Jaze is covering her mouth with both hands staring past her mother's glare, looking at her Grandmother.

"This is not over with little girl." Whit says as she gets out of the car, slamming the door closed behind her.

Once she's gone Mama Cole turns around to look at her frightened granddaughter.

"Baby, who is Uncle L..." she asks. Jaze continues to look at her but she doesn't respond. "Jazemene baby this is your Mama Cole,"
Mama Cole says, "you know you can tell me anything. grandma is going to help you, love you, and always protect you."

A tear rolls down the baby's pretty yellow face. Mama Cole unfastens her seat belt. Then she steps out of the car, walks around to the back-passenger side door, and takes Jazemene out of her car seat.

Holding her sweet grandbaby tight in her arms she walks along the sidewalk in the opposite direction from the way Whitney went to go inside the clinic.

"*Jazemene*..." Mama Cole says in a sing-song voice.

"Yes, Mama Cole..." the baby whimpers.

"Stop crying love," Mama Cole pleads, "We don't want to upset your mother. She's going through a lot right now. Now let me wipe your tears away so she won't know you've been crying."

"Okay Mama Cole..." the baby agrees. With her soft aging fingers Mama Cole dries Jazemene's delicate face.

"There all better," she says, "Now tell me who Uncle L is..."

"No Mama Cole, I promised." Jaze says.

"You promised who baby?" she asks.

"My Uncle L..." Jaze replies. "You promised him

what hunny?" Mama Cole asks.

"I promised I wouldn't say his name or…" Jaze hesitates.

"Or what baby?" Mama Cole prods. Jaze looks away from her grandmother, crossing her arms and poking out her bottom lip. Mama Cole laughs. "Girl if you aren't your daddy's twin I swear," Mama Cole smiles, "Look, unlike your mother I read the entire police report so I know whoever Uncle L is, he's the one who kidnapped you. Am I right baby?" Jaze doesn't respond.

"That's all the confirmation I need baby." Mama Cole says kissing Jaze on her tiny yellow forehead.

As they make their way back to the car, Whit is walking out of the clinic reading some papers. The look on her face is void of emotion. Mama Cole opens the door to the back seat and straps Jaze back in her car seat.

Then she and Whit get in the car at the same time. Once inside the car Whit doesn't speak a word. Staring silently at the paper her facial expression is still blank.

"Whitney, whatever it is girl…" Mama Cole starts. "Mama Cole, don't…" she says, "just drive." "Yes ma'am…" she responds as she cranks up and drives away.

(Love's apartment)

Every room in Love's lonely apartment is dark. The air has been running full blast for the past three days. But Love is too sick to get up and cut it off. Instead he just lay sideways in the middle of his bed, wrapped in multiple blankets staring at the T.V.

The volume on the television was muted days ago, about the same time he stopped paying attention to what was actually on the screen. The only noise in the room is coming from an old radio his big brother gave him when he was about twelve.

Love, could have bought a new radio years ago but this radio is the only thing his older brother ever gave him so he refuses to throw it away.

Love reaches up towards the head of his bed for his cell phone. He detaches it from the charger and begins to type a long text message.

"Why won't she respond to me," he mumbles to himself, "I lost my man and my girl in the same week. Sadly, this feeling isn't alien to me. This pain is the only comfort zone I knew growing up. Nobody wanted to hang with the little red sissy. And it was so much worse, because I didn't have a dad. Back then I wasn't even sure if I was gay, but everybody else seemed to be. I hated living in the shadow of my perfect big brother. How was I supposed to even appear masculine next to a beast like him?"

Love's phone vibrates. The text is from Whitney. It says,

"Love, I thought you were the man for me. I thought you were good for me, and maybe you could have been. But your lifestyle is too dangerous for me. I love you, but I can't be with you."

Love yells out loudly, as if he just got stabbed in the back with a sharp knife.

"Nothing makes sense, nothing matters," he yells out, "The whole world is closing in so fast. How does she not know she's the only light in my dim life? She can't know my darkness... if she did she would never leave me like this. She knows what she means to me, it just doesn't matter to her. At least she bought me some time though."

"We always knew what it would come to…" a dark voice says.

"I battled and hid the voices for too long," Love whispers, "Now they're all I have. The voices in my head give me no rest. There's only one way to shut them up for good."

With what little strength he has left in his body, Love rolls himself out of his bed onto the floor. Inch by inch Love crawls slowly to his bathroom. Inside the bathroom he uses the wall to pull himself up.

He reaches over to the light switch, but quickly decides to leave them off. He opens his medicine cabinet and begins pouring every pill he has into one large bottle. His whole body is in pain. Love stumbles twice as he makes his way back to his bed.

As he sits back down on his large empty bed all of his emotions attack him at once. With his face down on his bed he smells his sheets, as flashbacks of steamy nights long past crowd his mind.

He smiles blankly. Loves looks glumly down at the bottle still clutched tightly in his hand.

"Pussy," Love whispers in the darkness, "that's what my big brother used to call me constantly. I started to feel like it was my real name. Well I'm not gonna be a pussy this time. I'm going to swallow every one of these pills. I'm gonna take myself out of everybody else's misery."

He opens the bottle with shaky hands. With two hands, he brings the bottle to his mouth.

He turns it up. His phone vibrates violently beside him. He panics and clumsily spills every pill on his bedroom floor. It's Whitney calling him.

"Baby…" he answers.

"What am I doing, I um… was about to take a nap. Your test was negative too? I'm so relieved, baby I was nervous for both of us. I don't know how it's possible either, but just thank God it is. Corey and I never did have sex, I uh… Just wanted to make sure I didn't have it. No, baby I understand that. I understand. Whitney, I said understand! But I'm telling you I'm not gay anymore, all I want is you."

Love stops talking to listen to what Whitney is saying. He doesn't like what he hears.

Love stands up both of his brows furrowed tightly. "What do you mean," he says into the phone, "How would you know if I can stop being gay or not Whitney? Have you ever been a gay man? I doubt it. Well I have, and it's not easy. It's a choice that I don't want to make anymore. I can live without the stress, and the secrets. But what I can't live without Whitney… is you. Did you just hear me? You're the only reason I'm still breathing right now. Whitney… I'm not good right now. I swear I seriously need help. I'm completely broke and I'm drowning in debt. I already lost everything… all I have left is you baby. So, I don't have you? Ok, that's fine. Can we at least talk before, wait, don't just hang… Whitney? You're going to his family reunion this weekend? So, you're back with him? No, but that's the plan, right? Yeah don't lie to me. Well it's cool baby, you can be with him… over my dead body."

Love smashes his new cell phone, on his bedroom floor into multiple pieces.

"Damn it," Love screams out, "What now? Do I kill her, or him, or myself? Or do I just kill every damn body? Where is that damn gun?"

Love begins scrambling around his bedroom frantically.

The entire room in spinning, but we have to find that gun. One step at a time Love... Where did that bastard hide it? We told him to get the damn thing out of the house.

"I know but he never listens." Love whispers. *"He does what he wants," the voice in Love's head says, "with no regard for either one of us."* Love looks around his room, from wall to wall, and corner to corner. There is no one there but him.

"I remember..." Love whispers as he drops down on his stomach close to his bed and begins reaching under it, as far as he can.

Shoe box, shoe box, board game, cold hard steel... got it!!

Love snatches the old rifle out from under the bed by its cold barrel. Corey bought this military assault rifle off the street, and insisted on keeping it in the house.

Love has never shot a real gun in his life, but he's ready to try now. He sits at the edge of his bed, with the gun positioned between his legs pointing up at him.

"I told Corey to get this gun out of here," Love says, "I told him to unload it and get it out of my apartment."

"What are you going to do with it Love, kill yourself?" the dark voice asks him.

"No," Love replies, "I'm going to kill Keldrick, and kidnap Whitney."

"What about Jaze?" the dark voice asks.

"Oh, little Jaze," Love cries, "She's my princess, of course she will come with us."

"Then what Love?" the voice inquires.

"Then we live," Love whispers into the darkness, "We

288

live, as if K.C. and her old life with him never even existed."

"You're not even man enough to do it though Love." the voice assures him.

"I am a man." Love claims.

"No, you're a pussy." the voice tells Love.

"Never call me that!" Love screams into the darkness. *"That's what you are Love," the voice insists, "a pussy."*

"I'm a man." Love claims.

"Then go kill him now Love, don't wait." the dark voice provokes him.

"I will." Love says.

"Then get up," the voice taunts Love, "What are you waiting for pussy?"

"Wait," Love says, "I can't kill him or her. They're both a part of me."

"Just like I thought," the dark voice says, "you're a pure pussy. So, since you won't kill him or her, who are you going to kill then Love?"

"You..." Love replies.

Love hears psychotic laughter in his head. *"Me," the voice says, "you can't kill me..."* "Yes, I can." Love replies.

"The only way to kill me is to kill yourself you idiot, I am you." The voice explains.

"Exactly…" Love says. Then he rests his yellow chin on the end of the gun's barrel and closes his eyes. He has one hand on the barrel and one finger on his opposite hand on the trigger. His entire body is soaked with sweat.

Love stands up, and lays the gun on the bed. Then he

quickly takes off all of his clothes. After Love sits back down on the bed he puts the gun back in its deadly position. Love closes his eyes again.

"You're not going to do it Love…" the dark voice whispers.

"Be quiet!" Love screams out.

"Be quiet or what pussy?" the voice inquires.

"I'm trying to concentrate Lance," Love yells, "Please shut the hell up!"

"Oh my," the dark voice says sounding louder to Love than ever now, "you've been talking to me since you created me over ten years ago, and now you finally gave me a name."

"You have always been Lance." Love explains to himself.

"Right before we die huh," Lance asks, "that's when you show me the decency of giving me a name, right before you kill us? Lance and Love, so I'm guessing Lance is the man who lives inside you. The man you were never man enough to be!"

"Shut up Lance!" Love screams.

"You owe me," Lance screams desperately, "I was your only friend…"

"Friend," Love says, "we were never friends. You tortured me Lance!"

"I was all you had," Lance claims, "You created me when he started touching you. I was there, I comforted you."

"No," Love screams, "you made it worse!"

"I encouraged you to destroy him!" Lance yells.

"That wasn't good advice Lance," Love yells, "My mother loved him, and he's my only brother's father."

"And he raped, and molested you for years," Lance

290

reminds Love, "He was a monster. He made you the way you are."

"And what am I Lance?" Love asks.

"A pussy!" Lance screams out.

"I'm ready." Love says.

"Ready for what boy," Lance inquires in a completely demonic tone, "We both know you're not going to pull the trigger."

Love opens his eyes one last time. With his chin still resting on the end of the gun, he stares up at the ceiling and tries to pray.

"Lord," Love cries, "Please, forgive me for I know this is a sin…"

"That's it Love say your little prayers pussy!" Lance screams.

Love closes his eyes, holds his breath, and then pulls the trigger.

Everything goes black.

Chapter 12
The Proposal

As K.C. pulls up to the church, he's not sure what to do next.

(Kel)

It's been years since I visited my old childhood church. I stopped praying and believing in God when my dreams of football stardom died. Football was my life, and I was the best receiver in the country.

I couldn't understand why God would take my dream away from me. My pastor tried to explain to me years ago, that God didn't purposely ruin my dream.

But he did allow my injury to occur for a reason. None of it made sense to me though so I never came back. I'm here now, and I don't really know why.

I don't know after everything I've been through I guess I just need some more answers. I already spoke to Pastor Jackson, now it's time for me to talk to my head pastor. It's Monday morning and I know Pastor White is always here at the church every Monday morning checking the books. He'll be happy to see me. He used to call me the prodigal son...he knew one day I would come back. And I'm back...

Kel laughs to himself. Hesitantly he steps out of the car. The air around the church smells so sweet. As he makes his way to the side door, of the church Keldrick feels a slight chill down his spine.

He looks down at his clothes, and straightens himself up a bit. He takes a deep breath. Kel reaches up and knocks twice on the church door. No response. Kel knocks again. He turns to leave.

"Just a minute…" a voice says from the inside. Kel hears the door being unlocked from the inside. The door opens. A tall dark-skinned man in his sixties, with gray hair is standing in the doorway staring at Keldrick.

The old man squints, then he pulls his gold rimmed glasses to the end of his nose to get a better look.

"Keldrick… Keldrick Cole… Boy is that you?" the old man asks grinning from ear to ear. Pastor White is missing several teeth but his smile is the most pleasant sight Kel has seen in a long time.

"Yes sir," Kel replies, "it's been a long time Pastor White." Pastor White hugs Kel tightly. With a hand on each of Kel's shoulders, he steps back to get a good look at him.

"Yes, it has been a long time," he agrees, "the **prodigal son** has finally returned. How are you my boy?" "To be honest Pastor White, I've been better." Kel tells him.

"Say no more son step into my office." the pastor says. As they walk down the halls old memories of various childhood experiences he had at the church flood Kel's mind. Pastor White looks back at Kel as they walk.

"What's so funny Keldrick?" he asks. "I was just thinking about that time you and Ms. Fitzpatrick caught me and Whitney kissing in the fellowship hall."

"Yeah you and Whitney were always up to

293

something," the pastor joins Kel in laughter, "How is Whitney by the way?" Kel takes an exaggerated deep breath as they enter the pastor's office.

"From what I hear she's happy." Kel replies.

"Wait," Pastor White squints, "you two aren't together anymore?"

"No sir, we broke up about a month ago." Kel tells him. "Now that is crazy son, I thought you two would be together forever." the pastor admits. "Yeah," Kel replies, "everybody did sir."

"Well we'll get to that in a minute son," the pastor tells him, "What really brings you here to me today?"

"I'm lost Pastor White," he says, "nothing is going right for me. I've been working really hard, and I've recently been given the opportunity to do something very special."

"That sounds good son," the pastor smiles, "Did you get a new job or something?"

"Yes sir," K.C. confirms, "but it's not guaranteed yet. I have to go in and be productive from the jump, or they're going to let me go quick."

"What kind of job is it son?" the pastor asks. "I can't really talk about it yet sir," Kel tells the pastor, "But my life is finally transitioning into something good. I wanted the girl I fell in love with to be a part of it."

"Whitney…" the pastor asks. "No sir, her name is Cameron," Kel says, "she is the most beautiful, intelligent… strongest black woman I know. I put her through a lot because I had to be sure she was the one. But I messed up. I pushed her too far this time."

"It's never too late son," he says, "A *moment* can only end… when you decide to stop living in it. Control your happiness son, hell it's yours."

"I asked her to marry me in front of the entire mall, and she left me standing there." Kel explains.

"She hurt your pride." the pastor says. "Yes sir, she crushed it." Kel replies.

"Did you ever cheat on her?" Pastor White asks.

"What…" Kel replies.

"You heard me son," the pastor says, "I said did you ever cheat on Cameron?"

"Yes." K.C. admits.

"Did she find out?" Pastor White asks. "Yeah but…" Kel starts. "No buts Keldrick," he interjects, "you cheated on her. How do you think that made her feel to know that? She may have broken your heart in public, but you shattered hers in the privacy of her own home. How's your mom son?"

"She's… to be honest I don't really know sir." Kel says. "Still not speaking?" the pastor inquires.

"No sir, not really…" Kel tells him.

"I remember you two stopped talking not long after your injury, your senior year I believe." the pastor reflects.

"That's a shame," the pastor continues, "Look, this is my advice to you son… I want you to mend all the good bridges you've burned. I don't care what each person did or said to you, you are a man Keldrick. You are a black man, and we are an endangered species son. Your family needs you, *all* of your family. Go home Keldrick. Mend all your bridges, and go home. You know where home is."

"Yes sir." he replies.

"Now come Sunday morning," the pastor tells him, "I wanna see you and your mother at church. Don't let me down boy."

"Yes sir, I'll see what I can arrange." Kel replies.

K.C. thanks the pastor for his time, and then makes his way back to the car. As he pulls away his phone starts ringing. It's Jay calling. "Hello," he answers, "What's up bro? Yeah, I'm good. Are you back in town? Yeah, I just left the church. Don't ask, it's a long story bro. Ok, just meet me at the McDonalds on Sandlake Road."

Ten minutes later Keldrick pulls up at the McDonald's where he finds Jay sitting in his rental car with his head down. Kel immediately gets out of his car and approaches his friend.

"You good bro…" K.C. asks. "No, not really fam…" Jay replies. "Well come inside bro, are you hungry?" K.C. asks.

"I could eat." Jay replies. Jay slowly steps out of the car, and the two men make their way inside.

"You still eat the two cheese burger meal bro?" K.C. asks with a friendly smirk on his face.

"Man, that was years ago bro, I'm a grown ass man now K.C." Jay says. They both laugh. "So, you telling me your little ass don't eat the two cheese burger meal anymore?" K.C. asks teasingly. Jay hesitates. "Yeah nigga I still eat it," Jay admits reluctantly, "but I get two extra burgers now though."

K.C. laughs loudly. "I knew it," he says, "but look, don't eat too much, my family reunion starts in a few hours and my people gone be grilling all night."

"Cool," Jay says, "It's gone be at your mom's crib?"

"Yeah, we're gonna be in her backyard." K.C. says.

"Welcome to McDonalds, may I take your order?"

the pimply faced Puerto Rican cashier says.

"Yeah," K.C. says, "Let me get two number 2's that's all."

"Ok your total is $12.48." Jay reaches in his pocket. "I got you bro don't worry about it." K.C. says as he pulls out a crisp hundred-dollar bill and pays for the food.

Jay watches K.C. as he places his change in the middle of a roll of all new hundred dollar bills.

"So, are Whit and Jaze coming to the reunion?" Jay asks.

"Yeah," K.C. replies, "they live with Mama Cole now."

"What… When did that happen?" Jay asks.

"She got into it with her boyfriend or something," Kel says, "so she moved out, and went to stay with Mama Cole."

"Why didn't Whit just move back into ya'll's old apartment?" Jay asks.

"Whit broke the lease on our apartment when she moved in with her boyfriend," K.C. explains, "So she couldn't go back there."

"Wait," Jay says, "I thought you were back home with Mama Cole too Kel. Where you been staying at?"

"Extended Stay hotel." he tells his friend.

Jay hesitates. "Kel," he says, "it's not my business so you ain't gotta tell me nothing. But, where are you getting all this new cash from bro? You must have started back slingin' dope?" K.C. laughs.

"No sir," he says, "I'm never going back to that life. Let's just say my future is looking brighter these days. But enough about me, we're supposed to be talking about you bro."

Jay hesitates again, and then takes a bite out of his burger. Keldrick can tell he's thinking as he chews.

"Kel..." Jay says. "Yeah bro..." K.C. replies.

"You ever wish you had a dude you were close to that you could talk to about anything?" Jay says.

Kel leans in close to his friend. "Jay, are you trying to come out of the closet to me in the middle of McDonald's bro?" K.C. asks teasingly.

"See that's what I'm saying," Jays says hitting the table, "how come if a man wants to be honest and open with another man he gotta be gay?"

"So, you're *not* gay," K.C. says, "cause if you are bro it's cool I'm not trippin'."

"No, I'm not gay nigga," he says, "and if I was I wouldn't tell you."

"What's that supposed to me Jay?" K.C. asks with a straight face.

"Are you serious," Jay says, "nigga... in high school you tortured your baby brother just because people said he *acted* gay. I'd hate to see what you would do to a non-family member."

Kel holds his head down for a moment. After a silent prayer, he looks back up at his old friend.

"You're right bro," K.C. says, "You're *absolutely* right. I did my little brother wrong, but I'm going to fix it today."

"How the hell you gone fix it," Jay asks, "Nigga that man hates you, he ain't gone talk to you period."

"I still gotta try Jay," K.C. says, "I burned a lot of good bridges in my past, and before I can move on to the next phase in my life I have to mend them all."

"So, what are you going to do?" Jay asks.

"I already told Mama Cole to invite my little brother to the reunion," K.C. tells Jay, "She told him I want to speak with him."

"That's love K.C.," Jay says, "that's real love bro. You know, you always had it so good but for some reason you could never see it."

"Don't start that Jay," K.C. says laughing lightly, "I'm gon have to bring up that movie theater in yo folks crib."

"Seriously though bro," Jay says, "it was never about the money. You had people who loved you, and looked up to you. People like me, and Ty, and even your little brother. We all idolized you K.C. Then you had the perfect girlfriend. Good ole Suga Mama."

They laugh together. "That's what we're all living for," Jay continues, "those moments that we all grew up watching you live out. But it never mattered to you, because you were K.C., the big man on campus, the ladies' man, the future NFL star. You took it all for granted bro. I'm not trying to down you. All I'm saying is I'm struggling right now bro. I can't find myself, no matter how hard I try. I'm gonna be thirty in a few years and I still don't have a record deal yet."

"It's okay bro." K.C. says.

"No Kel," Jay says, "It's definitely not okay. What's next for me? Huh… This is all I know. I can't continue to let my parents sustain my income. I have to be a man. That's why I said I wish I had another man, somebody I'm close to, I could talk to about all of this. I get stressed out fam."

Jay puts his head down hard on the table trying to

hide his emotion. K.C. puts a caring hand on his back. Jay sits up quickly.

"**Don't pity me bro**," Jay says, "I don't want your pity. I just need your guidance fam. Just…tell me what to do bro."

"What are your options bro?" K.C. asks.

"My dad said if I'm not signed to a record deal by Christmas I gotta go to the military." Jay tells him.

"The military," K.C. says, "that's not a bad idea. Is that what you want to do?"

"Hell, no bruh…" Jay says wiping a tear away.

"What do you wanna do fam?" K.C.

"First off, I want a good woman like you had," Jay tells him, "then all I wanna do is travel the world forever, rapping my heart out, and giving my music to the world."

"Do it," Kel says, "don't accept any other options, do what you really wanna do bro. And real soon I'm gonna be in a position to push you like I want to, and I'ma do everything I can to get you signed. You got my word. And for the record there ain't nothing wrong with two guys talking to each other about their problems. That's what brothers are for."

(Mama Cole)

"Baby, bring that potato salad outside for me please." Mama Cole tells Whitney. "Okay mama." she replies. Mama Cole's back yard is filled with hundreds of her close and distant relatives.

They're all wearing the bright yellow Cole family reunion shirts. The shirts depict a diagram of a detailed

Cole family tree. The air smells sweet from all the baked pies, cakes, and cookies she's been slaving over all day.

K.C.'s Uncle Que, is manning the grill because he says, "can't nobody on the planet make *barbeque* like **Uncle Que** do."

So, everybody pretty much stays out of his way when it comes to the grill. Cousin Jeff brought some huge speakers from the church and hooked them up to Mama Cole's old entertainment system.

Since he brought the speakers he feels like he's a real DJ today. He's playing everything from the **Temptations** and the **Isley Brothers**, to **Nicki Minaj** and **Chris Brown**. Some of the younger cousins are shooting some hoops on K.C.'s old basketball goal in the driveway.

Mama Cole didn't want to move her car out of the way, but did anyway after the youngsters got on her nerves enough. Jaze and Whitney are both wearing the Cole family reunion shirts as well.

They've been back and forth, and in and out of the house all day helping Mama get everything set just right. Whitney thought the reunion might be awkward for her, and so she elected to just stay inside all day.

Mama Cole wouldn't hear of it, she insisted that Whitney wear a shirt and act as if she's family, because she is by way of K.C. and Jazemene.

Whit is glad she decided to participate because K.C.'s family is surprisingly fond of her. Some of them even know about the circumstances in which she left K.C., when he needed her the most.

But they contend that she's still young, and she's entitled to make mistakes. Aunt Luella told her,

"Everybody makes mistakes baby, but the trick is admitting to our mistakes, fixing them, and learning from them."

She insisted that Whitney and K.C. would end up back together by the end of the reunion. She said, "Intimate events like this, have a funny way of showing you who you really love."

This didn't make much since to Whitney, but she just smiled and hugged Aunt Luella anyway. Whitney looks down at her beautiful daughter, who's been attached to her leg all day.

"Jazemene, baby why don't you at least try to go meet some of your cousins…" Whit says. "No Mama, I don't want to. I wanna stay here with you…" Jaze replies.

"Look over there Jazemene," Whit says pointing close by, "the twins Monica and Victoria look really nice. And ya'll are about the same age too."

"When is my daddy coming?" Jaze asks. Whitney looks towards the door at the back of the house, as she was just thinking the same thing. As Whit is looking at the door, Ty walks out with Cam on his arm.

"There's your Uncle Ty," Whit says, "so your daddy can't be far away. Wait, is this nigga with Cam?" Whitney quickly picks up Jaze and rushes over to Mama Cole at the Spades table.

"Mama Cole…" Whit says. "What baby, I'm in the middle of a game." she replies. "Ty is here…" Whit says. "That's good baby," Mama says, "send him over I want to see him."

"He's not alone Mama…" Whit whispers. "Well who's with him,

K.C. and Jay?" Mama Cole asks never looking away from the card game.

"No Mama," Whit says putting Jaze down and placing a hand on each hip, "he has Cam with him."

"What Cam baby," Mama asks, "not K.C.'s Cam…" "Yes Mama." Whit tells her. "What the hell," Mama says laying her cards down, "just a minute ya'll cause it's about to be some mess and I'm not gone have it. I wonder how those two got so close. K.C is gonna kill Ty."

"Why," Whit asks, "I thought you said they were done for good this time." Mama Cole looks at her solemnly.

"They are," Mama Cole says, "but you don't know everything that's going on with them Whitney."

Whitney crosses her arms tightly. "Then tell me Mama so I will know," Whit says, "I know you're K.C.'s mama, and not mine but don't act like ya'll have always been the best of friends Mama Cole."

"Don't go there Whitney." she says.

"What? It's true Mama," Whit insists, "now Mama Cole please, tell me what's going on between Cam and my… I mean K.C."

"He proposed to her," Mama Cole says, "at the mall in front of hundreds of people. He spent more money than you can imagine just to, make that one moment perfect for her."

"Are you serious?" Whit asks. "Yes ma'am." Mama Cole replies nodding her head slowly. "So, what happened?" Whit asks.

"Well," Mama Cole starts, "after all the singers and

dancers were finished performing, they had a flash mob you see… All of the dancers got down on one knee and…"

Jaze steps forward. "Me, and my daddy walked through the crowd," Jaze says, "then we got down on one knee and asked Ms. Cam to marry us. But she ran away with Uncle Ty. My daddy cried."

"Mama Cole." Ty says. "Tyboonie, how you doing baby…" Mama Cole says.

They hug each other tightly. After they hug Ty can tell by the way Mama Cole is looking at him, he's in trouble.

"Come here Ty." Mama Cole takes him by the hand. She leads him a couple feet away. Whitney and Jaze go sit back at their table. "Ty," Mama Cole points at him, "what you do on your own time, in your own world, is your own business. But why the hell would you bring her here?"

"Too soon…" Ty says with a smirk on his face.

"That's not funny Ty," Mama Cole says, "K.C. is on his way here now. He's not going to be pleased son."

"He's not coming Mama." Ty says still smiling.

"How do you know that Tyboonie…" she asks.

"I was there at the mall," Ty says, "Cam crushed him Mama. Kel is not coming here with all these people. I'm sure his pride is still hurt." Mama Cole puts her hands on her hips.

"If you know Cam crushed your best friend," Mama Cole says, "then how the hell can you be with her like nothing happened?"

"Because..." he says.

"Because what Ty?" Mama Cole asks.

"Because I love her Mama Cole…" Ty claims.

"K.C. loved her first Ty," she says, "You're wrong son…"

"Well to be honest Mama at this point I really don't care." Ty says.

"What do you mean at this point Ty," she asks, "What point are you at, and why?"

"I'm not going to be in his shadow any damn more," Ty says, "I'm tired of it, and Jay can have that spot being Kel's lap dog. I'm a man Mama Cole."

"Ty what the hell are you even talking about?" Mama Cole asks with her old brows wrinkled heavily.

"K.C. has always been the star," Ty says, "nobody else mattered, not me, not you, nobody but Keldrick. He always had everything, including the beautiful girlfriend. Well now I got one of his girls, and I'm not going to let her go she needs me."

"That girl doesn't need you Ty," Mama says, "She doesn't even really want you. You're just a rebound. You're living a lie Tyboonie."

"Well I'm going to live this lie as long as it lasts," Ty says, "Look I gotta get back to Cam Mama Cole."

Ty walks back to her angrily. Taking her by the hand he leads her toward the food. Mama Cole shakes her head as she makes her way back to the card table.

Whitney watches Mama Cole as she takes her seat back at the table. Whitney feels her temperature rising, and her entire face is bright red.

She picks Jaze up and rushes towards the house. Inside the house she lays Jaze down in her daddy's old bed, and then lies down next to her.

"What's wrong Mama," Jaze asks, "Is it nap time…"

"No baby," Whitney replies, "Mama is just doing some thinking." "Thinking about what…" a smooth baritone voice says from the doorway.

"Daddy," Jazemene screams, "Daddy I missed you." Jaze jumps out of the bed and runs into her daddy's strong arms. Whitney tries to hide her smile.

"Why are you late?" Whitney asks him.

"Well hello to you too Suga Mama…" K.C. flashes his perfect white smile at her. Whitney rolls over and sits up at the head of the bed staring at the wall.

"Uh oh," Kel wrinkles his brow, "I know that look. Who's been messing with my Suga Mama?"

With Jaze still in his arms he approaches the bed, and sits next to Whitney. "Talk to me Suga Mama," he says, "What's wrong? You know Big Daddy's gone fix it."

"Ty is outside hugged up with that… with Cam." she replies. "I know," he replies with no emotion, "My Mama text my phone to warn me before Jay and I got here."

"So, what are you going to do?" she asks. "I'm just going to live and let live," Kel says, "I'm here to mend all the good bridges I burned over the years, before I move on to this new season in my life."

"So, you're telling me, when you walk outside, it's not going to bother you to see your best friend with your ex?" Whitney asks.

"Nope," he says with a genuine smile on his face, "because I'm going to have the two prettiest girls here with me."

"Who daddy…" Jaze asks. K.C. looks down into his

306

daughter's eyes and says, "You Pumpkin, you and your mommy."

Jaze looks around her daddy's massive shoulder at her smiling mommy.

Whitney pulls her legs around on the bed from behind K.C., and then sits up next to him on the side of the bed. She grabs his left arm tightly.

"Well, *we* are going to be on the arm of the most gorgeous man here." Whit says kissing him on the cheek.

"And the most gorgeous daddy…" Jaze says kissing K.C. on his other cheek. K.C. stands up with Jaze still in his arms, and takes Whitney by the hand.

"Let's do it ladies." he says as he leads them out of his old bedroom. Stepping out of the backdoor as a unit, as a team, as a family the three of them have never felt as complete and powerful as they do right now.

Luther Vandross' *"Dance with my father,"* is playing loudly on the speakers. K.C. kisses his baby girl on the forehead and says, "Jazemene Cole may I have this dance?"

"Yes, you may daddy." Jaze replies through a huge smile. He gently swings her down so that she can stand on top of his feet as he leads her step by step.

Whitney is mouthing every word of the song as she happily watches them dance together from a chair close by.

"Come here baby." K.C. says looking at Whitney with those eyes she can't resist. Standing behind Jaze, Whitney has one hand on K.C.'s back, and her other hand in his, as Jaze holds on to her daddy's swaying legs.

The three of them dance the rest of the song together,

never noticing the angry man watching them. He's standing in the corner of the yard close to the house. He's been there for over an hour propped up on the wall, with a handgun in his pocket.

"Come on y'all I'm gonna go see Mama." K.C. says. As they approach the card table Mama Cole turns around smiling. It's like she could feel the happy family's presence.

"Baby," she says, "have you eaten?"

"Not yet Mama," he says, "but you know I will." "Oh, I know you will," she says laughing to herself, "that's why I told everybody to eat before you got here. You've always have been a bottomless pit; boy you eat like you'll never eat again. But anyway, Pastor White said you came to see him."

"Yes, ma'am I did." he replies. "That's good son," Mama Cole tells him, "he was glad to see you. Oh, your brother is here somewhere. I didn't want to invite him but I did because you begged me too. Why don't you go find him and leave Whitney and Jaze here with me?" K.C. laughs thinking her words are a joke.

"No, Mama Cole," Whitney says, "Jaze and I want to see him too. I don't remember much about Kel's brother. I just know he was short, quiet, and had really bad acne."

"Yeah well, he doesn't look like that anymore trust me child," Mama Cole says, "People do grow up... and out."

"It'll be fine Mama," K.C. says, "My brother and I, are going to turn over a new leaf today. No fighting, no animosity period, just brotherly love."

"Boy," Mama Cole says, "I ain't ever told you anything wrong. Listen to your mama. I didn't get old by accident. Leave Jaze and Whitney here with me…"

"Keldrick…" a familiar voice says from the rear. K.C. turns around with Whitney holding one hand and Jaze holding the other. "Baby bro…" he says, "Whitney, Jaze I want you both to meet somebody I should have introduced y'all to a long time ago… my little brother *Lance Vinson Cole*." Whitney looks into his green eyes as her heart drops to the pit of her stomach.

"*No*…" Whitney whispers to herself. K.C. hugs Lance tightly.

Lance looks down at a smiling Jaze and winks at her.

"Bro," K.C. says, "let me start by saying I was so wrong for the way I treated you, and for keeping you out of my life and my child's life. If you will give me the chance I want to start over today and be the big brother you deserve."

"Hey that's cool with me bro." Lance replies with a big smile.

"Cool," K.C. says, "Well give my girls a big hug and a kiss bro."

Whitney squeezes K.C.'s hand tightly. He turns around to look at her. He can see the fear in her eyes.

"What's wrong baby?" he asks.

"Big Daddy…" Whit says falling down on one knee, "*will you marry me*?"

Every eye at the reunion is on Whitney and K.C. He looks around at everyone and he knows what he must do. It hurt him so badly to be turned down by Cam at the mall in front of all those people. And he wouldn't dare have Whitney feel the way he did that day, especially not in front of Jazemene. K.C. looks back at Whitney.

Jazemene quickly drops down on one knee next to her mommy and looks up at her father.

He hesitates because he knows something's not right, so he can't just say yes. To him her proposal seems forced, and almost desperate.

Looking up at the crowd again K.C. immediately locks eyes with Cam still holding Ty's hand. He looks back down at Whitney immediately and says, "Suga Mama, I love you and of course I'll marry you."

Almost everybody at the reunion begins to rejoice about the engagement, everybody except Cam and Lance.

"What," Lance says, "bro you can't be serious." "What do you mean?" K.C. asks helping Whitney and Jaze back up to their feet.

"Marriage," Lance says, "I mean it's too soon. I mean why don't you two wait awhile… or a few months?"

"We will," K.C. replies laughing curiously, "we will wait until the wedding is planned and then we will get married. Is that a problem little bro?"

"You can't marry her bro!" Lance exclaims wildly.

"Why not Lance?" K.C. asks pushing Whitney and Jaze safely behind him. "Because bro," Lance says, "She's not good enough for you."

"This is the mother of my child," K.C. feels his temperature rising, "What exactly are you saying little bro. And whatever it is you're saying be very careful…"

Lance looks past K.C. into Whitney's nervous eyes. He swallows hard. "You can't marry her… because she's a hoe!" Lance yells for the whole world to hear.

"Boy I'm going to kill you," K.C. says, "have you been

drinking?" "She's three months pregnant now,"Lance exclaims,"she has no clue who the baby's father is," he continues, "It might be you bro, it might be the good doctor Carlos Sanchez, or the baby may even be mine. I've been smashing this hoe for…"

"Lies…" K.C. screams as he punches Lance hard in the face knocking him several feet away from where he was standing. Whitney immediately runs to Lance's side.

"Baby, are you okay?" she asks him.

K.C. and everybody else look on in awe. Lance flashes a bloody smile at his big brother. "I told you." he says spitting out bright red blood. Whitney freezes as she realizes what she just did.

She feels K.C.'s eyes burning a hole right through her. K.C. steps forward with Jaze close on his heels.

"Baby," he says, "Did I hear you just call my little brother baby? What the hell is going on here, and how do you two even know each other?"

Lance sits up on his elbows still too weak to stand up.

"We've known each other for a while Keldrick,"Lance says,"Every time you snuck off to be with Cam, *"the queen of the ghetto",* Whitney called me. She begged me to come give her everything you never could…"

Mama Cole steps forward. "Lance," she says, "you were always the cancer of this family."

"Mama Cole," Whitney says, "why didn't you tell me who Love was? How could you hide that from me Mama?"

"It was too late little girl," she replies, "You were already too deeply involved with him." K.C. turns to look at his mother.

"Mama," he cries, "you knew?"

Mama Cole tries to hold his hand, Kel snatches away from her. "I just found out a couple of days ago." Mama Cole says unable to hide her shame.

"What is your point Mama?" Kel asks.

"You were so excited about reconnecting with your little brother," Mama Cole says, "I didn't want to… I was afraid if I told you, you would think I was trying to sabotage your reunion with him."

"*Mama Cole*," Lance says, standing to his feet finally, "how you been Mama?"

"Boy don't you play with me." she tells him with venom in her speech.

"Of course, not Mama," he says wiping blood away from his sadistic smile, "You know it's really hard living in a world with *no mother* and *no father*."

"*Boy don't start no mess…*" Mama Cole says raising a nervous hand up at him.

"Yeah Mama," Lance continues, "you know if a young boy grows up in a house without a father figure it's very possible he can get the wrong ideas about the world. What a man is supposed to do… and what a man is not supposed to do." Lance smiles at K.C.

"What are you getting at Lance," K.C. says, "stop beating around the bush. My father was in both of our lives when we were growing up. He may not have lived here with us every day and night but my father was around if we needed him."

"Keldrick, you poor fool," Love says, "You really never had a clue, did you?"

"Lance," Mama Cole screams, "shut up, and just go home!"

312

"No Mama," K.C. says, "I want to hear him out. What do I not have a clue about Lance?"

"Your father…" Love says. "What about my father," Kel asks, "what the hell are you saying?"

"You said he was around," Love starts, "you're right Keldrick, he was around. He was there a lot more than you ever knew. Those late nights when Paul would come stumbling in our house drunk…I remember those nights well. My old room was right by the back door. I used to hear him outside the door fumbling with the keys Mama gave him to *our* house, even though he didn't actually live there or pay any bills."

"*Lance, leave my house now!*" Mama Cole, demands pointing towards the gate.

"No Mama," K.C. says, "Finish what you were saying Lance."

"Thank you, dear brother," Love says, "after a few tries he would finally unlock the door and stumble inside. Mama's room was all the way in the back, but it didn't matter he never made it that far anyway. At first, I would always keep my door locked but he always got in anyway so after a while I just stop locking it. He would come in my room, as quiet as he could. I think it turned him on more when he thought I was asleep."

"You're sick," Mama Cole says, "you *crazy* little red *sissy*, that's all you ever were. You used to sit in the closet and talk to your damn self all day and night."

"*Who the hell else was I supposed to talk to Mama,*" Love asks, "*not you, damn sure not Keldrick… Nope all I had was the voices in my head and good ole Paul!*"

"*You leave him out of this,*" Mama Cole demands,

"Paul caught you in my closet wearing my underwear, that's when this started. It was your own fault. You were born a faggot!"

Love's old tears begin to fall like new. He's heard those words all his life, but it hurts the worst coming from the one who gave him life. A mother's words are the most powerful to their children.

"Mama, be quiet," K.C. says, "or I'm going to ask you to go inside. Keep going Lance…"

"*Okay* good brother… he would come in my room," Love says, "and prop himself up on my dresser where I used to keep my socks and underwear. He would just lean there and stare at me as he groped himself. He would come closer to me, the more aroused he became and then he would do things to me that made me wish I wouldn't survive them. The pain that man inflicted on me was unspeakable…" Love wipes more tears away.

"I was so scared and embarrassed," he continues, "I didn't know what to do, or who to tell. So of course, I told my Mama."

Love points at Mama Cole in dramatic fashion. Keldrick turns to look at his mother again.

"He told you Mama," K.C. asks, "And what did you do?"

Love laughs out loud as he wipes more real tears away. "What did she do," Love says, "she handled it. She handled it the only way she could as not to lose the man she loves and not to disrupt your perfect life big bro. When I told Mama, she beat me. She beat me so good I swear my entire body was numb and throbbing at the same time. She told me if I ever told anybody else what I

314

told her she would kill me." "Mama you didn't... Tell me you didn't Mama." K.C. says wiping away tears of his own now.

"Since my Mama didn't have a problem with it," Love says, "I thought that what Paul was doing to me must have been the way things were supposed to be. So, I started to accept it, I even began to enjoy it, and seek that same thrill from other men when he wasn't around. Paul made me this little red sissy Mama, because you let him!" Love screams out in pain.

"And Keldrick..." Love Continues, "you and all your friends at school... you picked on me every single day of my life. I never had a friend. You never protected me or stood up for me. But as soon as somebody did or said something you didn't like to Tyboonie or Jay you were ready to kill them. But not me dear brother I was just the little red sissy, the faggot! I hated you so much, and I envied you more than anything... I looked at Whitney back then and decided if I had a girl like her, I could be normal like you... and maybe even popular. But back then I was too short and ugly to get any girl. I was invisible to Whitney back then, unless she was helping the rest of you torture me. So, when I saw her that day walking down the sidewalk it was no accident." Love looks at Whitney.

"I planned it all," he says, "I knew you would be there that day because I had watched you for weeks and I knew your entire schedule. I knew because of the way I look now, you would notice me and give me a chance. That's all I needed was a chance, and of course you looked into my eyes and gave it to me. I wanted to take you from Keldrick, break his heart and then make you fall madly in love with me, and then break your heart as well."

"That's cruel Love." Whitney tells him. "I didn't care," he replies, "the two of you caused me so much pain over the years I really just wanted to destroy you both. But… at some point I saw who you really were Whitney. I saw through your exterior, and our past, I found you. And I fell in love with what I found."

Love steps close to Whitney and kisses her passionately on the lips. "Everything is out now Whitney," Love tells her before kissing her again in front of everybody, "What's it gonna be baby girl? The ball is in your court."

"What do you mean Love," Whitney asks, "are you asking me to choose between you and K.C.?"

Love laughs snidely. "No," he says, "*I'm not asking, I'm telling you to choose now*! Do you want me… or my dear brother *the deadbeat dad*? That's what you call him right, *a deadbeat*?"

"That is a lie I never called him a deadbeat ever!!" Whitney screams.

K.C. looks at Whitney. "Who do you choose Suga Mama?" he asks through his blurry tears.

"I'm sorry K.C., I choose Love." Whitney says with no hesitation.

Love smiles at his mama and then at K.C. "I told you Keldrick, she loves me." Love says. He kisses Whitney hard on the lips and then he pushes her down to the ground. Love pulls out a high-powered hand gun and points it at her.

"I'm sorry Whitney," he says, "I did love you, but you broke my heart. After the Corey situation, you wouldn't answer my calls or text me back. I was locked in my room trying to kill myself, trying to kill myself for you! And you didn't even care!"

"Love, I didn't know you were going to kill yourself!" Whitney screams too scared to try to move.

"Uncle L, please don't hurt my Mama." Jaze pleads with her Uncle from her daddy's side. Lance looks down at his niece inadvertently swinging the gun in her direction.

Once the gun is no longer pointed at her Whitney finds strength deep inside her. She stands up and rushes Love, tackling him to the ground.

"You're Uncle L," she screams between punches and slaps, "Really Love? You kidnapped my daughter? I'm going to kill you!"

"It wasn't me," Love screams, "It was Lance…"

"***You are Lance you crazy fuck***!" Whit screams.

The gun is lying next to Love's head. He sees K.C. looking at it. Love dodges a couple of Whitney's blows and throws her off of him. Whitney falls back and hits her head hard on a nearby table.

When she hits the ground, her body goes limp. Love rolls over and grabs the gun. He aims the gun at Jaze who is standing twenty feet away from him frozen, staring at her mother's still body.

K.C. tries to rush Love. Before K.C. can reach him, he shoots Jaze in the stomach.

"Mama!!!!" Jaze screams out just before the bullet hits her. The baby flies back and falls to the ground just as limp as her mother.

K.C. jumps on Love and begins to strangle him. Ty and Jay run up and also begin beating Love.

K.C. leaves them to handle his psychotic brother. He looks at Whitney's limp body, then over at his crying Mother quickly carrying his daughter's bloody body to her car. He doesn't know which way to go.

"Go Keldrick!" Ty exclaims. K.C. rushes to Whitney and carries her to Mama Cole's car as well. Mama Cole jumps in the driver's seat, as K.C. positions himself on the backseat with both of his girls lying limp side by side in his lap.

Back in Mama Cole's backyard every person left at the reunion is crowded around Ty and Jay as they continue to beat up Love. "Somebody call the cops now!" Ty yells out between punches.

"I'm on it." Uncle Que replies. "We need to tie this fool up…" Jay says. "With what…" Ty asks.

"Welp back to getting raped…" Lance whispers to Love.

"What the hell are you talking about lance?" Love asks. Love can hear Lance laughing menacingly at him. "Speak you bastard!" Love screams.

Jay and Ty stop beating on Love and stare down at him in horror as he begins to physically fight with himself.

"I'm just being honest." Lance whispers to Love. "You're being honest," Love says aloud, "Being honest about what you bastard?"

"Right," Lance continues to laugh at Love, "What do you think is going to happen when your pretty ass goes to prison?"

Love doesn't respond to his dominant second personality instead he just punches himself again.

"They're gonna call you Goldie Lox," Lance taunts Love, "Or Honey Blonde. You'll be everybody's bitch! You little faggot!"

"No!" Love screams out.

"You're such a pussy Love!" Lance screams in Love's ear.

"No," Love shouts, "I'm a man!" Ty looks at Jay and nods his head in approval. Jay bends down and slaps Love hard across the face. "You ain't no man you a punk!" Jay assures him.

"Yeah," Ty agrees punching Love hard in the stomach, "Real men don't kidnap and shoot innocent little girls you evil little fuck!" "The police will be here any second fellas!" Uncle Que yells out to Jay and Ty. "Good," Jay replies, "Thanks Unc."

"No!" Love screams. "No what?" Ty asks.

"Just get the gun Ty!" Love screams from the bloody ground. "Game over Lance," Ty replies, "You are not getting out of this. Forget that gun fool."

"You don't understand, you idiot," Love says spitting out blood, "I want *you* to get the gun! I want you to shoot me. I want you to kill me Ty... Jay, one of ya'll. Please kill me, don't send me to jail! I'm not gonna make it in there..."

"Tell it to the judge!" Ty shouts punching Love hard once more, knocking him unconscious.

Chapter 13

Back in the Game

(Kel)

*T*oday is a magical day for me. My name is

Keldrick Jermaine Cole Sr., and I'm writing this letter to let the world know that dreams really do come true. This marks the end of one rocky chapter in the book of my life, and the beginning of a new wonderful chapter.

With all the criminal charges my brother Lance has pending against him, he will never see day light again. I used to say I would never wish prison on anybody because I know how bad prison is first hand. But Lance tricked the mother of my child into falling in love with him, and then he tried to kill her. He also kidnapped my daughter and hid her in a dark dusty old storage shed for days, and then he shot her at the family reunion.

Both of my girls made full recoveries, and they're doing well. My baby will carry that scar on the right side of stomach forever but it's okay I told her the scar gives her character. She has a story to tell her friends when she's older, and they'll all think it's cool that she survived a gun shot at such a young age.

So, my baby has learned to embrace her battle scar. Whitney has been working extra hard to be the perfect fiancé' and mother. I haven't brought that day up again, and I'm not going to punish her for it. It's my fault too. If I had been there for her she never would have entertained Lance.

I haven't seen Cam since the family reunion. I saw on Facebook awhile back that she and Ty had a house together in Atlanta. Then we found out my father Paul was an even bigger hoe than we thought. It turns out Tyrone is my brother too. After Cam found out, she left Ty and disappeared. Nobody has seen her since. I wish her the best though. Dr. Sanchez quit his job at the hospital, and word is he's off traveling the world, trying to mend his broken heart. Mama Cole has been perfect. She's the one who nursed both of my girls back to full health.

She helped us get moved into our new five-bedroom house in Miami as well. That's right baby, "Big Daddy" brought his talents to South Beach. I'm the biggest thing to hit the city since the king LeBron James.

The Miami Dolphins had been scouting me throughout high school up until my injury, after that I kind of fell of the map. They wrote several letters of interest over the years, stating that they wanted me to attend some camps over the summer.

I always ignored the letters because after I healed physically, I was still crippled mentally. Then after I got locked up, I was sure they would lose interest. They never did so finally Whitney wrote them back expressing interest in their programs. I didn't have a clue what she had done. She just cooked a huge dinner one day, and asked me to dress nice. We had dinner with the Dolphins Offensive coordinator Mike Sherman.

It was nice, and after hours of video, actual play diagrams, and talk about a sizeable signing bonus I was sold.

I immediately started secretly training with the coaches. Whitney didn't have a clue that I signed with the Dolphins. They saw my potential and decided to go ahead and give me the opportunity to walk on and play for them.

I signed on the dotted line, deposited my three hundred thousand dollar signing bonus, and started practicing in full pads the next week. At that point, nobody knew but my mom. I didn't want to get anybody's hopes up, because I still had my doubts that I could continue to perform at the level they expected me to.

If I failed to deliver, I knew that with the stipulations in my special contract I would owe the organization every penny back. So far everything has been lovely though, I'm slowly becoming the face of the franchise.

They need a new face after the huge scandal they just went through with Richie Incognito. My mom also lives with us at our beach front home in Miami, she has her own room and she takes care of Jaze and our new son Keldrick Jr. for us.

Mama's happy because I'm happy, and she's finally living the life she feels she deserves.

We had to go through some extensive family counseling, but we're good now. I think everybody is good now, Jaze loves her baby brother, and Whit seems to be finally in her comfort zone.

I don't think we'll have any more problems like we had in the past. Our wedding will be next month. We decided to get married right here on the beach.

Our wedding colors are white and pink. I wanted blue but my baby is an A.K.A. so I had to let her have that. It's her day anyway. I want it to be Whitney's dream day come true. The honeymoon is all me though, I want a sexy private exotic island getaway for just my queen and I.

To all my fellas out there if you're ever lucky enough to find a woman that you know you can't live without, don't hesitate to treat her just like that. And ladies if you ever find a man who treats you like a queen, if you continue to act like one, he will continue to treat you like one.

Epilogue
Island Get Away

Whitney left home early this morning to catch her plane. The flight was long and peaceful. She didn't sleep at all. The anticipation was too much for her to doze off even for a second. She's been waiting her entire life for a real moment like this.

A weekend getaway on an exotic island in the Quirimbas Archipelago near Pemba in northern Mozambique; is the perfect engagement present. He's already been on the island for a day or so waiting for her to arrive.

Whitney had never even heard of the gorgeous island before she received the ticket he had delivered to her. Stepping off the small plane Whitney feels as if she's stepping into a new chapter of her life.

The driver was already there waiting for her when the plane landed. He got all of her luggage and loaded it into the back of the brand new fiery red Rolls Royce.

She's at a loss for words when they arrive at the exquisite Ibo Island Lodge. She can't believe any of this is real, and she's so happy guilt doesn't even cross her mind.

"Right this way Ms. Powell," the driver says, "he's waiting for you." A couple of young men from the island begin to carefully grab her luggage and follow her and the driver inside the luxurious hotel. Walking along the pristine halls of the lodge Whitney feels as if she's having and outer body experience.

She's being lead down each hall by her own personal chauffer, and being followed by ruggedly handsome local island men carrying her brand-new Hermes luggage set. He picked it out for her a week ago and had it delivered to her house. She feels like a powerful island queen headed to her royal chamber in her stunning castle.

She's lost in her own personal fantasy. As they approach the door to her room she can hear her heart beating fiercely in her ears. She reaches up and tries to make sure her hair is still perfectly in place. Nervously she grabs the driver's arm before he can open the door.

Then she takes a small mirror out of her honey orange Hermes clutch. Holding the mirror up in front of her face she truly believes she's looking at perfection.

After placing the mirror back in her clutch, she nods at the driver giving him permission to open her door. He immediately takes his hat off, opens the door and stands to the side as she slowly steps inside.

Her heart is no longer beating in her ears because it has now dropped to her stomach. The room is even more breath taking than she could have ever imagined. Almost every wall is pearly white, except for the accent wall behind the bed in the bedroom.

This wall is a pretty pale green color, the exact same color as the perfectly hand stitched comforter on the bed.

As she enters the bedroom she can hear the shower running. She figures she must have arrived a little earlier than he planned, and he must still be getting ready for her.

The wildly flowing white cloth canopy on the bed is swaying methodically as a nice warm breeze is wafting in from the veranda. There is a small gold antique lamp sitting on a small table on each side of the bed.

The hardwood floors have been buffed to perfection. The soft air smells like fresh mango fruit. On the right side of the bed a gorgeous red Alexander Wang summer dress with a white floral print on it has been laid out for her.

As she reaches out to carefully feel the material she feels a sudden chill and her arms are covered in tiny goose bumps. Whit sighs happily as the gorgeous dress is made of pure silk. Below the dress on the floor beside the bed is a light brown Christian Louboutin box. She can hardly wait to see what's inside the box.

She quickly kneels down to take the top off of it. Inside she finds a pair of exclusive red and white Christian Louboutin pumps with tiny rhinestones all over them. She can no longer contain herself. She begins squealing joyfully like a small child on Christmas.

Lying to the right side of the dress is a small Chanel box. Inside the box she finds a luxurious Chanel jewelry set, containing a thin gold watch, bracelet, anklet, and two diamond earrings.

As she looks around the room she realizes the driver and bag boys have been gone for quite some time, she's all alone now. She sits down on the bed.

"I wonder why he chose to buy so many different designers instead of just sticking to one…" Whit says to herself.

"Because," a voice says near the door, "You're going to acquire so much clothing and jewelry for the rest of your life… if you don't learn to mix them all up you'll probably never get around to wearing them all."

"Carlos," Whit says smiling from ear to ear, "Where

have you been?"

He smoothly struts towards her, never taking his eyes off her. Picking her up off the bed, she wraps her legs around him, as he kisses her deeply and passionately.

He allows her to lean back in his arms so he can look at her.

"You know Carlos," she says, "you're going to have to work a lot harder to keep me now."

Carlos furrows his brows. "Why is that?" he asks.

"Because K.C. is rich too now," Whitney explains, "So you have to find other ways to excite me."

"So, you're saying you want something different," Carlos says, "something exciting, like a twist, right?"

"Yes, baby yes!" she tells him, as she hugs him tightly. Carlos puts her down. He sits down on the bed with a mischievous smile on his face. He looks towards the bathroom door and claps his hands. Moments later the shower cuts off.

Whitney can hear movement in the bathroom. Frozen, where she stands Whitney awaits curiously for Carlos' next move.

The bathroom door finally opens. A woman walks out in a bright red Chanel bath robe, drying her hair with a velour towel.

Sitting down next to Carlos on the bed, the lady looks through the soft towel with a smile and says. "What's up boo?"

"Cam..." Whitney says. "The one and only..." she replies.

"Is this a good enough twist for you?" Carlos says laughing out loud.

"Ladies I'll be back."he says kissing them each on the lips.

"Make yourselves look like the queens you are,"he continues, "tonight… we start living the way we were born too."

The good doctor leaves the room. Whitney continues to stare at Cameron. "I can't believe we're both here, in the same room… together." Whit says.

"Well believe it girl," Cam replies, "girl, Carlos bought the hospital on this island. The man owns an entire hospital. I understand that Kel is playing football now, but that little NFL money is only a drop in the bucket of what Carlos is worth. This island is my home now Whit. And I'm hoping you decide to stay too."

"Wait, how long have you been here," Whitney asks, "I can't stay here… with both of you. Carlos told me I would be his wife."

Cameron smiles at Whitney. "You will be his wife boo," she says, "we both will. Come sit next to me. It's time we get to know each other." Whitney obediently does as Cam asked her to do.

"Your hair is gorgeous girl; it always has been." Cam says as she softly runs her fingers through Whit's blonde highlights.

"So," Whitney says enjoying her scalp massage, "you knew I was coming, and you didn't mind? You don't see anything wrong with this… at all?"

"Girl," Cam says with a real smile, "this is 2015 nothing surprises me anymore. Wait, weren't you and Love living with another man?" Whitney puts her head down as her face starts to turn red.

"Girl pick your head up," Cam says, "don't be ashamed.

When I heard about ya'll little situation I was jealous. I was like that girl had two men all to herself, damn." Whitney and Cam share their first laugh together ever.

"Look Whit," Cam says, "All I'm saying is… just relax while you're here. If you decide to stay cool, if not Carlos and I will miss you but we'll understand."

Whitney turns to looks at Cam. "What do you mean Carlos and I will miss you?" Whit asks. Cam starts to blush herself.

"Girl, are you serious," Cam says, "Whitney you are **_fine as hell_**. I never wanted to be with a woman until the very first time I laid eyes on you." Whitney kisses Cam softly on the lips.

*(The following passage was an alternate ending I
decided not to use)*

Epilogue (Version 2)
Island Get Away

W hitney left home early this morning to catch her

plane. The flight was long and peaceful. She didn't sleep at

all. The anticipation was too much for her to doze off even

for a second. She's been waiting her entire life for a real

moment like this.

A weekend getaway on an exotic island in the
Quirimbas Archipelago near Pemba in northern
Mozambique; is the perfect engagement present. He's
already been on the island for a day or so waiting for her
to arrive. Whitney had never even heard of the gorgeous
island before she received the ticket he had delivered to
her house.

Stepping off the small plane Whitney feels as if she's
stepping into a new chapter of her life. The driver was
already there waiting for her when the plane landed. He

got all of her luggage and loaded it into the back of the brand new fiery red Rolls Royce.

She's at a loss for words when they arrive at the exquisite Ibo Island Lodge. She can't believe any of this is real, and she's so happy guilt doesn't even cross her mind.

"Right this way Ms. Powell," the driver says, "he's waiting for you." A couple of young men from the island begin to carefully grab her luggage and follow her and the driver inside the luxurious hotel. Walking along the pristine halls of the lodge Whitney feels as if she's having and outer body experience.

She's being lead down each hall by her own personal chauffer, and being followed by ruggedly handsome local island men carrying her brand-new Hermes luggage set. He picked out for her a week ago and had delivered to her apartment. She feels like a powerful island queen headed to her royal chamber in her stunning castle.

She's lost in her own personal fantasy. As they approach the door to her room she can hear her heart beating fiercely in her ears. She reaches up and tries to make sure her hair is still perfectly in place. Nervously she grabs the driver's arm before he can open the door.

Then she takes a small mirror out of her honey orange Hermes clutch. Holding the mirror up in front of her face she truly believes she's looking at perfection.

After placing the mirror back in her clutch, she nods at the driver giving him permission to open her door. He immediately takes his hat off, opens the door and stands to the side as she slowly steps inside.

Her heart is no longer beating in her ears because it has now dropped to her stomach. The room is even more breath taking than she could have ever imagined. Almost every wall is pearly white, except for the accent wall behind the bed in the bedroom.

This wall is a pretty pale green color, the exact same color as the perfectly hand stitched comforter on the bed. As she enters the bedroom she can hear the shower running. She figures she must have arrived a little earlier than he planned, and he must still be getting ready for her.

The wildly flowing white cloth canopy on the bed is swaying methodically as a nice warm breeze is wafting in from the veranda. There is a small gold antique lamp sitting on a small table on each side of the bed. The hardwood floors have been buffed to perfection. The soft air smells like fresh mango fruit.

On the right side of the bed a gorgeous red Alexander Wang summer dress with a white floral print on it has been laid out for her. As she reaches out to carefully feel the material she feels a sudden chill and her arm is covered in tiny goose bumps. Whit sighs happily as the gorgeous dress is made of pure silk.

Below the dress on the floor beside the bed is a light brown Christian Louboutin box. She can hardly wait to see what's inside the box. She quickly kneels down to take the top off of it. Inside she finds a pair of exclusive red and white Christian Louboutin pumps with tiny rhinestones all over them.

She can no longer contain herself. She begins squealing joyfully like a small child on Christmas. Lying to the right side of the dress is a small Chanel box. Inside the box she finds a luxurious Chanel jewelry set, containing a thin gold watch, bracelet, anklet, and two diamond earrings.

As she looks around the room she realizes the driver and bag boys have been gone for quite some time, she's all alone. She sits down on the bed.

"I wonder why he chose to buy so many different designers instead of just sticking to one," Whit says to herself, "this stuff is so pretty I swear I would think a girl picked it out."

"Because," a voice says near the door, "a girl did pick it out." Whitney gasps, "What the hell?" she asks.

Standing there adorned in shimmering jewelry; wearing a pearly white linen suit, white sandals, and a sexy white fedora is Cameron Jiles.

"Cam, what the hell are you doing here?" Whit asks. "Who were you expecting," Cam asks, **"The good doctor?"**

"Yes," she replies, "so why are you here?"

"Long story girl..." Cam says walking closer to the bed to remove her sandals.

"*Damn it*," Whit says, "I got time." Cam looks at her as she sits down on the bed and smiles at her obvious anger."

"First of all, welcome to my island," Cam says, "I hope you like Whitney stands up and walks away from Cam to the other side of the room.

"Your island," Whit replies, "what are you talking about Cam?" Cam smiles again as she removes some of her glistening jewelry.

"The entire time I dated *the good doctor*," Cam says, "I was secretly transferring money from his accounts to an off-shore account of my own. I took the money and bought into a few spider stocks that did well, and I also own some oil down south back in the states."

"How did you steal so much money without him knowing?" Whit asks.

"The man is loaded Whitney," she says, "plus he fired both of his accountants and he's terrible with numbers himself. The timing was just perfect."

"What is Carlos doing now?" Whit asks. "I allow him to fly out to the island from time to time." Cam says.

"Wait." Whit says, "What am I missing here?"

"K.C. got me pregnant months ago," Cam says, "The same night he got his memory back. I told Carlos the baby was his, but I didn't want to be with him. So, he figured it would be cheaper to pay me to get an abortion now, than deal with child support later on. So, he gave me this island, and helped me buy the hospital on it."

"Are you serious?" Whitney asks.

"As serious as a 2.4-billion-dollar island," Cam says as she laughs, "with a 3.3-billion-dollar hospital on it..."

Whitney continues to stare at Cameron. "I can't believe we're both here in the same room together." Whit says.

"Well believe it girl," Cam replies, "girl, Carlos and I bought the hospital on this island. I own an entire hospital. I understand that Kel is playing football now, but that little NFL money is only a drop in the bucket of what I'm worth."

"I can't just forget about K.C. though." Whit says. "Girl you flew half way around the world to be on a private island with another man," Cam says, "Forget K.C. He played us both from the beginning."

"You're right." Whit agrees.

"Besides," Cam says, "If I had said yes that night in

334

the mall K.C.'s trifling ass would be married to me right now anyway not you."

"So, what now…" Whit asks. "This island is my home now Whitney," Cam explains, "And I'm hoping you decide to stay here with me."

"Come sit down next to me," Cam says as she takes a seat on the huge bed, "It's about time we get to know each other."

Whitney obediently does as Cam asked her to do.

"Your hair is gorgeous girl; it always has been." Cam says as she softly runs her fingers through Whit's blonde highlights and her entire head.

"So," Whitney says enjoying her scalp massage, "Let me get this straight. Carlos never sent for me… You did. But why Cam…" Whit asks.

Cam starts to blush. "Girl, are you serious," Cam asks, "Whitney you are *fine as hell*. I never wanted to be with a woman until the very first time I laid eyes on you. Is that weird?"

Whitney hesitates. Cam takes Whitney's face in her soft hands and says, "Girl those men played us both so bad. I mean they really did us wrong. But we don't need them anymore. I own everything we will ever need right here on this island. I can take care of you Whitney…if you let me."

Whitney licks her lips before she speaks. "To be honest Cam," Whit says, "You are the sexiest dark-skinned chick I ever met in my life. And I wanted you from day one too."

Whitney leans in close and kisses Cam softly on the lips.

Characters

Cameron Candice Jiles "Cam"

Keldrick Jermaine "K.C." Cole

Whitney Michelle Powell "Suga Mama"

Lance Orlandis Vinson "Love"

Carlos Luis Sanchez "Dr. Sanchez"

Jazemene Argelle Cole

Jacody "Jay" Miller

Tyrone "Tyboonie" Carter

Corey "C"

Linda Cole "Mama Cole"

Annette Powell

Josh Powell

"TAKE MY BREATH AWAY 2"

(When Love Calls)

De'Lure

(Prologue)

(Love is talking to a psychiatrist at a prison in Orlando)

Lance Orlandis Cole is sitting in a hard iron chair in a cold office near the infirmary, inside of the Central Florida Reception Center, a large prison facility in Orlando Florida. This is where he has lived for the past five years. Lance is in the middle of a conversation with one of his psychiatrists, Dr. Granger. "How do you feel today Lance…" the doctor asks.

"The same…" he replies blankly. "When you say the same what exactly does that mean Mr. Cole?" Love looks at the aging doctor and replies with malice in his eyes. "I told you *Kevorkian*, my name is Vinson, and I am not a Cole." "Don't call me Kevorkian, Lance. You don't have to be disrespectful." The doctor replies. "Don't call me Cole, respect goes both ways or not at all. Do I not deserve respect as well as you do? You and I are not the slightest bit different Doc." Love says with a sick smile on his face.

Dr. Bruce Granger removes his glasses calmly and

asks, "What are you referring to Cole?"

"My name is Lance Orlandis Vinson. I'm not going to correct you again verbally." Love tells him.

"Is that a threat Lance?" Dr. Granger asks. "Check my record Doc I don't make idle threats," Love says, looking as deep as he possibly can into the frightened eyes of Dr. Granger. "Where did the name Love come from," he asks," that's what you call yourself right Lance?"

"You've never met Lance Doc," Love replies, "and you don't want to meet him. So, it's best you leave him out of this conversation, because I like you Doc, I really do but Lance doesn't feel the same way."

"But you are Lance Mr. Co…Mr. Vinson I mean." The Dr. says. You *are* Lance, why do you speak of yourself in third person?" Dr. Granger asks.

"I am not Lance Dr. Granger. "He is here though, and he is a part of me but our thinking patterns contrast in a way that the two of us could never truly co-exist. When he's here… Love is not."

"I see," the doctor says, "so what do you think caused your initial break down?" "Why so many deep questions today Doc…" Love asks through his sadistic smile. "This is the most talking you've ever done in one session, so I'm hoping for a brea…"

"You want a breakthrough Doc, is that what you want?" Love stands up quickly. Dr. Granger flinches in fear. Love smiles, then he walks slowly towards a wall in the doctor's office filled with various awards in the medical field he has been given over the years.

With his back to the doctor he begins to speak. "Fine Doc… here's your breakthrough. From a very young age, I was alienated by my entire family because they thought they saw something in me that I eventually accepted as well to be true." "What did they think they saw?" Dr. Granger asks.

"Don't interrupt me again Doc." He says. "Like I was saying before you broke my thought…They thought I was unusually feminine for a little boy. I was unsafe in my own home. I was molested and raped repeatedly by my brother's father and… one other person. So, for years they told me I liked boys, that I was a faggot, and a little red sissy." Love laughs silently to himself.
"But look at me Doc, I'm all man. I run this damn prison. No moves are made in this camp unless they go through me. Looking back, I don't think I was ever gay."

"Son, you had a boyfriend… Corey. You were definitely gay." Dr. Granger says.

"Sex makes you gay, not companionship you idiot. The first time I ever had sex as a grown man was with my ex Whitney Powell."

"So, you and Corey Lewis never had sex?" Dr. Granger asks.

"Never," he replies, "not even once. Living a life that wasn't mine was destroying me. But I'm doing much better now over all Doc, which is as good thing since I'm getting out soon. I'll be able to use my new-found skills to be successful out in the free world."

"Getting out…" Dr. Granger "Love…You have a life sentence without parole. You're never leaving here."

"Oh, but I am Doc," he says, "and you have the keys I need to do so." "What are you talking about boy?" the doctor asks. Love turns to face him.

"Don't ever call me boy again, you disgusting pedophile!" Love screams. "What are you talking about

Vinson?" the doctor asks standing up from his seat.

"Sit back down right now," Love says with finality.

Love begins to pace back and forth in front of the doctor.

"Were you born and raised in Orlando, Doc?" he asks.

"I was but…" the doctor starts. "And did you ever own a private practice on Orange Avenue?" Love asks.

"Yes, but how…" the doctor tries to speak again. "You used to drive a beat up old station wagon. It had a cracked windshield and a spare tire on the front passenger side. Inside it always smelled of cigarettes and old rotting fast food dinners."

Dr. Granger stands up again.

"Wait… how did you know…?" Dr. Granger is cut off again as Love rushes around his desk and grips his throat as tightly as he possibly can. Love puts his angry lips close to Dr. Granger's fat face as he continues to squeeze his throat.

"Shhh… just, be quiet Doc," Love says, "I'm not going to kill you… even though I should. But I'm not because you're going to redeem your sins by getting me out of here next week." Love tells him. "Look son," the doctor says struggling to breathe, "I don't know what's going on, and I don't know how you know all those things about my past but I am not helping you escape this prison." Love releases his neck and forces him to sit back down.

Walking around the desk Love takes a seat himself facing the doctor. "Escape," Love says smiling at the doctor, "oh no, no, no Doc. There will be no need to break the law… we've both done enough of that for a lifetime. No, you're going to write Judge Whatley and have her release me based on your evaluation of me."

"I have *never* broken the law." the doctor says standing up yet again. Love stands up and pounds his fist on the doctor's desk.

"Rape is against the law Bruce, or Brucie that's what you used to like me to call you right?" Love licks his full pink lips, and then smiles his sick but handsome smile.

The doctor holds his hand over his mouth with his eyes bulging out of his head. Slowly he sits back down. Love walks around the desk. Standing behind the doctor he begins to run his fingers through his thin graying hair.

"You remember me now Doc," Love says, "I never told a soul. My mother Linda brought me to you, so you could fix me. See in her mind I needed fixing, I was a strange and disturbed little kid." Love laughs snidely.

"Hell, after my step father sexually abused me for all those years, I think I deserved to be a little disturbed, don't you? So, then… then she brought me to a shrink. But not just any shrink, the *great Dr. Bruce Granger*, born and raised in Orange County. Yeah, Linda left it up to you to fix her disgusting little baby boy. But you had other plans for me didn't you Doc? How many little boys did you do this to Bruce?"

The doctor feels completely numb he can't even feel the rough scalp massage Love is attempting to hurt him with.

"This can't be real." the doctor says. Love laughs. "Oh, it's very real Brucie. So now the ball is in your court, are you going to write that letter, and ultimately right your wrongs to me, or do I have to ruin your entire existence?" Love asks.

"No, no, no… you can't…" The doctor starts.

"I can't what Bruce?" Love asks. "You plan to ruin me," he replies, "I can't lose my license, my job… and my wife, what about my poor wife Rachel?" Love laughs loudly.

"What about Rachel…I can honestly say Bruce, I don't give a damn about Rachel," he says. "I'm about to be late to chow call," he continues, "You need to let me know something now, because I don't plan on missing out on the fried chicken and mashed potatoes. I'm sure Rachel has a wonderful meal waiting on you at home." Dr. Granger stares briefly into the eyes of the convicted inmate who holds his entire life in his very hands.

"What exactly do you want?" Dr. Granger asks. "The letter Bruce," he says, "all I want is Whatley to get the letter and then you walk away free. You can remain in your comfortable fairytale life without a worry in the world." Love exits Granger's office confidently.

Alone in his office, Granger tries to calm himself. Inside the pocket of his polo button down, he finds a small faded blue handkerchief. Trying to steady his shaky hand he wipes the sweat beads from his face and forehead.

"What's done in the dark…" he mumbles nervously to himself. After refreshing his laptop screen, he begins to delete all of the child pornography videos he's downloaded, and made himself over the years.

After the last video is completely gone from his computer, Granger tries to gather his thoughts about what exactly he plans to put in this letter to Love's judge. One thing's for sure it will be the most well posed letter he's ever written in his life.

(Shadows)

In the middle of the night Love wakes up and he can't move. He can barely breathe and he can see absolutely nothing. He tries to lick his dry lips, but he can't find them, and he can't touch them. He squirms in panic. A cool breeze floats across his body chilling him to the bone. He shivers. His body is completely naked.

I must be in Hell he thinks to himself. Is this how bad Hell is? You can't move, talk, or breathe. I can't even touch or see myself. And it's cold here, how is that possible. Hell is nothing like I imagined, I knew one day I would reside here, but I pictured it much different. Wait, how did I die?

A cold gloved hand is running down his perfect stomach. Now two hands are running up and down his thighs.

SMACK!! Someone or something slaps him hard across the face. He can feel some of his senses returning to him. He can feel his legs more now. He's standing up, and has been for quite some time. His legs must have fallen asleep.

Somebody is biting his left thigh softly. Now they begin kissing it as they make their way up towards his private center. As it begins to fondle him, he closes his eyes tightly. Love has no idea who or what is teasing, and tormenting his body right now, but it's been so long he really doesn't care at this point.

"THE RAIN IS CRASHING"
(Original Poetry)

THE RAIN IS CRASHING IN
FLAMES OF SWEET PASSION
LOVE IS EVERLASTING BUT THE FUTURE DOESN'T
JUST HAPPEN
WE DRAFT IT WITH THE PENS OF OUR LIVES OUR
DRIVE OUR EYES
WE STRIVE TO FLY HIGH ABOVE VANILLA SKIES
LOST IN EVER LUCID DREAMS OF MILK AND
HONEY
WE STRESS OVER MONEY
AND THE PERCEPTION OF
OTHERS
FIGHTING BLINDLY WITH EACH OTHER
KNOWING FULL WELL THAT NONE OF THESE SINS
WILL BE COVERED
UNLESS WE LOVE... WE
LOVE, IF WE LOVE EACH
OTHER ALL THE PAIN
FADES AWAY INTO AN
UNFAMILIAR SPACE AS WE
PRAISE HIS FACE
ALL THE DEMONS AND HATRED
BECOME DULL LIKE 50 SHADES OF GRAY
WE NEED SUBSTANCE IN OUR
LIVES ACTION AND PURPOSE
THIS SHOULD MAKE US THRIVE
NOT MATERIAL THINGS AND SOCIAL STATUS
WHO'S LEFT TO TEACH US WHAT REALLY MATTERS
WE NO LONGER HAVE T.V. DAD'S

LIKE WILL SMITH'S UNCLE
AND CARL FROM FAMILY
MATTERS
OUR DADDYS ARE 2 CHAINS AND FUTURE
AND OUR MOTHER'S BE BEYONCE AND NICKI

THAT'S WHY OUR HEARTS TIME BOMBS ARE
TICKING
DON'T GET IT TWISTED
I LOVE FUTURE, TITTY, B. AND NICKI
THEY'RE JUST ENTERTAINERS THEY WERE
NOT SENT
HERE TO TRAIN US HOW TO THINK
BUT WE FOLLOW THEIR LEAD
ANYWAY
ME... I'D MUCH RATHER BE LIKE JAY-Z OR DRAKE
AND THEY SAY DRIZZY DIDN'T START FROM THE
BOTTOM
BUT THAT STILL DOESN'T MAKE HIM FAKE
I DIDN'T START FROM THE BOTTOM EITHER
BUT I'VE BEEN THERE
AND THAT'S WHERE I FIRST SAW GODS FACE
I WANNA LIVE LIFE WITH A GODLY FAITH AND FATE
I'M BUILDING MY MENTAL ENDURANCE TO GET IN
PERFECT SPIRITUAL SHAPE
I ESCAPE TO THE STATE OF MIND
THAT THE ONLY LINES THAT EXIST
ARE THE ONES THAT I WRITE
MY BOOKS HAVE LIVES OF THEIR
OWN
AND THEY WELCOME ME
INTO A POWERFUL PEACEFUL
ZONE
THAT COULD NEVER BE CLONED
FIND OUT WHY YOU WERE
CHOSEN

AND CHOOSE TO BE SUCCESSFUL
BECAUSE ONCE YOU KNOW YOU
LIFE IS NO LONGER CONFUSINGLY
STRESSFUL
I NEVER WANNA *EVER BE* REGRETFUL
OR
DIRESPECTFUL
RESPECT MY
MIND
AND KNOW THAT MY BODY OF WORK

IS A BODY THAT WORKS
FOR THE GOOD OF OUR
NATION
I'M PATIENT AND WAITING ON AMAZING
MY PASSION IS EVERLASTING WHILE THE RAIN IS
JUST CRASHING

De'Lure

If you enjoyed this novel you should check out these other **AMAZING** titles by De'Lure

Onyx Cielo: Book 1 -The Tree of Transformation- (Fantasy)

Take My Breath Away 2: When Love Calls (Realistic Romance/ Drama/ Erotica)

Take My Breath Away 3: Save me from My Past (Realistic Romance/ Drama/ Erotica)

Passion Absolute –Radicon's Princess- (Realistic Romance/ Drama/Erotica)

De'Lure Shorts & Poem (Poetry/Drama/Short Stories)

De'Lure Shorts & Poems 2 (Poetry/Drama/Short Stories)

He Without Sin (Realistic/Romance/Drama)

Kissed (Realistic/ Drama/ Murder/ Mystery)

Mental Apex -Invisible Pyramids- (Poetic Perfection)

About the Author

De'Lure is a 10-time published career dreamer who writes with his heart and a very realistic imagination. His first passion was acting, but from that love spawned an even deeper passion for the art of writing. The imagery he uses to create stories is packed with all the components' legendary writing careers are made of. Expect great things from Dreamer De'Lure.

Facebook: Published De'Lure
Email: ceom.love@gmail.com

www.ingramcontent.com/pod-product-compliance
Lightning Source LLC
Chambersburg PA
CBHW061316170626
46817CB00001B/202